SIGNATURE PIECES

(SIGNATURE PIECES)

On the Institution of Authorship

PEGGY KAMUF

Cornell University Press

ITHACA AND LONDON

Cornell University Press gratefully acknowledges
a grant from the Andrew W. Mellon Foundation
that aided in bringing this book to publication.

First published 1988 by Cornell University Press.

International Standard Book Number 0-8014-2209-4
Library of Congress Catalog Card Number 88-47731
Printed in the United States of America
Librarians: Library of Congress cataloging information
appears on the last page of the book.

The paper in this book is acid-free and meets the guidelines for
permanence and durability of the Committee on Production Guidelines
for Book Longevity of the Council on Library Resources.

Contents

I'm Nobody! Who are you?
Are you—Nobody—too?
Then there's a pair of us!
Don't tell! they'd banish us—you know!

How dreary—to be—Somebody!
How public—like a Frog—
To tell your name—the livelong June—
To an admiring Bog!

       —Emily Dickinson

(Anyway I've had now to sing glad pleas for happy glad-dings of more endless pops & goes. I have signed my name but now I feel awfully frightened. Am I saying wisely in these solemn legalnesses) that any little murder, caused by here & there, has been quite let off by my names having been signed so beautifully!??

       —Stevie Smith

Preface

Like most books, this one "began" before it began. Its several preoccupations—signature, authorship, the gender of the writer or writing— had been dogging me for a long time. In particular, I was pursued by a persistent dissatisfaction with the way in which these terms tended to get confused or even collapsed into one another by most discourse concerned with the relation between writer and writing, and especially between the woman writer and her writing. That relation continued to be thought largely according to notions of representation, expression, the fully present intentionality of a subject, and so forth. I had been convinced for some time by demonstrations, most notably in the writings of Jacques Derrida, that such notions contributed essential elements to the metaphysical construction of women's exclusion, to the "phallocentrism" at the base of virtually all Western habits of thought. I was also convinced, therefore, that deconstructing this exclusion could not be a matter *only* of enlarging the field of expression to include "feminine" subjects, or writers, or writings. Unless this expansion is accompanied by a rethinking of some fundamental categories that have classified us *as* subjects, however discerning or changed the aspects of that subjectivity may appear, then the chances for displacement of the fundamental structures of exclusion are no doubt considerably lessened. Such rethinking, or rather thinking-beyond-the-subject, has been going on for some time now in many quarters and in many modes. This book merely gathers some of my own (halting and insufficient) attempts to give it its chance.

That these attempts or essays have come together under the single or singular title of "signature" may seem somewhat arbitrary at first glance. But, I would argue, it is the place of the signature that has been largely ignored, elided, or simply filled in by the presuppositions shaping much past and present discourse about the writer in/and his/her writing. The principal reason for this neglect is that this "place" is not a place at all, but an always divisible limit within the difference between writer and work, "life" and "letters." Signature articulates the one with the other, the one *in* the other: it both divides and joins. It is this double-jointedness of signatures that will be lost to any discourse that continues to posit an essential exteriority of subjects to the texts they sign.

If we ask: What happens when someone writes his or her name in the mode of a signature? we may begin to see that this everyday occurrence is supported by immense conventional systems that tend to hide the precariousness of a general understanding of that act. For the most part, these conventions allow us to perform, in a more or less reliable manner, operations of identification, attestation, verification, attribution of responsibility, and so forth. Indeed, many social institutions thoroughly depend, in one way or another, on the reliable functioning of signatures, and whole areas of law can be said to be concerned almost exclusively with the rights and duties guaranteed by signatures (e.g., contract, property, and copyright law). The legal signature signals that, usually on a certain date and according to certain formalities, the subject named was present and assented to, accepted, affirmed some accord with another party. "The subject named" is thus first of all assumed to be present to himself or herself for the accord to have taken place between the identifiable parties to it. This accord presumes, moreover, that the signature represents a particular person, the bearer of a certain proper name and no other. It presumes, in other words, the possibility of singling out one subject from all others. But since names circulate within the public domain of language, they can always be changed or borrowed or duplicated. Supplementary guarantees of the singularity of signature must therefore be given, such as the notion of the verifiable differentiation of its *mark*. When you sign, you do not merely write your name, which anyone could do in your place: you affix your name as a particular mark. The singularity of the autograph, however, cannot be absolute; on the contrary, verifiability or authentication relies on its reproducibility by "the subject named." If every time you sign your name, you deliberately make a significantly different mark, if no two of your signature acts resemble each other, then there is no telling after you have signed whether it was indeed you who signed. After a while, even you may forget having made some particular mark. Here the grounding assumption is that "the subject named" is not only self-identical with itself in the moment of signing but as well remains recognizably the same over time. By a seeming paradox, then, the singularity of the signature's mark depends on its limitation within recognizable parameters of reproducibility or iterability, which is to say of *generalizability*. The signature, therefore, is always detachable from the singular instance it supposedly designates. It can always be and in fact already has been detached from the signatory and expropriated by a field of general substitution. This is to remark that, within such a field of general substitution and exchange, "the subject named" is always finally a general subject, classified in a large but nevertheless limited number of ways. The particularization of this general subject through the functioning of signature is thus also always countersigned by the system of interchangeable likenesses, the system of the same in which singularity is but a necessary *concept*.

There are also, however, occasions when this conventional understanding is loosened and we are allowed to see the signature operating on its own, so to speak, as a particular use of the proper name. Such occasions are written works (literature in the general sense) bearing an author's signature which also make bare its uncertain operation. Yet the modern study of literature has largely contrived to look away from this exposed condition of the signature. To do so, it has dressed the signature in various guises: psychological, historical, formal, ideological. Working together, these constructs have produced what may be called the institution of authorship, an institution that masks or recuperates the disruptive implications of literary signature. Our investment in this institution is massive. All sorts of values are exchanged within its construction. There are enormous profits to be had, of course, and questions of what returns to whom, who gets what return, and who has rights over what—all these basically economic questions agitate the scene of the signature but also inscribe its unsettling otherness within an economy of the same. It is finally to this economy that the greater profits return; anyone can hold shares in it for the price of *identification* with authors via their written representatives, foremost and most essential among which is the signature.

By shifting some of the accumulated weight of authorship on the way we read and the way we act on what we read, this book attempts to recover some of the pieces that have fallen into the cracks of the identificatory economy. Three leverage points are used: the example of Rousseau's signature as a particularly lucid experience of dissociation between author and text; the signatures of Baudelaire and Woolf as demonstrations of how a signature's gender can also be interrupted; finally, two moments in a recent (but also long-running) theoretical debate over authorship, intentionality, and reading by identification. The first part is to be read as chapters in what I initially call a history of Rousseau's signature; the second and third parts each pair two essays with results that I hope are illuminating for both even though they may be read separately.

Despite the apparent or implied continuity from one chapter to the next, these pieces are not forced into a whole or made to yield some general theory of the signature. Indeed, it is the very possibility of generalizing in this domain of the singular that has to be put in question, even as it is also the signature's lot to suffer the constraints of the general laws limiting its singularity. That double exigency has been the constant companion of these pages.

I refer to published translations whenever such works are available. In all other cases, translations are my own.

Parts of this book have previously appeared elsewhere. A somewhat different version of chapter 5, "Baudelaire au féminin," was initially published in *Paragraph* 8 (1986), edited by Diana Knight; a shorter version of chapter 6, "Penelope at Work," first appeared in *Novel* 16 (Fall 1982); chapter 7, "Floating Authorship," was published in *Diacritics* 16 (Winter 1986); chapter 8, "Pieces of Resistance," was originally a contribution to the volume *Reading De Man Reading*, edited by Wlad Godzich and Lindsay Waters and published by University of Minnesota Press (1988). I here thank all the publishers for their kind permission to use these texts.

Peggy Kamuf

Oxford, Ohio

SIGNATURE PIECES

A Single Line Divided

Early in *Le Rouge et le noir*, when Julien Sorel enters the church at Verrières which will later be the scene of his attempted assassination of Mme de Rênal, the narrator explains that Julien "thought it might be useful to his hypocrisy to stop off in the church."[1] The excuse of the hero's hypocrisy is a clever one since it both names and camouflages the hypocritical agency of the narrative, which is—like Julien, we might say—interested only in its own advancement beneath the cover of some higher or at least different purpose. This brief interlude in the church is constructed entirely out of elements prefiguring Julien's *arrivisme*, crime and punishment. The novel thereby parades its foreknowledge that where it is going is where it has been, and it invites the reader to share in the irony that Julien alone remains ignorant of the fate prepared for him. Since, however, Julien's ignorance is a pretext for the narrative to unfold this twice-told tale,[2] the hypocritical detour needs to establish it in the clearest way. And what better way could there be than to show Julien as a failed reader of his own name on a death sentence?

[1]Stendhal, *Red and Black*, trans. Robert M. Adams (New York, 1969), 18.
[2]The crime and execution of Antoine Berthet, which had supplied the general outlines of Stendhal's plot, was a well-discussed scandal by the time the novel was published in 1830.

All alone in the church, he took a seat in the finest pew. It bore M. de Rênal's coat of arms.

On the lectern, Julien noted a scrap of printed paper, set out there as if for him to read. He glanced at it and saw:

Details of the execution and the last moments of Louis Jenrel, executed at Besançon, on the—

The paper was torn. On the other side were the first words of a line: *The first step....*

Who could have left this paper here? thought Julien. Poor fellow, he added with a sigh, his name has the same ending as mine. . . . He crumpled up the paper.

As he went out, Julien imagined he saw a pool of blood by the baptismal font; it was merely some holy water which had been spilled; the red curtains covering the windows made it look like blood.

At last, Julien grew ashamed of his secret terrors.

Am I going to be a coward? he said. *To arms!*[3]

Julien taking the place of M. de Rênal, signaled by his coat of arms, then rushing from the church with the cry of "To arms!" as he executes the first step toward what will be his last moments in Besançon: the irony accumulated with each of these traits sets the scene apart, lifts it out of the successive narration, or rather forms a loop in that narration, a point where the two ends of its thread cross and draw up in a circle. At the center of the circle, the fate of a name, torn from its reference, fragmented, left for anyone to read, a collection of letters that submits to the arbitrary principles of resemblance, repetition, combination. The name ends in *-rel*, but also it ends up by ending in *-rel*: its fate is to end up providing a rhyming syllable for Sorel. Julien decapitates the name and appropriates what is left: "his name has the same ending as mine." The irony is that Julien recognizes a resemblance between the names as a succession of letters but cannot see the resemblance between the fates of the names, their ending in decapitation. The Louis Jenrel named in the fragment has ended up as the name of someone decapitated; saying his name ends like mine, Julien says also

---

[3]Stendhal, 20.

without realizing it: his name ends as mine will end, detached from its bearer, naming finally only that detachment.

This fragment of text about a fragment of text is also about the fragmentation of names as arbitrary signifiers that, at any moment, can be cut off from their referent—the bearer of the name—and left to their fate, floating in the currents of chance encounters with readers who are free to associate a meaning with the name. Of course, Julien Sorel's encounter with the name of Louis Jenrel is one of chance only within the frame of the fiction. Stepping outside that frame, one finds a ready answer to his question "Who could have left this paper here?" in the other name—Stendhal that floats over this scene and calculates the placing of the exact anagram, "left there as if for him to read."

This loop in the narrative is what may be called a signature piece (as one says a signature tune), that is, a device repeatedly associated with a subject. The encrypting of proper names is such a device for Henri Beyle, who never signed with his proper proper name and who invented hundreds of pseudonyms or cryptonyms for himself and his relations. Because Beyle always signs by signing not "Beyle" but some other name, it is not so much his signature that is encrypted as an encrypting that is his signature. "Louis Jenrel," as one such anagrammatic encrypting, is also a barely disguised signature of Henri Beyle.

But the name(s) of the author—Stendhal/Henri Beyle—does not simply point to someone behind the scenes, pulling the strings. It too is displayed in the scene like a fragment of text set out in order to be read. The assonance or near rhyme of those two names—Louis Jenrel/Henri Beyle—signals that the proper name of the signatory has not simply been left out of the loop to be replaced or protected by the device of encrypting. What is more, the name Rênal, which is also circulating in the scene, ends like Stendhal. Both pairs of names—Jenrel/Beyle, Stendhal/Rênal—are paired in their final syllables according to the principle of resemblance that Julien remarks. This effect, one suspects, can no longer be read simply within the calculation of Beyle's signature, its deliberate veiling, or its disrespect for orthography that makes possible the ironic distance installed in the narration. The name Beyle/Stendhal has itself gotten caught up in the textual network through a fragmentation that can always divide any name from itself and associate it with fragments of other names which spell the end of proper reference to an integral subject. The name functions already as the subject of a death sentence. No less than Julien Sorel, the name Henri Beyle/Stendhal ends by prefiguring its own end in the text it cannot sign from any safe distance. The signature piece, then, when inserted in the field of fragmenting forces which is a text, leaves the signature in pieces.

These pieces of the signature Beyle/Stendhal can serve to introduce what has been "left there as if to be read" in the following essays. In particular, they point to the necessary detachment of the signature from the signatory, of the sign from any singular, historical referent. The process by which Henri Beyle can take Stendhal, the proper name of a place,[4] as signature is the same process that has to allow "Stendhal" to become detached again from the signatory. It is already detached and the signatory is already outlived by the signature even when, at the moment he signs, his death is only announced or prefigured as a still future event. The structure of this *already*, or, in another idiom, of this *déjà*, marks every signature, as Jacques Derrida observes, taking the example of his own abbreviated name:[5]

[4]From Stendal, now a town in East Germany.

[5]*Derrida, Jacques is already déjà.* Once remarked, the dissemination of this proper name through the temporal adverb (or the spatial adverb *derrière*) seems to have as well the effect of appropriating the common use, diverting public funds for private benefit. Derrida elsewhere has commented on this effect: "playing with one's own name, putting it in play, is, in effect, what is always going on. . . . But obviously this is not something one can decide: one doesn't disseminate or play with one's name. The very structure of the proper name sets this process in motion. That's what the proper name is for. At work, naturally, in the desire—the apparent desire—to lose one's name by disarticulating it, disseminating it, is the inverse movement. By disseminating or losing my own name, I make it more and more intrusive; I occupy the whole site, and as a result my name gains more ground. The more I lose, the more I gain." *The Ear of the Other*, ed. Christie McDonald (New York, 1985), 76. As I make clear later on, *Glas* is concerned with precisely this uncertain economy of loss and gain which it would be illusory to think could somehow balance out for the signatory, or make any difference, finally, in the structure of signing. Perhaps less

read the *déjà* [*already*] as an abbreviation. When I sign, I am already dead. I hardly have the time to sign than I am already dead, that I am already dead. I have to abridge the writing, hence the siglum, because the structure of the "signature" event carries my death in that event. Which means it is not an "event" and perhaps signifies nothing, written out of a past that has never been present and on the basis of [*depuis*] the death of someone who has never been alive.[6]

When I sign, I am already dead because, according to the inexorable logic of the deictic or shifter, its singular referent—me—will have already submitted to the requirement of its generalization in order to signify itself. I cannot say—or sign—what I mean, and I say precisely what I do not mean.[7] By the same token, "I" spells the death of me; it is already the effacement of a singular nature in a common sig-nature.

The phrase "the death of the author" ought to come to mind here. And indeed, the pages that follow will frequently encounter that figure, although not always in the same guise. The phrase has gained a certain currency among literary theorists both as a shorthand for a nonhermeneutic thinking about texts and as a label against which to react in the name of the historical subject. The brandishing of the phrase as a token in some struggle has not helped to illuminate its possible import because the question of whether one is for or against the "death of the author" obviously makes little sense in itself. For this reason, it may be helpful to review one of the sources of the controversial slogan: the brief essay by Roland Barthes titled, precisely, "The Death of the Author."[8]

---

clear is what happens when that signature is cited, as it is here, to back up claims being made about signatures in general.

[6]Derrida, *Glas*, trans. John P. Leavey, Jr. and Richard Rand (Lincoln, Nebr., 1986), 19, right col.; translation modified; further references will be included in the text.

[7]See Paul de Man's reading of the phrase from Hegel's *Encyclopedia* "so kann ich nicht sagen was ich nur meine" as first "I cannot say what I make mine," then "I cannot say what I think," and finally "I cannot say I." "Sign and Symbol in Hegel's *Aesthetics*," *Critical Inquiry* 8 (Summer 1982), 768.

[8]Barthes, "La Mort de l'auteur," in *Le Bruissement de la langue* (Paris, 1984); English translation by Stephen Heath in the collection *Image-Music-Text* (New York, 1977). Page references will be to this translation.

First published in 1968, this essay bears the stamp of Barthes's association with the "avant-garde" journal *Tel Quel* through its notion of a break that divides literature's modern history between the age of the author and the age of the text, or, in Barthes's terms, between the ages of the writer and the scriptor. In particular, the name Mallarmé, whose "entire poetics consists in suppressing the author in the interests of writing," situates the break. While Barthes characterizes this break in several ways, there is also a recognition at the outset that "in ordinary culture" the image of literature remains "tyrannically centred on the author. . . . The *explanation* of a work is always sought in the man or woman who produced it, as if it were always in the end, through the more or less transparent allegory of the fiction, the voice of a single person, the *author* 'confiding' in us" (143). Seeing in the positivism "which has attached the greatest importance to the 'person' of the author" "the epitome and culmination of capitalist ideology," the *telquelien* argument advances "nonordinary" culture's role as an avant-garde overturning the ideological supports that have made authors into the owners of their texts. The analogy with property is itself closely linked to an analogy with filiation, as Barthes reminds us:

> The Author, when believed in, is always conceived of as the past of his own book: book and author stand automatically on a single line divided into a *before* and an *after*. The Author is thought to *nourish* the book, which is to say that he exists before it, thinks, suffers, lives for it, is in the same relation of antecedence to his work as a father to his child. In complete contrast, the modern scriptor is born simultaneously with the text, is in no way equipped with a being preceding or exceeding the writing, is not the subject with the book as predicate. (145)

Rather than the romantic expression of an Author, the modern text's mode is inscription of "a field without origin—or which, at least has no other origin than language itself." Barthes goes to Flaubert and to the "profound ridiculousness" of Bouvard and Pécuchet for a confirmation that the "text is a tissue of quotations drawn from the innumberable centres of culture [in which] the writer can only imitate a gesture that is always anterior, never original" (146).

This brief essay concludes by a shift that replaces the distinction Author/scriptor with its parallel distinction Critic/reader. The shift is motivated when Barthes observes that the ideology supporting the position of the Author has had one clear beneficiary: the Critic.

> To give a text an Author is to impose a limit on that text, to furnish it with a final signified, to close the writing. Such a conception suits criticism very well, the latter then allotting itself the important task of discovering the Author (or its hypostases: society, history, psyche, liberty) beneath the work: when the Author has been found, the text is "explained"—victory to the critic. (147)

The Critic's "victory," if it could ever be won, would operate a check on the text's "anti-theological activity, an activity that is truly revolutionary since to refuse to fix meaning is, in the end, to refuse God and his hypostases—reason, science, law." The scriptor/text's counterpart cannot, therefore, be a Critic. Rather, it is "simply that *someone*" called "the reader":

> a text is made of multiple writings, drawn from many cultures and entering into mutual relations of dialogue, parody, contestation, but there is one place where this multiplicity is focused and that place is the reader, not, as was hitherto said, the author. The reader is the space on which all the quotations that make up a writing are inscribed without any of them being lost; a text's unity lies not in its origin but in its destination. Yet this destination cannot any longer be personal: the reader is without history, biography, psychology; he is simply that *someone* who holds together in a single field all the traces by which the written text is constituted. (148)

The final sentence of the essay places the future of writing in the balance between "the death of the author" and the "birth of the reader."

There is not far to go from "The Death of the Author," the essay, to the quotation of that title as a polemical slogan.

Barthes is already writing in a polemical style, favoring reductive summary and rapid judgments to any more patient procedure. His stance here is somewhat that of spokesman representing to a broader readership (broader, that is, than the readership of *Tel Quel*) the results of the more patient work that he and others were carrying out elsewhere. (The essay begins, in fact, with a reflection on a passage from *Sarrasine* which would later be expanded into the line-by-line reading of that story in *S/Z*.) Once this situation of address is recognized or admitted, and there is no reason it should not be admitted, then any dispute with its accepted limitations would be misplaced. Yet, to the extent the essay also represents or anticipates the polemical form that was to develop as an accompaniment to certain changes taking place in the practice of literary criticism, and because that accompaniment has tended to grab center stage,[9] there may be reason to go back over some of this ground more slowly.

Barthes deploys two seemingly contradictory senses of his title in the essay. On the one hand, the "death of the author" would refer to the eidetic law of any writing:

> Writing is that neutral, composite, oblique space where our subject slips away, the negative where all identity is lost, starting with the very identity of the body writing. *No doubt it has always been that way* [italics added]. As soon as a fact is *narrated* no longer with a view to acting directly on reality but intransitively, that is to say, finally outside of any function other than that of the

[9]The role of this polemical accompaniment may have assumed the particular shape it has in the United States because literary critical practice is there more confined within the single institution of the university and consequently more apt to mistake institutional effects for criteria of critical evaluation. For a discussion of some effects of "market" on American literary theory, see Jonathan Culler, "Criticism and Institutions: The American University," in *Post-Structuralism and the Question of History*, ed. Derek Attridge, Geoffrey Bennington, and Robert Young (Cambridge, 1987). On the other hand, in France, for example, precisely because "literature" is less institutionalized, fundamentally the same polemic has been taken up by the "mass media" to a far greater extent, but with even less circumspection. Barthes's essay bears the stamp of this journalistic mode.

very practice of the symbol itself, this disconnection occurs, the voice loses its origin, the author enters into his own death, writing begins. (142)

On the other hand, the phrase has a specific historical reference to the activity of certain late-nineteenth and early-twentieth-century writers (Flaubert, Mallarmé, Valéry, de Quincey, Proust, the Surrealists are mentioned) who sought to loosen the hold of the Author, itself a concept with a specific history, on writing.

> The author is a modern figure, a product of our society insofar as emerging from the Middle Ages with English empiricism, French rationalism and the personal faith of the Reformation, it discovered the prestige of the individual. . . . In France, Mallarmé was doubtless the first to see and to foresee in its full extent the necessity to substitute language itself for the person who until then had been supposed to be its owner. (142–43)

Considered together, the two senses of the phrase imply a certain narrative of truth in which the second, historical sense acts to retrieve the first, nonhistorical sense that had been lost or covered over through the aberrant historical invention of the Author. The problem with such an implied narrative is that it can easily come to resemble the theological narratives of the very sort "the truly revolutionary" activity of writing is supposed to refuse. Furthermore, the problem is not just dormant in the essay but fully awakened when Barthes closes on the figure he calls the reader, described in the terms we have already quoted:

> The reader is the space on which all the quotations that make up a writing are inscribed *without any of them being lost* [*sans qu'aucune ne se perde*]; a text's *unity* lies not in its origin but in its destination. Yet this destination cannot any longer be personal: the reader is without history, biography, psychology; he is simply that *someone* [italics in the original] who holds together *in a single field all the traces* [*dans un même champ toutes les traces*] by which the written text is constituted. (148)

Nothing in the scheme of this description comes forward to hold off the ultimate collapse of this unity of destination, the single totalizing field, into the theological terms it is supposed to refuse or defeat.[10] The necessity that posits an original theological principle is finally the same necessity that projects a destination where "all the traces" of a text are gathered "without any of them being lost."

How did this essay end up saying almost precisely what it does not want to say, having perhaps done nothing else than exchange the "tyranny" of the idea of the Author for that of the reader? One answer lies in the form of the denegation that dictates the notion of a space of inscription ("the reader is the *space* on which . . . are *inscribed* . . ."; "le lecteur est *l'espace* même où *s'inscrivent* . . .") where there is no loss. To make such an assertion, Barthes has to forget—lose track of—the loss that he named at the outset of the essay and that he made coincident with the beginning of writing: "Writing is that neutral, composite, oblique space where our subject slips away, the negative *where all identity is lost, starting with the very identity of the body writing* . . . the voice *loses* its origin, the author enters into his own death, writing begins."[11] When, at the end of the essay, the reader is said to be a space of inscription *without loss*, then either this inscription is not a writing (but what could that mean?) or else there is indeed loss registered by the assertion that nothing is lost in such an inscription for gone is all trace of the loss of "the very identity of the body writing."

Backtracking to the divided sense of the title phrase, "the death of the author," we can perhaps isolate not the loss "itself"

---

[10]If we were concerned with the complexity of Roland Barthes's thinking, rather than with the way in which this essay installs a more general polemic, we would point out that this notion of the totalizing reader is activated by *S/Z* only to be abandoned for the partialness and partiality of reading described in *Le Plaisir du texte.* In other words, Barthes seems to have jettisoned the concept of a totalizing "reader."

[11]Elsewhere Barthes situates the beginning of writing and thus the death of the author in the absence of the other to whom one addresses a "lover's discourse": "To know that writing compensates for nothing, sublimates nothing, that it is precisely *there where you are not*—this is the beginning of writing." *A Lover's Discourse: Fragments,* trans. Richard Howard (New York, 1978), 100.

(for its loss is, precisely, irretrievable), but the loss of the loss, the juncture at which one trace or track converges with another, larger path and disappears into the general direction—or destination—of meaning. Recall that with that phrase Barthes designates both a necessary condition and something like a historical event, one that, however, tends to find itself inserted in a timeless narrative of theological, teleological revelation. This "event," in other words, merges with a general structure. But there is another event that the phrase is turning around without ever naming as such: not the death of the author in general, nor as an age in the history of either literature or a theory of literature, but the death of *this* author or *that* author, the one named (Stendhal during the night of 22 March 1842) or the one who signs, who, nevertheless, even as s/he signs is already dead before the event. The disappearance of this event, of, that is, "the very identity of the body writing," in the "always already" of its general occurrence is the loss that no writing or reading can recuperate, for that is the condition of possibility of those activities. "I" cannot say what I mean. There remains a remainder lost to the destination of sense.

It cannot be a question of whether one is for or against this remainder. In either case, the remainder remains. Whatever the apparent stakes of a polemic about "the death of the author," however welcome may seem a "return to the subject" (even a "changed" subject) or to history, the loss is not to be remedied, just more or less buried beneath appeals to a radical break or to a return.

The loss of the "very identity of the body writing," Mallarmé's "disparition élocutoire du poète," does not disappear without a trace, however. What is called a signature, its trait or its contract, traces the disappearance and marks the division of the proper name where it joins a text. Although Barthes's essay never names the signature as such, it designates a certain line of division between author and book where one might expect to read a signature: "The Author, when believed in, is always conceived of as the past of his own book: book and author stand automatically on a *single line divided* [italics added] into a *before* and an *after* [*une même ligne, distribuée* comme un *avant* et un *après*]" (145). It is this conception of a temporal division or filial derivation which must succumb to the activity of the "modern scriptor [who] is born simultaneously with the text, [who] is in no way equipped with a being preceding or exceeding the writing." But already, one might say, before this "event" in Barthes's implied narrative, there is the curiously ambivalent image of "une même ligne, distribuée," an ambivalence that Stephen Heath accentuates by translating with the phrase "a single line divided." The logic of Barthes's description requires one to think this singular division or distribution as *both* an erroneous, past conception of the Author preceding what comes after *and* as the implied temporal frame of this narrative which sets off premodern from modern writing, which distinguishes between the filial concept of the work's derivation from its author and the simultaneous birth of scriptor and text. This passage at the center of the polemic, from the death of the author to the birth of the scriptor, depends, in other words, on the *erasure and reinscription* of a "single line divided." It is thus not a simple passage, but itself divided by the traces of the author whose death it announces. The "single line divided" *names without naming the signature.* There where a concept divides the line between writer and text, before and after, outside and inside, at the point of division that Barthes's essay supposes but elides in something like a syncope, a piece (but a piece of what?) falls through the crack.

A signature is not a name; at most it is a piece of a name, its citation according to certain rules. But neither is it simply a piece of common language that can be picked up and used by just anyone to any purpose. Like a dash or a hyphen—a trait— the signature spaces out, joins, and dissociates. It is not, however, a line of division, nor a dividing line— unless one hears that phrase as a line that is at every point dividing itself (but, since a point is precisely the indivisible unit of this figure, better not to try to measure the signature geometrically or to plot its position in this way in the textual space). As a piece of proper name, the signature points, at one extremity, to a properly unnameable singularity; as a piece of language, the signa-

ture touches, at its other extremity, on the space of free substitution without proper reference. At the edge of the work, the
dividing trait of the signature pulls in both directions at once:
appropriating the text under the sign of the name, expropriating
the name into the play of the text. The undecidable trait of the
signature must fall into the crack of the historicist/formalist
opposition organizing most discourses about literature. Its case
is that of the rest, which remains unclassified by either determinations of agency (biographical, historical, political, economical) or determinations of formal, arbitrary structures of language.

Jacques Derrida's *Glas*, without doubt the most sustained
and intricate work yet undertaken on this case, must therefore
be of two minds in its approach to the question "What remains
of a signature?"

> First case: the signature belongs to the inside of that (picture,
> relievo, discourse and so on) which it is presumed to sign. It is in
> the text, no longer signs, operates as an effect within the object,
> has its part to play within that which it claims to appropriate to
> itself or lead back to its origin. Filiation is lost. The signature
> [seing] deducts itself.
>
> Second case: the signature holds itself, as is generally believed,
> outside the text. It emancipates as well the product, that can get
> along without the signature, from the name of the father or the
> mother which it no longer needs in order to function. The filiation
> again gives itself up, is still betrayed by what remarks it. (4R)

The two cases represent two modes of denegation of the remains of the signature. As attempts to bury these remains, they
describe a labor of monumentalization or memorialization, a
work that can never complete its task of mourning the "death
of the author." The difference between the cases is topical, that
is, it depends on a spatial metonymy to situate the signature
either inside or outside the work. That difference, however, is
finally reabsorbed by the failure of either topographical trope to
dispense with the other. In the first case, which is that of
formalism, the signature is supposed to sign from within the
work; the text thus encloses it and erects it as monument. If,

however, the signature belongs to the inside, it can no longer appropriate the work, the monument remembers nothing outside itself, filiation is lost, and the thread of memory cannot be retraced. In the second case, which is that of historicism, the signature is supposed to sign from outside, the work stands apart and on its own, as if no singular, finite, or limiting existence had had a hand in its realization. But the filiation that the conceptual system must overcome if it is to stand as a truly general one is betrayed by the mark of the signature it cannot quite get out of its system. The first case represents the major stakes of literary discourse: the monumentalizing transformation of the proper name into things, into names of things (11R). Derrida takes the name, the signature "Genet," as an intrepid guide to this work of nomination. The second case represents the stakes of scientific or philosophical discourse for which the name "Hegel" is at once the indispensable guide and the half-effaced remains of a patrilinear descent. Shuttling between the pair of names (which are almost mirror images of each other: twice -*e-e*-) and between their alternating cadences, *Glas* proposes itself not as a discourse, but as an instrument (a surgical instrument but also a musical one, for example, a clanging clapper ringing its knell) with which to *unnerve* discourses about textual authorship, to unsettle the institution of the author's rights to some property:

> to insinuate the delicate, barely visible stem, an almost imperceptible cold lever, scalpel or *stylus* in order to unnerve [énerver: literally, to remove the nerve, hence to deprive of force; more colloquially, to get on someone's nerves, to annoy] then delapidate enormous discourses that always end up, even though they deny it more or less, by attributing an author's rights [droit d'auteur]: "that comes (back) to me," the signature [seing] belongs to me. (3R)

There is indeed something unnerving about a signature that remains to return to no one.

The essays gathered here are not surgical instruments, nor do they claim to apply the instrument that *Glas* has forged. The reference to texts on signature signed by Jacques Derrida is more often than not a chagrined admission that there is much more to be said than has been attempted.[12] At best, some pieces of deconstructive levers have been inserted at diverse points without any overall calculation of the best way to go about shifting the weight of the critical monuments that support the institution of authorship.

If, however, there is one concern that may be read as uniting these various interventions, it would be the necessity, perhaps more apparent now than ever, to redistribute the revenue or returns of literary "property," or of all that which is upheld by the instance of signature. The institution of authorship has shown a remarkable capacity to return even after being pronounced dead, and its resuscitated form may bear a remarkable resemblance to the ideological construct whose epitaph Barthes wrote too soon. The lesson should be that the authorial institution and the critical attitudes it fosters are not to be simply opposed or thrown over. Such oppositional "strategy" has proved to some extent to be but an anticipation of its own reversal in a new valorization of the "author," the "historical subject," or a "new subject," "intentionality," and so forth. Nor can simple opposition take into account the critic's necessary inscription within the very institution she or he would oppose. For these and other reasons, a deconstructive strategy is called for and is in fact already at work wherever the logic of supposed contraries or oppositions has been instituted on the ground of the differences, contaminations, repetitions, and citations of

---

[12]Within Derrida's oeuvre to date, signature is one of its most constant preoccupations. Besides *Glas*, *Signéponge/Signsponge*, trans. Richard Rand (New York, 1984), *The Truth in Painting*, trans. Geoffrey Bennington and Ian McLeod (Chicago, 1987), and *The Post Card: From Socrates to Freud and Beyond*, trans. Alan Bass (Chicago, 1987) all work on the signature from various angles. While our own analyses remain altogether indebted to these works and others, we will not propose here a reading of Derridean signature theory. Such a reading, however, has been admirably undertaken by Gregory Ulmer in *Applied Grammatology: Post(e)-Pedagogy from Jacques Derrida to Joseph Beuys* (Baltimore, 1985), especially in chaps. 4 and 5, and again in his essay "Sounding the Unconscious," included in John P. Leavey, Jr.'s remarkable *Glassary* (Lincoln, Nebr., 1987).

general textuality. The general text returns to no one; no signature closes it off or gives it its *coup d'envoi*. Rather, it inscribes and limits of what we call signatures; that is, it gives them at once the law of their possibility and impossibility.

It is not a question here of proposing a theoretical program with which to effect the redistribution of textual agencies. The point is precisely that such a "program" is already in effect and already makes its effects felt. While these effects may be structurally determined, there is nonetheless a marked historical tendency for them to accelerate in the age no longer of mechanical, but of electronic, reproduction. Positive copyright law is but one symptomatic area of the general incapacity of a conceptual framework to support or contain the author function disseminated by computer-aided modeling and composition, video reproduction, hypertext data banks, nanotechnology, and so forth.[13] This too is not altogether new, but the institution of authorship has been showing for some time now the strain from the increased pressure on all the profound habits of thought protected by that institution. The choice may seem to be between tearing down its weakened structure to make way for some new construct or patching its too-evident cracks with new materials whose constructive virtues have been overlooked heretofore. Both of these projects, however, risk overlooking once again the nontotalizability of the structure which, like the Tower of Babel, must fall before it can impose the name of its authors, builders, or architects.[14] Thus, such structures are already necessarily deconstructing themselves, displacing

[13]For enthusiastic predictions about the future of such technology, see K. Eric Drexler, *Engines of Creation* (New York, 1986).

[14]"The 'tower of Babel' does not merely figure the irreducible multiplicity of tongues; it exhibits an incompletion, the impossibility of finishing, of totalizing, of saturating, of completing something on the order of edification, architectural construction, system and architectonics. What the multiplicity of idioms actually limits . . . is also a structural order, a coherence of construct. There is then (let us translate) something like an internal limit to formalization, an incompleteness of the constructure. It would be easy and up to a certain point justified to see there the translation of a system in deconstruction." Jacques Derrida, "Des tours de Babel," in *Difference in Translation*, ed. and trans. Joseph F. Graham (Ithaca, N.Y., 1985), 165–66.

themselves around certain pivots which, like levers, are at once inside and outside the systems they fracture. Deconstruction, as the word says, is not just a destruction of an old program, or the putting in place of a new one. Its force is precisely not that of a program or a project, but of an unprogrammed newness that arises there where the old has worn out without yet yielding the ground to a stable and recognizable structure. Its form, if it has one, is pieces that are at once fragments of a totality that never was and parts of a whole that cannot cohere. That, at least, is the wager of these signature pieces.[15]

We have touched on some of the deconstructive levers to be applied in the form of denegations organizing a polemic around the phrase "death of the author." Other touchstones will come into view as the shaping principles of the three sections that make up the book.

Part I, "Rousseau and the Modern Signature," proposes that one historical phase of the "author" concept finds an emblem in the problematic name Rousseau. To a great extent, the tyranny of the Author that Barthes refers to has survived in the form installed by the Rousseauian notion of the writer's expression of "inner self." This is not to say that the tyranny thus unleashed should be traced to a tyrant-subject, for example, Rousseau, who, if he was not exactly authorship's victim, was also hardly its beneficiary. The signature "Rousseau" indicates rather a spectacular encounter between the appropriation of the

[15]One may find pieces of the signature visibly scattered by the effects of that other borderline, the one supposed to divide painting and writing, image and meaning. In "Esquisse d'une typologie," *La Revue de l'art* 26 (1974), Jean-Claude Lebensztejn concludes his typology of the "motivation or non-motivation of signature in paintings" with the example of Paul Klee's *Zerbrochener Schlüssel* (Broken key), which puts this division of intentional from involuntary signature radically in question: "The whole painting, including its title, constitutes a signature-rebus: broken Klee. Broken key [clef] of broken Klee. . . . Among the signs of the painting, one may read what look like exploded letters: K, L, fragments of E. . . . To reach this point, the semiotic opposition between image and writing had to be canceled. They are no longer opposed, and need no longer be isolated from or integrated with each other. A same space of non-representation merges them; and that space from then on engulfs the typology of signature" (55–56). See as well the rest of this issue of *La Revue de l'art* devoted to signature in painting.

text to the name and the expropriation of the name by the text. The expropriating text, moreover, has to be read both in the limited sense of the works Rousseau wrote and signed, but also as the general text on which those works and that signature had themselves to be inscribed. In particular, it is to the emerging concepts of "literary property" and "droit d'auteur" (author's rights) that the signature "Rousseau" must be referred *by law*, a law that itself bears all sorts of signatures as so many marks of appropriation/expropriation. The question arises (most pertinently regarding *Of the Social Contract*) of the signature that validates the law concerning signature in an analogy with property. By considering the establishment of the legal determination of literary property, I am interested in questions not only of historical or "historicist" significance. Rather, this consideration would constitute as well the prolegomenon to a necessary reelaboration of the problematic "literary property" which modern legal treatment continues to understand (despite the ever more obvious insufficiency of the model) according to the conceptual apparatus of authorship as ownership guaranteed by signature.[16]

But it is as well the condemnation of *Emile* and the issuing of a warrant for its author's arrest that underscore the expropriated condition of his signature. In its wake and with the breakup of the name "Rousseau" which is that signature's ambiguous legacy, it becomes possible to read, if not yet a Mallarmean affirmation of the author's dispersal, then at least inescapable intimations that signature occurs, if it occurs, in a difference from itself and an address to the other.

These intimations are explored in terms of sexual difference in part II, "No One Signs for the Other." The breakup affecting the property of Rousseau's signature has already shown up the system of exclusions which determine the name and the voice of woman as outside the law, as outlaw. Two essays, on Baudel-

---

[16]Critical Legal Studies could provide an opening for such a reelaboration in conjunction with the questioning already begun there of the legal models of contract and property. For an overview of this mode of questioning, see Robert Mangabeira Unger, *The Critical Legal Studies Movement* (Cambridge, Mass., 1986).

aire and Virginia Woolf, test further the necessary deconstruction of this system by considering works that are themselves shaped by its demands. For one and the other, the very possibility of signature is its divisibility by the excluded outside: a woman's voice in Baudelaire, a man's law in Woolf. The functions of address or apostrophe for Baudelaire and of interruption for Woolf are, it is suggested, instances of signature where no *one* signs, where singularity is traced in the encounter with the finitude that already partitions it. Not far in the background of both of these essays one may read certain questions posed to the establishment of women's writing as determined by the identity of signature, to "the explanation of a work . . . sought in the man or woman who produced it" in Barthes's twenty-year-old phrase.[17] The unnerving of a discourse that (once again) identifies its major stakes with the subvention of property and the classification of subjects constitutes, therefore, something like the horizon of these essays.

Part III, "Resistance Theories," engages with that discourse in a more direct attempt to unnerve it. It juxtaposes readings of two essays whose titles announce a struggle: "Against Theory," by Robert Knapp and Walter Benn Michaels, and "The Resistance to Theory," by Paul de Man. The openly oppositional or polemical term of "against" in the first title is shifted by the second title, which repositions the debate over theory on a ground that is more like an underground, the unconscious underpinnings of "resistance." The stakes in the struggle, however, are situated precisely in the admission or denial of such an underground as a force of meaning which does not necessarily return to human agency. When it can be shown that the denial of nonintentional meaning must construct its argument out of all sorts of unintentional meanings, then an unnerving effect is indeed the result. The effect is that of a discourse haunted by the ghost of the author whose disappearance has been covered over or denied.

[17] I have addressed these questions more directly in "Writing Like a Woman," in *Women and Language in Literature and Society*, ed. Sally McConnell-Ginet, Ruth Borker, and Nelly Furman (New York, 1981), and in "Replacing Feminist Criticism," *Diacritics*, Summer 1982.

While the author's ghost assumes several names here (Baudel-aire, Woolf, Wordsworth), one among others comes back and insists: Jean-Jacques Rousseau. Having been "caught" in the attempt, in part I, to engineer his own return and dispersed in the remains of his signature, Rousseau returns in the final pages like a ghost (in French, a *revenant*), having perhaps never really left the scene of these readings. His specter resurfaces, precisely, in the scene of reading, told allegorically (and retold by de Man) as the specular scene of encounter between two intentional subjects, two men. Perhaps Rousseau *names* the experience of reading signatures, that is, he both describes the identificatory mechanism that drives this reading act and puts his own name to the figure of Author who appears in the mirror.

But is there not always something ghostly about a signature written "on the basis of the death of someone who has never been alive"? It is an unnerving remainder or reminder, a frag-ment that was never wholly of the whole, be it author or work. Reading signature pieces cannot, therefore, offer a method of exorcism, restitution, or any other rite performed in view of some eternal life. The wager is of another order which puts on the line not life and death but, precisely, the line of their separa-tion, the "single line divided."

PART I

ROUSSEAU AND THE MODERN SIGNATURE

Barbarus hic ego sum, quia non intelligor illis.
—Ovid

CHAPTER ONE

The Name of a Problem

What if one were to read "Rousseau" as signature, and the works signed by that name as support for the signature? Is such an order tenable, does it hold together, will it get us anywhere to think an inversion or a literalization of the figure of the signature? Let us say Rousseau wrote what he wrote so as to have something to do with his signature. This is not to suggest a psychological motivation that we would pretend to be able to detect. The "logic" we want to isolate is both before and beyond "psycho-logic." Indeed, it is this lack of coincidence—at once an excess and a lack—between the signature and the proper name which installs the problem we want to consider in the case of "Rousseau." As to why that signature before any other, we can do no better than refer to Jacques Derrida's answers to a similar question.

The second part of *Of Grammatology* opens with a series of questions about the choice of the "age of Rousseau" as exemplary of the West's logocentric metaphysics: "Why accord an 'exemplary' value to the 'age of Rousseau'? What privileged place does Jean-Jacques Rousseau occupy in the history of logocentrism? What is meant by that proper name? And what are the relationships between that name and the texts to which it was underwritten?" Several pages of introduction propose a preliminary form for the answers that Derrida will work out at length in his following chapters. Rousseau's work, he writes, "seems to me to occupy, between Plato's *Phaedrus* and Hegel's *Encyclopedia*, a singular position." This singular situation is ascribed to a new model of presence: "Rousseau is undoubtedly the only one or the first one to make a theme or a system of the reduction of writing profoundly implied by the entire age . . . but [he] starts from a new model of presence: the subject's self-presence within *consciousness* or *feeling*." But the "privilege" that is accorded here—the privilege of being first—goes less to Rousseau than to "Rousseau," that is, to the name: "The names of authors or of doctrines have here no substantial value. They indicate neither identity nor causes. . . . The indicative value that I attribute to them is first *the name of a problem"* (italics added).[1] "Rousseau" is the name of a problem, the problem of the idealist exclusion of writing—of materiality, of exteriority—in the name of the subject's presence to itself. *Of Grammatology's coup de force* against this exclusion has meant, first of all, that one can no longer approach Rousseau's text with complacent disregard for the supplementary writing that takes the self-present concept beyond itself.[2] Rousseau will have been transformed, reinscribed as "Rousseau." Second, therefore, the transformation will have made of Rousseau's problem not an isolated aberration nor an individual case. Rather, the name "Rousseau" can now be said to supplement the signature on any text and to make of its property, its identity, a problem.

And it is in this sense that we can speak of "Jean-Jacques Rousseau" as the first "modern" signature. We take "Rousseau" to name the problem of a signature that cannot sign for itself, by which we mean both that it carries no guarantee of authenticity and that it cannot sign on its own. This is not just Rousseau's problem, but for reasons to be explored one may say that his texts uncover the structural limits on the properness of

[1]Derrida, *Of Grammatology*, trans. Gayatri Chakravorty Spivak (Baltimore, 1976), 97–99.

[2]Or it means that one can no longer be satisfied with such disregard when it is encountered in "new" readings of Rousseau, such as Tzvetan Todorov, *Frêle Bonheur, essai sur Rousseau* (Paris, 1985), as well as his presentation of an anthology of essays on Rousseau's political writings, *Pensée de Rousseau* (Paris, 1985).

any signature. In Derrida's reading, Rousseau's notion of truth as self-presence is made to depend on the reliable authenticity of a subject's expression of some "internal feeling." In this expressive relation between the interiority of feeling and the exteriority of discourse, only the subject can say what only the subject feels, but his word is no guarantee that he indeed feels what he expresses or expresses what he feels. Having once engaged his word to speak only the truth that he feels, Rousseau will find himself constrained to multiply the acts of guaranteeing with another signature what he has already signed. Yet no single act of signing can ever sign for itself, and this leaves the door open to all sorts of improprieties and expropriations.

By the "modern" signature we also understand one that compels a certain fascination for the living author or the life of the signatory. It is a fascination exercised in the wake of texts like the *Confessions* or the *Rêveries*, the autobiographical writings with which Rousseau tried to pin down his own signature on such volatile works as *Du contrat social* and *Emile*. The fascination that compulsively substitutes the narrative of a life for the disjunctions and disruptions of a work found its first or at least its most receptive repository in Rousseau himself. Rousseau's writing "career" (by which we mean the career of the signature "Rousseau") is, we might say, emblematic of what was to become the *sense* of signature in a postclassical age, the age of the writing subject writing about itself or in its own name. Since "Rousseau," it has seemed only natural to ask: In whose name? The demand to know who signs, the move to authenticate the signature are gestures that Rousseau was, to a significant extent, the first to perform and he performed them on "himself" in somewhat the same way that Freud, the founder of another institution of self-reflection, had to perform his own analysis. To an important extent unlike both Augustine and Montaigne (his apparent precursors), Rousseau wrote his *Confessions* to justify and authenticate a signature already circulating widely so that, at a certain point in its career (after the ban on *Emile* and the pursuit of the author), his signature is entirely concerned with *countersigning* what had already been signed. And it is this necessity of doubling itself that marks a certain turn (or turnover) in the history of signature. Indeed, one could justifiably speak of a historicization or narrativization of the signature. Doubling itself, the signature "Rousseau" uncovers what must always divide it; it exposes the limit at which one signs—and signs again.

Two moments of Rousseau's signature display this limit in a very economical way. Provisionally, we will call them the first and last instances of "Rousseau." We can also, therefore and just as provisionally, call the narrative they bracket its history.

Rousseau the First, Rousseau the Second

In book IV of *The Confessions*, a remarkable tangle occurs that crosses the name "Rousseau" first with a pseudonym, then with a homonym. To straighten things out, Rousseau signs.

During the winter 1730–31, Rousseau is living in Lausanne under the anagrammatic name of Vaussore de Villeneuve and passing himself off (although not too successfully) as a Parisian music teacher.[3] In April 1731, he travels as Vaussore to the border town of Soleure where he is cornered by the French ambassador (who must have had his reasons for suspecting the young man's story) and led to give up his masquerade. In this brief account of his confession of his identity to a representative of France, one may already read a *mise en abîme* of *The Confessions* as a whole:

> Having given myself out as a Parisian, I was, as such, under his Excellency's jurisdiction. He asked me who I was, and exhorted me to tell the truth. I promised to do so, and asked him for a private audience, which was granted. The Ambassador took me to his study, and shut the door. I threw myself at his feet and kept my word. I should not have confessed less, even if I had made no promise; for a continual need of opening my heart brings it at every moment to my lips.[4]

---

[3]Christie McDonald has analyzed some elements of this episode with particular attention to the musical improvisation/impersonation in "En-harmoniques: L'anagramme de Rousseau," *Etudes Françaises* 17 (October 1981).

[4]*The Confessions of Jean-Jacques Rousseau*, trans. J. M. Cohen (London, 1953), 161. Translations are from this edition with pages noted in parentheses.

The episode impresses the ambassador, who is so "pleased with my little story, and with the way he saw I poured out my heart in telling it to him [et de l'effusion de coeur avec laquelle il vit que je l'avais contée]," that he intervenes to straighten out the young man's affairs and set him on the road to Paris, where, indeed, Rousseau will endeavor to make his fortune as a musician. No sooner, however, has the young man left his private audience with the ambassador, no sooner has Vaussore the musician changed places with Rousseau the Genevan watchmaker's son, than this Rousseau aspires to change places with the other Rousseau, the poet.

> M. de la Martinière, secretary to the embassy, was, in a manner, entrusted with the care of me. While showing me to the room which was intended for me, he said: "This room, in the time of the Comte du Luc, was occupied by a celebrated man of the same name as yourself; it rests with you to supply his place in every respect, so that it may one day be said *Rousseau premier, Rousseau second.*" This similarity, of which at that time I had little hopes, would have flattered my ambition less, if I had been able to foresee how heavy would be the price I should one day have to pay for it.
>   M. de la Martinière's words excited my curiosity. I read the works of the writer whose room I occupied; and, having regard to the compliment which had been paid me, and believing that I had a taste for poetry, I composed a cantata. (162; 1:157)

For as long as he thought his chances for renown—for making a name for himself—lay in that direction, Rousseau practiced more or less systematically his imitations of Jean-Baptiste Rousseau. In a prefatory note to one of the few published poems,[5] the editor of the journal invokes the same homonymy

---

Modifications to the translation are not noted. When no published translation of a work of Rousseau's is available, translations are my own from the *Oeuvres complètes*, ed. Bernard Gagnebin and Marcel Raymond (Paris, 1959–69); volume and page numbers of this edition will also be included in parentheses (e.g., 1:157).

[5] Rousseau, "Epître à M. Bordes," *Journal de Verdun*, March 1743; see 2: 1130–33.

to compliment the young poet: "You will see . . . that he is able to support the renown of the great name he bears, and that if he continues to practice Poetry, and to perfect his practice, it may well happen one day that the inhabitants of Parnassus will say: Rousseau I, Rousseau II."[6] Rousseau himself makes a somewhat different prediction in a fragment written long after he had given up his aspirations as a poet:

> Neither Homer nor Virgil was ever called a great man although they were very great Poets. Some authors have gone to great lengths during my life to call the Poet Rousseau the great Rousseau. When I die, the Poet Rousseau will be a great Poet, but he will no longer be the great Rousseau. While it is not impossible for an author to be a great man, it is not by writing books, whether in verse or in prose, that he will become one. (Fragment 38; 1:1129)

This fragment makes clear a structure at work in the first encounter with the homonym at Soleure: to sign "Rousseau" is to take the name of the already monumentalized Poet, but also already to see one's name as a monument left to stand in the place of life, after death.

The Telltale Heart

These various crossings of Rousseau's identity, the slipping from pseudonym to homonym, can be traced to the structure of what passes as the one moment of true naming. At the heart of this truth, which stands between a fraud and a copy, is the metaphor of a heart made manifest. In confessing his real name, Rousseau had, he writes, his heart on his lips, "son coeur sur ses lèvres," and the ambassador was moved to generosity (even though he had just heard the confession of a fraud) because of the "way he saw I poured out my heart in telling it to him." Having promised to tell the truth of who he is, Rousseau honors his word but he gives even more than he promised: not just his word, not just his name, but the truth of both word and name which is the heart.

[6]Cited by the editors in a note, 2:1893. This quotation suggests that Rousseau might have misremembered or simply invented M. de la Martinière's remark, attributing to him the formula that another had used much later.

To tell the truth when one has promised to do so is to leave open to question whether one is telling the truth or keeping a promise. Rousseau seems to anticipate this question because he writes: "I should not have confessed less, even if I had made no promise" ("Je n'aurais pas moins dit quand je n'aurais rien promis").[7] What would be at issue is whether this truth comes from the subject, who gives his name of himself and to himself, or whether the truth of the name lies outside the subject which it names in a contract with some other. The movement of the "coeur" from inside to outside appears to decide this question because it gives the name its seal of truth from within and makes of the contractual promise to the other an external and unnecessary circumstance. With his heart on his lips, Rousseau has a reinforced instrument with which both to tell the truth *and* to tell that he is telling the truth. If this episode might be taken as a model of the felicitous or successful confession of identity (which is also an excuse for the false identity "Vaussore"), it is because it leaves no room for doubting the truth of what is being told. The gap into which such doubt might have slipped is closed off when the heart moves to the lips and puts its seal on what is spoken.

Rousseau's "effusion de coeur" seems to have a unidirectional sense, from inside to outside. But that phrase itself occurs in an ambiguous syntactic location between the two parties to this speech act. The ambassador was, we read, "content de ma petite histoire et de l'effusion de coeur avec laquelle *il vit* que je l'avais contée [with the way *he saw* I poured out my heart]." No doubt the ambassador saw many things in the course of the scene in his office—tears or gestures (Rousseau writes that he threw himself at the feet of his interlocutor, although that may be just another manner of speaking). To say, however, that he *saw* an "effusion de coeur" is to compound a metaphor of expression by a metaphor of reception. The effect of this use of the verb *to see* is to blind one to the first metaphor and to lend a phenomenal appearance to the heart's invisible metaphoricity.

---

[7]In the first version of *Du contrat social*, Rousseau insists that "there is a great difference between executing what one had promised, because one has promised it, and still wanting it even if one had not previously promised it" (3:315–16).

The second metaphor, in other words, covers and covers for the first. A complicity links the mode of recounting his identity ("mon coeur sur mes lèvres") to the mode of receiving that account.

And, in fact, in the phrase "l'effusion de coeur avec laquelle il vit que je l'avais contée," a second syntactic possibility designates the "effusion de coeur" as coming from the ambassador, more precisely as that *with* which the ambassador "sees" Rousseau's account of his name: the outpouring of the heart *with which he saw* that I had told it. This eccentric reading goes against the sense of the story—Rousseau's interiority made manifest—because it situates the metaphor of the heart in a space between its emission and reception. It also complicates considerably the scene we are trying to read because, instead of an interiority made manifest, it now seems that the heart is a metaphor for the interval of meaning—its pulsing rhythm—between intention and reception, and that that metaphor has been internalized. To say Rousseau's confession of his name interiorizes the metaphor of interiority is but to remark once again that it literalizes the figure by closing a gap within the subject who speaks "from the heart." Rousseau, we could say, has been literally taken in by the metaphor that represents the meaning of meaning as an interiority to be poured out. When, therefore, he pours out his name, the metaphor acts itself out and carries its interval over to the very heart of the truth the subject can speak about himself. The heart seals or signs the account only when it has been doubled in the heart-to-heart, only once the ambassador can "see" with his heart all the heart Rousseau put into his story. This is to say that the confession is signed "Jean-Jacques Rousseau" from the place of the other as represented in the story by that representative of the French sovereign, the ambassador.

But is it also to say that anyone can sign in Rousseau's place?

Double Trouble

To begin to measure the pertinence of the latter question, we must let this history of Rousseau's signature continue to unfold. For, in fact, the confession at Soleure is not sealed off by the scene in the ambassador's closed office, but goes on duplicating itself. We have already remarked this condition when we pointed to the *mise en abîme* of *The Confessions* in the episode. The account in book IV marks a folding back on itself of the text of *The Confessions* to that point. Because of this duplicating structure, a reader might fail to notice that Rousseau reports nothing whatsoever of what he said to the ambassador during their private audience. The assumption is perhaps too easily made that he confessed to some abbreviated version of his life and adventures as recorded in books I–IV. That assumption, however, merely comes to fill the place left vacant in the account. All one can really affirm is that Rousseau claims that he spoke passionately and that his speech was received sympathetically. Nothing in the account excludes the possibility that the ambassador heard yet another story from Rousseau alias Vaussore, and indeed several details suggest that the young man may have presented himself as an aspiring poet in need of a benefactor. This would explain, for example, why M. de la Martinière, who had not been present to hear the boy's story, wanted to see a sample of his style: "M. de la Martinière wanted to see how I could write [voulut voir de mon style], and asked me to give him in writing the same details as I had given to the ambassador. I wrote him a long letter [Je lui écrivis une longue lettre] . . ." (163; 1:157).

Whatever may have been the secretary's reasons for requesting it, this letter, which duplicates an act of confession, acquires an authenticating function. Or at least it is to such a virtual function that Rousseau points when he cites the continued existence of the letter: "I wrote him a long letter, which I hear has been preserved. . . . I have asked M. de Malesherbes to try and get me a copy of this letter. If I can procure it through him or through others, it will be found in the collection which is intended to accompany my Confessions." This letter, if it could be produced, would supply the account of Rousseau's confession to the ambassador that is missing from *The Confessions*. Or rather, since nothing can guarantee that Rousseau did not give different accounts of himself to the ambassador and to the secretary, producing the letter would tend to substantiate at least one of these accounts. But this would not seem to be the principal concern here. Rather, the concern is with a guarantee for the signature "Jean-Jacques Rousseau" on a text— *The Confessions*—that is itself but the explanation or description of its signature. If one were to put this guarantee in writing, so to speak, it would have to read something like this: I, the signatory of *The Confessions of Jean-Jacques Rousseau*, declare that this is a true account and, as proof of that statement, I submit a copy of a letter in question there in which the signatory, Jean-Jacques Rousseau, declares that he is Jean-Jacques Rousseau and no other. By doubling and redoubling itself, Rousseau's signature would attempt to sign for itself. One can easily see, however, that this structure cannot be closed off and that, having signed once, Rousseau cannot sign once and for all. Every signature, including the "first" signature from the heart, depends on, is constituted by the possibility of its repetition, for example, the repetition in its reception by the ambassador in Rousseau's account. But this is also to say that every signature includes a deviation from itself which may also be an opening for error, falsehood, or duplicity.[8]

Rousseau, it seems, never received the copy of his letter to M. de la Martinière which he requested. Others continued the search, however, and in 1824 the Musset-Pathay edition published for the first time the text of a letter from the copy submitted by a certain M. Dubois of Geneva. It begins thus: "To M. de la Martinière, Secretary to the Embassy at Soleure: I have recounted to you my foolishness and my errors. You have asked me to put them in writing; I obey your orders. Here is a summary."[9] There follows a rapid telescoping of books I–IV of *The Confessions*, which hits all the high points of decision along the road leading from Geneva to Soleure via Annecy, Turin, Lyon, and Lausanne. This letter, in other words, corresponds neatly to the assumption with which the reader might have already filled

---

[8]See below, pt. III, chap. 7, for a further discussion of iterability and possible deviation.

[9]Rousseau, *Oeuvres inédites*, ed. V. D. Musset-Pathay (Paris, 1824), 1:3–6.

the gap left in the account. The unbroken succession of briefly declarative sentences that make up this résumé resembles more a procès-verbal than the pathetic outpouring that was supposed to have so impressed the ambassador. Subsequent editors and scholars have concluded that the letter is a forgery.[10]

This postscript to the confession at Soleure, which is only one of the many frauds perpetrated in the name of "Rousseau," would be of limited interest if it did not seem to act out, in a perverse manner, the principle of iteration and deviation dividing Rousseau's signature. The episode of the signed confession of his identity contained already in embryo the counterfeit that "M. Dubois de Genève" merely brought to term. Or, put another way, the false letter arrives because it was dispatched along with the missing original that it imitates. At the origin, already, Rousseau cannot sign "Rousseau" without engaging the doubling mechanism that reproduces, with machinelike indifference, both "true" and "false" copies.

Declaring Something

We suggested earlier that the episode at Soleure may be taken as a first instance in the history of the signature "Rousseau." The artifice of such a positioning—it was just a place to begin—should now be clear since an account of the signature at Soleure cannot remain within the strict limits of a historical narrative inaugurated by a designated firstness. The "first" signature reproduces itself long after the signatory has ceased to be able to sign. The artifice is no less evident when we close the brackets within which this "history" was suspended and cite the opposing term: Rousseau's "last" signature. This time, however, it is the signatory who would declare that he has signed for the last time.

[10]"One senses that it has been fabricated after a reading of *The Confessions* and nothing about it recalls Jean-Jacques's style at any period of his life," writes Théophile Dufour in *Correspondance générale* (Paris, 1924), 1:4. See also Pierre-Maurice Masson, "Le Séjour de J.-J. Rousseau à l'Hospice du Spirito Santo," *Revue d'Histoire Littéraire de la France* 21 (1914), 63, n. 5.

[Declaration concerning various reprintings of his works][11]

When J.J. Rousseau discovered that certain people were hiding themselves from him in order to print his writings secretly in Paris, and that they asserted publicly that it was he who directed these reprintings, he quickly understood that the principal aim of this maneuver was the falsification of these same writings and he wasted no time, despite all the care that was taken to prevent his awareness, from convincing himself with his own eyes of this falsification. . . . Thus, since his writings, in the form that he composed them and published them, no longer exist except in the first edition of each work that he prepared himself, and that have long ago disappeared from public view, *he declares all former and new books printed or that will be printed from now on under his name, in any place whatsoever, to be either forged or altered, mutilated and falsified, with cruelest malignity, and he disavows them as being either no longer his work or falsely attributed to him* [*il déclare tous les livres anciens ou nouveaux, qu'on imprime et qu'on imprimera désormais sous son nom, en quelque lieu que ce soit, ou faux ou altérés, mutilés et falsifiés, avec la plus cruelle malignité, et les désavoue, les uns comme n'étant plus son ouvrage, et les autres comme lui étant faussement attribués*]. Since he is helpless to bring his complaints to the ears of the public, he has been led to try as a last resort distributing to various persons copies of this declaration, written and signed by his hand [écrites et signées de sa main], certain that if among their number there is a single honest and generous soul who has not sold itself to iniquity, then such a necessary and just protest will not remain stifled, and posterity will not judge the sentiments of an unfortunate man on the basis of books that have been disfigured by his persecutors.

Paris, 23 January 1774   J. J. ROUSSEAU

(1:1186–87; italics added)

Although the date on this declaration situates its composition close to the end of Rousseau's life and although, in fact, after that date he would authorize no other first edition of his signature (*Les Confessions, Rousseau juge de Jean-Jaques,* and *Les*

[11]"Déclaration relative à différentes réimpressions de ses ouvrages"; this title is the editor's.

Rêveries were all first published posthumously), these punctual facts do not of themselves suffice for one to read this "Declaration" as carrying Rousseau's "last" signature. They do not, that is, suffice for a reading of the relation between this declaration about a signature and the signature that signs it.

To declare is to make manifest, to make something known, for example, to declare one's intentions or feelings, to declare love or enmity, or to declare that something is in fact the case. In this latter instance, the declaration functions on one level as a statement or constative, an utterance that, in theory at least, can be verified. But a declaration is often a particularly marked constative, a statement of fact that states that it is a true statement of fact. For example, a customs declaration of the sort one completes before entering or reentering the United States is incomplete if one neglects to sign the form in the space following the printed words: "I have read the above statements and have made a truthful declaration." Even if one has "nothing to declare," there is no crossing the symbolic border until one has signed. The constative declaration is incomplete unless accompanied by a performative, an act of signing. Other examples could be cited that would show that this kind of declaration always implies a signature or a subscription to a statement that is being made. If a declaration of this sort is made in someone's name, then to verify it is to check not a general order of fact but a *correspondence* between some state of things and a particular instance of declaring something about that state assumed by a signatory in his or her name. That is, the signature, in these instances, is first of all an instrument for the particularization of a law's application to those who are subject to the law.

While, however, this declaration implies or requires a signature, it is also the case that the signature implies a declaration of the sort: I declare that I am in truth s/he whose name I here sign. There is, in other words, a mutual implication of constative declaration and the performance of signature—each resting on and implying the prior establishment of the other. Such implications are not to be easily sorted out even by the most rigorous customs regulations. The "Declaration concerning various reprintings of his works" applies this logic of the mutual implication of constative and performative declarations to the breaking point. The signatory, J. J. Rousseau, known to the public at large as the author who has also signed a number of highly provocative works, declares that he is not the author of any work printed under his name "désormais," from now on. This temporal marker or deictic is the mark of a performative force since it situates the effective date of a revised state of affairs: "from now on." In principle, only a dated signature can validate this act, but it is precisely the validity of that signature which has just been canceled by the decree denouncing from now on the signature "J. J. Rousseau" as false. The declaration is not valid unless signed, but how can it be signed without invalidating what is declared—to wit, that from now on the signature "J. J. Rousseau" is false? Thus, the question this text poses would be the following: How can a signature declare its own termination, put an end to itself, and yet still hold in reserve one last place and time to sign so as to validate the act of termination?

This problem will not in the least be resolved when, instead of printing his declaration, Rousseau distributes *in person* copies that are, as he writes, "écrites et signées de ma main."[12] To find in Rousseau's person an ultimate support for the signature that rescues it from the divisions imposed by the text is to try to take refuge in an *absent* term of presence or "lived experience." To be sure, this model of extratextual verifiability is variously invoked in the text of the declaration (principally through the several figures of bodily organs),[13] but this only tends to confirm that no presence outside the text speaks for the signature. Nor will it suffice to assert that Rousseau *meant* to sign his declaration with his person or his presence. The prob-

---

[12]As to why and how Rousseau distributed his declaration "à diverses personnes" instead of publishing it, see the editor's note 3, 1:1872. One cited source claims that various journal editors refused to publish it; another that it was published in *La Gazette de Littérature, des sciences et des arts,* but this reference cannot be verified. Both of these sources would seem to be contradicted by the internal logic of the text.

[13]For example, "par ses yeux," "par ses propres yeux," "aux yeux du public," "aux oreilles du public," "de sa main."

lematic signature in and on the text cannot be dispelled by such an assertion.[14]

Why not just overlook all this and read Rousseau's gesture as having a meaning despite or beyond these problems of execution? His declared disavowal is but an understandable attempt to distinguish between his signature and its various simulacra. But what even this common sense explanation cannot overlook is that the attempt to save the signature from simulacra takes unmistakably the form of condemning it to disappear *from now on*. Only the original signature on the first edition "which he prepared himself" ("qu'il a faite lui-même") would escape this general condemnation, but it is precisely that signature "that has long ago disappeared from public view" ("qui depuis longtemps a disparu aux yeux du public"). Inexorably, the logic that would enforce or legislate an unbridgeable separation of original from reprint, of true signatures from simulacra, can do so only by suppressing what it wants to preserve. This logic demonstrates, therefore, that the only chance for the survival of "Rousseau" as a true signature lies in the perpetuation of an undecidable relation to its simulacra. But its only chance, of course, is as well its greatest risk because the condition of its survival is the lack of any guarantee as to its truth, and it is only on such a condition that we can continue to read "Rousseau." Consider what would have to happen if Rousseau's signature were not so suspended but could somehow have the effect of enforcing the "Declaration" as one made in the name of truth. The name "Rousseau" would no longer truly sign works that are either false attributions or deliberate distortions of lost originals. It would thus survive as the name of an author whose works can be known only through imitations or simulacra.[15]

---

[14]See Derrida, *Of Grammatology*, pt. II, chap. 2: "And one cannot abstract from the written text to rush to the signified it *would mean*, since the signified is here the text itself. It is so little a matter of looking for a *truth signified* by these writings (metaphysical or psychological truth: Jean-Jacques's life behind his work) that if the texts that interest us *mean* something, it is the engagement and the appurtenance that encompass existence and writing in the same *tissue*, the same *text*" (150).

[15]The suspension of the signature on the "Declaration" is made evident when that text can be allowed to take its place in the *Oeuvres complètes de Jean-*

Instead of insisting on the dilemma posed by this quirky gesture, why not just acknowledge that when Rousseau made his declaration he was mad and that such a text can only be read as a symptom of that madness? The declaration poses a false problem because it presupposes a malevolent plot to falsify the signature "Rousseau." To take it too seriously, as I have done, is to credit the persecutory delusion of a conspiracy against him which prompted Rousseau to devise such a defense. It is, in other words, to adopt "madness" as a critical point of view. Once one rules out the mad hypothesis on which is constructed this paranoid theory of the signature, then the declaration may be seen for what it is: a document that could only have been written by someone no longer in his right mind, as one says.

This argument makes sense, by which I mean not only that it is reasonable to doubt Rousseau's universal conspiracy theory. Beyond that, however, it makes sense of what otherwise must continue to trouble our sense of meaning. A "Rousseau-not-in-his-right-mind" explains the aberration of a signature that has to preserve the simulacrum—that may be false—as the only place from which to sign its disavowal of false simulacra. To say what it means—"J. J. Rousseau is no longer a valid signature"— the declaration has to put itself in the position of not meaning what it says, a position of falsity—"signed J. J. Rousseau." This is madness, perhaps, but who is to say it is Rousseau's? Rather than imposing aberrations on his text, this madness would be a madness of the text, the madness of words, of names, and of that special use of names called signature. Rousseau's career as a signer of texts would have displayed a progressive uncovering of the illogical logic of that act, culminating, in a profoundly necessary way, in the declaration we have been reading. Despite the infelicity of its performative, the very fact it is unable to do what it says points to a certain truth that the "Declaration" does not so much declare as leave to function as textual effect. By protesting that his signature is not his, Rousseau is mistaken

---

Jacques Rousseau. It would seem that either the "Declaration" is truly signed by Rousseau, in which case it denounces any "Complete Works" as a fraud, or else the "Declaration" does not really bear Rousseau's signature, in which case one has to ask why it has been collected among his other writings.

only insofar as he understands that condition to be contingent; but *precisely because he is right* in saying his signature is not his, no declaration on his part can reappropriate it from the state of its dispersion by the texts he signs.

The order of meaning according to which a tortured psychological condition dictates an aberrant text, insofar as that order repeats or reflects a unidirectional sense of general meaning, is precisely what is in question in Rousseau's "madness."[16] The error, then, would be to trace the aberration of a text like the "Declaration" to a psychological source and thereby to repeat the very error of paranoia imputed to Rousseau that consists in psychologizing the disfigurement his signature has suffered. The declaration closes in exactly this sense: "posterity will not judge the sentiments of an unfortunate man on the basis of books that have been disfigured *by his persecutors*" ("que la posterité ne [juge] pas des sentiments d'un homme infortuné sur des livres défigurés *par ses persécuteurs*"). The error makes sense by giving the process of disfiguration an Author—an intention, a will, a motive, a cause. The unreadable, produced by contraries that imply rather than exclude each other mutually, becomes readable through the movement of interpretation of a signature, a *supposition d'auteur* that orders all the disparate and discrete marks into the text or *trame* of a plot.

Border Incidents

A signature, however, is not an author or even simply the proper name of an author. It is the mark of an articulation at the border between life and letters, body and language. An articulation both joins and divides; it joins and divides identity with/

---

[16]See Michel Foucault's introduction to *Rousseau juge de Jean-Jaques* (Paris, 1962) which ends in dialogue with an interlocutor who wants to judge the text as mad:

—So you're saying the *Dialogues* is not the work of a madman?

—This question would only matter if it had a meaning; but the work, by definition, is non-madness.

—But surely the structure of a work can allow the figure of illness to appear.

—The decisive point is that the reciprocal possibility does not exist. (xxiii) from difference. A difference from itself, within itself, articulates the signature on the text it signs. This is another reason it cannot be a question here of a *history* of the signature "Rousseau," for that would suppose a possible identification of the signature *itself* as distinct from what it is not. It would also suppose a dating of the signature, an identification of the term of its validity. And, as we have just seen, the signature cannot date itself for the same reason it cannot sign for itself. The signature "Rousseau" can be said to have a history only to the extent that its term is unfinished, yet to be terminated. To put this another way: readings of a signature, which are always more or less the function of some identificatory fascination, are part of its history and, in the case of "Rousseau," not necessarily the least significant part. Nor would such a history be easily distinguishable from the larger political, social, intellectual histories that have, periodically in France, attempted to rewrite themselves through some kind of reading of "Rousseau"—appropriating, expropriating that name's relation to the functioning of subjectivity in the French language and to the position of the individual in the state. Indeed, it would seem that most of the major revisions of French political discourse since the revolution have been accompanied by a reading of Rousseau and a repositioning or reevaluating of the truth of his "je."[17]

Instead of a history of that signature, then, "Rousseau" would offer something like a screen onto which history "itself" has been projected. What perhaps has always been at stake in that

[17]Two recent studies have attempted to specify elements of the political history of transference onto the subject of Rousseau's signature. Georges Benrekassa, in *Fables de la personne: Pour une histoire de la subjectivité* (Paris, 1985), reviews in great detail some nineteenth-century readings of Rousseau that culminated in the French Third Republic's celebration of the centenary of his death in 1878 and the bicentenary of his birth in 1912. In a more familiar mode, Carol Blum, in *Rousseau and the Republic of Virtue: The Language of Politics in the French Revolution* (Ithaca, N.Y., 1986), takes up Robespierre's and Saint-Just's appropriations of Rousseau. For a brief analysis of how Rousseau was read by the reactionary nationalists of the Action Française, see my "Rousseau's Original Language," forthcoming in *The Harvard History of French Literature*, ed. Dennis Hollier.

name is the very possibility of inscribing its truth. "Rousseau" exhibits a problematization of the border and a divisibility of the mark that joins/divides the two poles of the signature—the historically singular subject to which it refers (or seems to refer) and the formal generality of language. Rather than a borderline marked out by the signature, or a line on which the signature signs, this border is itself divided by a line passing somewhere between "Jean-Jacques" and "Rousseau." A text like *Rousseau juge de Jean-Jaques*, for example, seems entirely concerned with soldering the pieces of the signature into a whole, but the double articulation cannot be reduced beyond the line of the hyphen or the *trait d'union* that maintains the interval of difference between the terms it unites. The dividing line, however, has only been displaced because the text that would finally authenticate the signature "J. J. Rousseau" by reducing its duplicity to a single trait has itself to be left unsigned or, more precisely, has to be left for another to sign.

Not a history, then, but a series of border incidents traversing the text "Rousseau" can never quite finish signing. *Rousseau juge de Jean-Jaques* is only the most sustained and self-reflexive of the series, but the scene staged there has been programmed by many other border confrontations. One of these we have already encountered at Soleure, the town on the border between two national states. To cross this symbolic line between two symbolic entities, a signature is required. But in what language does the stranger sign his name? "I have read the above statements and have made a truthful declaration." To cross the line a translation is required. But how is one to translate a signature? "Barbarus hic ego sum, quia non intelligor illis" (I am considered a barbarian here because they do not understand me) is the epigraph Rousseau placed on *Rousseau juge de Jean-Jaques*. It is a citation from Ovid's poem of exile, *Tristia*. The same epigraph appears on the work that was the first to make a name for its signatory: the *Discours sur les sciences et les arts*. Bracketing the two extremes of his work, the Latin verse is like Rousseau's signature which here speaks the despair of its untranslatable condition. A signature cannot be translated, but its trait is still marked in the other's language.

CHAPTER TWO

Contracting the Signature

It may easily be overlooked that Rousseau's most widely read text has as a first title *"Du* contrat social." The preposition in the title tends to disappear, leaving only the definite article, so that one commonly refers to *"Le* Contrat social," or *"The* Social Contract." The truncation is frequently required by the syntax into which the title is inserted: it is clumsy, if not altogether ungrammatical, to speak of *"Of* the Social Contract." The encounter of the two prepositions interrupts the syntactic flow and creates a rift in the fabric of the sentence. Thus a curious effect is set up as soon as one speaks of *Of the Social Contract*: either one quotes or translates the title precisely, disregarding the faulty syntactic articulation, or else one quotes imprecisely, preserving syntactic order. It is as if, to make *Du contrat social* fit certain modes of reference, an excess particle had to be cut off. This uneasy fit would not be too worrisome if one could be certain that only the form of the work's title was being tampered with. But, precisely, the title's form should warn us that nothing is less certain.

In the foreword introducing his text, Rousseau refers to it as a "traité" or treatise. Adding this term to the title yields "un traité du contrat social," or "un [écrit où il est] traité du contrat social."[1] Such a formula seems reassuring as to the stability of

---

[1] See *Oeuvres complètes*, 3:1431, n. 1, for other references to the "traité du contrat social" in the correspondence.

the referential system one is about to enter. This stability, however, begins to tremble once one notices that "traité" and "contrat" are basically the same word put to only slightly different uses. Indeed, "traité" in the sense of "treaty" may be used more or less interchangeably with "contrat" as meaning a convention or agreement between parties. If the "traité du contrat social" is a "contrat du contrat social," then "contrat" is doubly in question as both that which is designated and that which designates it. The term to be defined is included within the defining term. What Paul de Man has shown to be the incompatibility between the constative and performative functions of the contract is thus in place in this text from the very first word of its title.[2] The "du" of *Du contrat social* would mark the articulating joint of these two functions which cannot be closed by the totalizing mechanism that would be the social contract.

This remark implies another reading of the troublesome particle in the title: as the mark that exceeds or prevents a totalizing reference, it signals a certain partialness or partition and suggests the use of "du" as a partitive article. *Du contrat social* might thus be better translated as "Some Social Contract" or even "A Piece of the Social Contract." What one reads would have been "tiré du contrat social," drawn from or taken from a large—we cannot say whole so let us say nontotalizable fabric or texture.

Weaver/Writer/Ruler

With the words *contrat*, *traité*, and *tirer* we remain within the semantic field of *tractum*, the tuft of wool drawn first into a thread before being twisted with other threads (to form the woof) and drawn through the warp. The crossing of these properly textile threads with a textual activity forms one of the most well worn and familiar of patterns. It is, so to speak, woven into the language of contract, treaty, treatise, and text. Contracting to treat the contract, then, Rousseau could hardly have avoided being drawn into a network that, on the other hand, never

[2]De Man, "Promises," in *Allegories of Reading* (New Haven, Conn., 1979).

becomes an explicit theme or analogy. There is, in other words, no attempt to extract from the network some figure of weaving which could then serve as a model or point of reference for the contract to be defined and the contract defining it. Such a model, nevertheless, was clearly available in a text to which *Du contrat social* refers throughout: Plato's dialogue *The Statesman*.[3]

There, it is the paradigm of weaving, the art of interlocking the warp and the woof, which seems to allow the interlocutors to extract the art of the statesman from all the other activities of the city and to place it in the ruling position. The royal weaver is said to command all the other arts that together produce the fabric of the city: his supreme art is to assemble the other arts, which can be classified as arts either of separation and selection or of assemblage and combination. The dialogue, an exercise in dialectics, draws distinctions and draws together in the portrait of the king. But this portrait cannot mask the necessity for the royal weaver's art to be not yet one, not the total art that brings the city together as a whole, but two—assembling *and* separating. In his final traits, which combine all those of his subjects, the weaver/ruler must know how to discard as well as integrate the elements at his disposal:

—Eleatic: Is there any science of combination which, if it can help it, will construct even the meanest of its products of bad materials as well as good? Is it not true universally of every science that, so far as it may, it discards the bad materials and retains the appropriate and good, whether they are alike or unlike? It is by working them into one whole that it fabricates a product of single quality and form?
—Socrates Junior: Why surely.
—Eleatic: Then we may be sure that neither will true natural statesmanship ever, if she can avoid it, construct a city out of good men and bad alike. . . . Hence those who prove incapable of any share in the brave and the modest temper and the other dispositions which tend to virtue, but are driven by their native evil

[3]There are references to this dialogue in bk. II, chaps. 7 and 8, and bk. III, chap. 6, as well as in the "Manuscrit de Genève," bk. I, chap. 5.

constitution to irreligion, violence, and crime, she expels by the punishment of death or exile, or visits with superlative infamy.[4]

This double art is reflected so closely in the procedure of the dialectician that from time to time he stops and asks his pupils whether their aim is to learn the traits of the weaver king or the traits of their own art. Weaving is a metaphor for ruling, which is a metaphor for writing, which is a metaphor . . .

Fringe Benefits

Yet, as we said, despite the metaphoric field into which the *tractum* draws Rousseau's text, Plato's paradigm of weaving finds no explicit echo in *Du contrat social*. The double arts of assembling and separating, gathering and discarding are given no single and totalizing point of reference outside their contrary, contracting movement through the text. The movement extends beyond the text's limits: it is not set in motion at its outset, nor does it conclude where the text concludes. Both of these limits are but arbitrary cuts made in the chain of the social contract. That the work titled *Du contrat social* had to be cut from a larger fabric, that the treatise is a contraction and an extraction, is remarked at either edge of the text. These pieces of *Of the Social Contract*, neither simply inside nor outside the treatise, would be like the fringe on a woven fabric, the slight extension of the chain or the warp necessary to prevent an unraveling along the line of the cut.

(A question we hold in reserve: If one must sign at the edge of the text, how can these fringelike extensions support a signature?)

We have already mentioned one of these pieces: the *avertissement* or foreword from which we drew the term "traité." It is very brief, but its brevity does not rule out a certain complexity.

Ce petit *traité* est *extrait* d'un ouvrage *plus* étendu, entrepris autrefois sans avoir consulté mes forces et abandonné depuis

---

[4]Trans. A. E. Taylor (New York, 1971), 308 D–E, 339–40.

longtemps. Des divers morceaux qu'on pouvait *tirer* de ce qui était fait, celui-ci est le *plus* considérable, et m'a paru le moins indigne d'être offert au public. Le reste n'est déjà *plus*. (3:349; italics added)

(This little treatise is part of [extracted from] a longer work, which I began years ago without realizing my limitations, and long since abandoned. Of the various fragments that might have been extracted from what I wrote, this is the most considerable and, I think, the least unworthy of being offered to the public. The rest no longer exists.)[5]

The trait of the *tractum* insists in these several lines that confirm the partial status of this treatise extracted from a more extensive work which we had already begun to read in the title. Also, despite the conciseness and the apparently limited functionality of these lines, a note of pathos is struck which warns one to read this warning label carefully. The extraction and setting apart of a part of the social contract may not have been such a simple operation. The very least one can say is that it does not cut out a piece from some larger cloth along a clean, indivisible line, but rather the cut itself takes on a certain extension or breadth that is contained by neither the part nor the whole even though it is produced by nothing but their differentiation. This "nothing but," in other words, is not simply nothing: the differentiation of partial text from more extensive text has been negotiated in yet another text that sets the terms of the division or extraction. And these terms describe a zigzagging pattern in the space of just three sentences.

Besides the three different inflections of *tractum* ("traité," "extrait," "tiré"), the word "plus" occurs in each sentence and each time is pulled in a different direction. From the comparative "un ouvrage plus étendu" to the superlative "[le morceau] le plus considérable," the movement of the signifier goes counter to the movement of the signified from larger extension to smaller piece. This double movement negotiates the terms by

---

[5]Trans. G. D. H. Cole (London, 1973), 164. Further references to this translation are included in parentheses in the text.

which the smaller unit—"ce petit traité" called *Du contrat social*—can be considered "le plus considérable" and taken as a part to represent the whole. The displacement of a "plus étendu" by its lesser but most considerable representative is completed and rendered irreversible by the final use of "plus" as a temporal adverb: "Le reste n'est déjà plus."

The syntax of this latter sentence demands that it posit the very remains that it states no longer exist. The predicament can be rendered if one translates the phrase as "There remain no remains," where, in spite of what is declared, something remains. But it is this sentence as well that gives the little hors d'oeuvre its predominant note of pathos, and one has little difficulty picturing the somewhat pitiable scene of Rousseau, his strength exhausted on a work he could not finish, forced finally to destroy the greater part of it. Besides being unlikely,[6] this scene may be diverting one's attention from the drama on the page which follows a somewhat different scenario.

What is pitiable there is that the movement—put in motion by a desire—to represent the whole comes up against the obstacle of an excess of articulation that cannot be incorporated into the representative part or made to disappear with the rest. This surplus would be something like the contract of the *Of the Social Contract*, that is, of a text in which the issue is the contract between a particularity and a more extensive generality. We could thus say that, in or at this fringe, *Du contrat social contracts itself*: on the one hand, it contracts with itself, negotiating an incorporation of whole into part; on the other hand, this act of incorporation is effected only by means of a contraction or constriction of the larger extension. These are

---

[6]To be sure, one cannot produce evidence that Rousseau did *not* destroy something of this larger work that he several times refers to as *Institutions politiques*. Such an action would, however, have gone counter to his habits, which tended toward an accumulation and conservation of the least fragment. What is more, a number of fragments concerning political institutions do survive and have been collected in the *Oeuvres complètes*. Finally, there is as well the "Manuscrit de Genève," the first version of *Du contrat social*. One of its most important sections, "De la société générale du genre humain," was never integrated into the final version. On the question of destroyed manuscripts, see 3:1431, n. 3.

the terms that allow a work titled *Du contrat social* to be "offert au public." In that work, however, what is described is a social contract that contracts itself in apparently the opposite direction: particular will incorporated into general will, part contracting itself into the whole. To put it another way, *Du contrat social* is the result of a contract whose terms reverse those of the social contract to be defined and described within. This reversal is the fold of a textuality that can never incorporate the surplus of its performance in what it can say about itself. A remainder will remain, even or rather especially when it is stated that nothing remains.

A Signature Surplus

This is already to read an entire program in the three sentences of the *avertissement*. Specifically, we are reading a textual program that exceeds and, to some extent, overturns the terms of the contract it also allows one to describe. But we have not yet exhausted all one may read there. It is implied that the contraction of the "ouvrage plus étendu" into "ce petit traité" is due to an outside constraint rather than an internal necessity, internal, that is, to the logic of the work. The outside constraint is "mes forces," which were exhausted before I, Rousseau, could complete the whole work. The limits of *Du contrat social* correspond, then, to the limits of "mes forces," whereas the unrealized "ouvrage plus étendu" would have corresponded to a desire that exceeds those limits. Such a description of a constraining exteriority fits more or less with the conventional representation of author as simply external to the work signed, somewhat in the manner of cause and effect. By remarking the place of the signature on *Du contrat social*, however, the *avertissement* renders this simple representation of exteriority inadequate to account for the notion of a forced signature, for the resignation to a force of contraction. The signature of *Of the Social Contract* is here described as contracted by a force exercising a limiting constraint on the extension that that signature would embrace if it were carried only by desire. But there is a problem with this description, the problem precisely of the place of the signature, which arises from the unmistakable resemblance between the signature *on* the text and a signature *in* the text, between the signing of *Of the Social Contract* and a signing in *Of the Social Contract* of the social contract.[7]

The air of resemblance is most striking in the following passage, which was deleted in the final version:

> Let us begin by enquiring whence the need for political institutions arises.
>
> Man's strength is so strictly proportionate to his natural needs and to his primitive state that when this state changes, or these needs increase, be it ever so slightly, the help of his fellow-men becomes necessary to him. When, finally, his desires encompass the whole of nature, the co-operation of the whole human race is hardly sufficient to satisfy them. (155; 3:281–82)

This general description of the disproportion between a limited quantity of force and an unlimited extension of desire concurs with the particular version of that disproportion which Rousseau gives in the *avertissement*. There is as yet nothing too problematic at this level of resemblance: the condition of a particular man, divided by the difference between his force and his desire, is the same as the condition of every man no longer in "his primitive state." Yet it is also this principle of resemblance between the particular and the general, between *man* and *whole human race* (*le genre humain*), which, it is implied, is responsible for the divisive disproportionality of a desire to embrace "the whole of nature." With the power to conceive the generality of "le genre humain" (the power of the principle of

---

[7]Geoffrey Bennington has remarked that the aporia of performance of the contractual promise described by de Man ("Promises," in *Allegories of Reading*) draws into it the very possibility of a signature. "The immediate effect of this aporia is to threaten any possible empirical 'happiness' of the performance of the contractual promise by splitting open the instant in which any such performance must be assumed to take place. De Man writes, 'every promise assumes a date at which the promise is made and without which it would have no validity' (273); but the aporia in the structure of the contract makes such dating (and its corollary, signing, not mentioned by de Man) strictly speaking impossible." *Sententiousness and the Novel: Laying Down the Law in Eighteenth-Century French Fiction* (Cambridge, 1985), 161.

resemblance) comes the desire to have power over that generality, a desire that quickly encounters the obstacle of one man's limited strength.[8] There are two possible exits from this impasse: some form of enslavement, in which the force of a multitude of men is made to serve the desires of one man; and the social contract, in which the parties agree that the only way they will realize their desires is through the medium of what will be called the general will. In the definitive version of this moment, which Rousseau restates in preamble to the precise terms of the contract in book I, chapter 6, the choice of enslavement has been effectively eliminated. The only alternative to the social contract is quite simply the end of the human species:

> I suppose men to have reached the point at which the obstacle in the way of their preservation in the state of nature shows their power of resistance to be greater than the resources at the disposal of each individual for his maintenance in that state. That primitive condition can then subsist no longer; and the human race would perish unless it changed its manner of existence. (173; 3:360)

Few readers of *Du contrat social* have failed to notice that the distinction of a just from an unjust social order at every point threatens to collapse around the lack of a stable referent for the general will. But it is not this internal instability that I will pursue at this point. Rather, I want to return to the question of resemblance between the signing of the social contract—an act that, in the literal or historical sense, never takes place, that is itself structurally impossible—and the signing of *Of the Social Contract*. As we have already remarked, the resemblance between these two acts seems at first motivated by a structure of inclusion: Rousseau's particular condition is included within a general condition of humanity. The shift that is evoked from the equilibrium of a state in which "men's strength is . . . pro-

---

[8]Farther on in the same part of the text, one reads: "It is clear that the word *genre humain* creates in the mind only a purely collective idea that supposes no real union among the individuals who constitute it" (283).

portionate to his natural needs" to the disequilibrium engendered "when this state changes . . . be it ever so slightly" joins
what is perhaps the most consistent motif in Rousseau's work,
a thread that connects the earliest anthropological and political
texts to the last autobiographical ones and that finally overrides
their clear generic distinction.[9] And this is to remark that the
general structure within which the particularity of Rousseau's
signature is inscribed here—the divided condition of force/
desire—has been reinscribed under that signature with such
insistence that their traits are interchangeable. Instead, therefore, of a resemblance based on a simple structure of inclusion,
a double inclusion is implied in the uncanny topology of a part
comprehending the whole of which it is a part. The topology is
uncanny because the comprehension of the whole by the part
can proceed only by a division of the part from itself, by a
repetition of its mark outside that of which it is part of the
inside. A coincidence of the whole with its conceptualization,
which alone could remedy the division between force and desire, is deferred indefinitely along the line of this repetition.
Dividing itself from itself, standing outside itself, the most
familiar becomes the most estranged. Rousseau's signature is
the uncanny mark of a desire to cure the very division it remarks.

But the social contract bears no signature because it is contracted in the name of no one in particular and everyone in
general. In his very precise terms, Rousseau defines an instrument that at one and the same time abolishes and reinvents the
signature or, if you will, that replaces an illegitimate appropriation by force with a legitimate ownership by right. "The pecu-
liar fact about this alienation is that, in taking over the goods of
individuals, the community, so far from despoiling them, only
assures them legitimate possession, and changes usurpation
into a true right and enjoyment into proprietorship" (180; 3:
367). Before the social contract is signed, the proper name could

---

[9]It is this motif of a lost original unity that comes apart under the deconstructive pressure of the supplement as applied in *Of Grammatology*; see in particular 229ff.

only be the mark of a desire to subsume something or someone to the bearer of the name. After the social contract, the name's right to signify ownership is guaranteed; it is given its properness but only by convention and constriction. This is to say that the condition of "having" a name is not having it but receiving it from somewhere else. One can put one's name on one's property because the name is not anyone's property. Between these two versions of the name, between illegitimacy and legitimacy, the name imposing itself and receiving itself, the contract takes place in the absence of any name, in the name of the proper name in general or the idea of the proper name: the Sovereign. In the Sovereign, the concept of a generality would coincide at last with the desire to have power over that generality, which is to say over itself *over* which there is, by definition, no higher will that can give it the law. "It is consequently against the nature of the body politic for the Sovereign to impose on itself a law it cannot infringe. . . . The Sovereign, by the simple fact that it is, is always all that it must be [Le Souverain, par cela seul qu'il est, est toujours tout ce qu'il doit être]" (176–77; 3:362–63).[10] By the simple fact that it is (but is it? and where is it?), the Sovereign is always all that it must be. And what it must be is all, *tout*. The least subtraction from the totality or limitation of its power and the whole idea of Sovereignty collapses. The Sovereign, then, cannot and need not sign any contract because a signature contracts. Subjects subscribe to the Sovereign, which subscribes to no one:

> Sovereign power need give no guarantee [garant] to its subjects, because it is impossible for the body to wish to hurt all its members . . . it cannot hurt any one in particular. . . . This, however, is not the case with the relation of the subjects to the Sovereign, which, despite the common interests, would have no security that they would fulfill their undertakings [engagements] unless it found means to assure itself of their fidelity.

The engagement between two parties in which only one of them signs, or rather in which everyone signs, on the one hand,

---

[10]See Bennington, 158–59, for a reading of this phrase as announcing a solution to the "problem of the undecidability of descriptive and prescriptive senses of the word 'law.'"

and no one signs, on the other, reverses precisely the illegitimate terms of the slavery contract in which one signs for everyone:

> It will always be equally foolish for a man to say to a man or to a people: "I make with you a convention wholly at your expense and wholly to my advantage; I shall keep it as long as I like, and you will keep it as long as I like. (172; 3:358)

The senseless discourse establishing the right of slavery is, writes Rousseau, "null and void, not only as being illegitimate, but also because it is absurd and meaningless [parce qu'il ne signifie rien]." The denial of any meaning essentially voids the convention pronounced by an "I" subject with a "you" object who is manifestly nothing other than an instrument for "I's" pleasure. If there is to be a coming together in a convention of meaning, "I" and "you" cannot be subsumed into only an "I." By itself, in other words, "I" makes no sense. There is no meaning, no contract without the more-than-one of an "I/you" articulated by their difference. As the inversion and negation of the social contract, the senseless convention of slavery is separated from the meaningful convention only so long as the Sovereign never says "I."[11]

"Je veux . . ."

Rousseau, on the other hand, both signs and says "je." We are asking about the place of this particular signature in the general structure of nonsigning sovereignty. What, for example, is one to make of the place of a certain "Je veux . . ." immediately following the *avertissement* in the opening clause of *Of the Social Contract*, which reads: "Je veux chercher si dans l'ordre civil il peut y avoir quelque règle d'administration légitime et sûre" (I mean to inquire if, in the civil order, there can be any sure and legitimate rule of administration) (165; 3:351). Everything that is to follow follows from this "je veux," which we

[11]Paul de Man has shown why this constraint cannot be respected and how the "je" of the lawgiver must lend its voice to the mute sovereign (*Allegories of Reading*, 273–75).

will not rush to pin on Rousseau in particular, even if that reference is implied a few lines later in one of the rare auto-biographical remarks to be found in the text.[12] Rather, we take this "je veux" to be the necessary position from which *Du contrat social* is forced to set out in order to arrive at the terms of the social contract, terms that "although they have perhaps never been formally set forth [énoncés] . . . are everywhere the same and everywhere *tacitly* admitted and recognized" (174; 3:360; italics added). The "Je veux chercher . . . quelque règle" of the *incipit* establishes the text's governing rule to be the explicitation of the tacit rule. Its explicitation—that is, its framing by the terms of a text.[13] But how can the tacitly or silently recognized rule be made explicit by a "je veux" that breaks the silence and thus breaks the rule that imposes silence on the "je"? It is this double exigency that situates the "je" on the enigmatic edge of *Of the Social Contract*, an edge that does not so much wrap around the work as traverse it from end to end, as we shall see.

The incipient "je veux" has an uneasy balancing act to perform. Where it stands, the ground that supports the rectitude of its *volonté* has to be carefully posed. This placement takes place along yet another fringe, which this time is internal to the work because it extends between the heading "Book I" and its first subheading, "Chapter 1." The "je veux" in fact inaugurates three paragraphs that are within the book but outside any of its subdivisions. It is here that "je" responds to a question about its place in a treatise on politics: "I enter upon my task without proving the importance of the subject. I shall be asked if I am a prince or a legislator, to write on politics. I answer that I am neither, and that is why I do so. If I were a prince or a legislator, I should not waste time in saying what wants doing; I should do it, or hold my peace [je le ferais, ou je me tairais]" (165; 3:351). These lines distinguish a writing on politics from a doing of

[12]There has been no thorough census of the use of "je" in *Du contrat social*. The available concordance, by Michel Launay and Gunnar Von Proschwitz (Paris, 1977), unfortunately does not index this pronoun, which falls into their category of omitted "utilitarian words[!] of one or two letters" (25).

[13]In paleography, *incipit* and *explicit* designate the first and last words of manuscript parts.

politics and imply even that the two activities are mutually exclusive. If one writes on politics, it is because one is in no position to do politics, and if one can do politics one does not waste one's time talking and writing about how to do it. According to this schema, the political text would even be generated by a powerlessness to do what it says, since doing and saying exclude each other. Yet this structure is made to tremble in its final position, in the punchline: "je le ferais, ou je me tairais." If writing on politics and political action excluded each other, then one could also reasonably expect to find a conjunctive "and" here rather than an alternative "or": I would do it *and* I would be silent. Instead, the phrase as it reads implies that "doing" politics is an alternative to being silent, and thus puts politics in a category that includes rather than excludes speaking, saying, writing.

It may therefore be naïve to assume that the force of the text's incipient "je veux" is contained within some purely definitional limits of a "je veux *dire*," I mean or I mean to say. What is more, it may be precisely because saying and doing cannot be definitively dissociated or predictably associated that there are politics and political texts.[14] But the very least one can say is that the distinction that identifies the "I" writing on politics with a "saying" rather than a "doing" shows itself to be less than totally reliable.

The State of the Signature

In the next paragraph of the section we are examining, more solid ground is placed under the feet of "je," who claims the

[14]See de Man, *Allegories of Reading*, 277: "The redoubtable efficacy of the text is due to the rhetorical model of which it is a version. This model is a fact of language over which Rousseau himself has no control. Just as any other reader, Rousseau is bound to misread his text as a promise of political change. . . . To the extent that it is necessarily misleading, language just as necessarily conveys the promise of its own truth. This is also why textual allegories on this level of rhetorical complexity generate history." Most attempts to account for Rousseau's influence on the Revolution neglect this "rhetorical complexity" and its power to generate history. For this reason, Carol Blum, in *Rousseau and the Republic of Virtue*, for example, is forced to fall back on conjectures about patterns of psychological identification which remain thoroughly contingent.

birthright of the "citizen of a free State and member of the Sovereign." One is reminded that Rousseau's signature on this text carries the apposition "Citizen of Geneva," and that here, as elsewhere, he signs with the name of a political, geographical state. "Je," then, is also "Geneva" according to a metonymy of place.

There would have been, of course, another reason that Jean-Jacques Rousseau signed *Du contrat social* as a citizen of Geneva. Rousseau published this text, like most of his previous ones, in Amsterdam. The principal aim in doing so was to protect his work from certain strictures of the French jurisdiction. It therefore could not hurt to remind the Parisian authorities, on the title page of this text, that not just the work but its author, a foreign national living in France, was not strictly subject to French laws. It is often forgotten that it was not France but—ironically—Holland and Geneva that banned *Du contrat social*.[15] French authorities banned only *Emile*, but then they also pursued its author with an arrest order (*une prise de corps*), thereby thoroughly undermining the notion that Rousseau's citizenship could offer any protection from the overzealous watchdogs of public order. The circumstances of the banning of *Emile* and of *Du contrat social* are at the very least reminders that the politics of the signature in the 1760s were bound up with the situation of nation-states that did not often respect one another's borders.

Rousseau underscores the irony of these circumstances in his polemical *Letter to Christophe de Beaumont*. (The latter was

[15]Both *Emile* and *Du contrat social* were condemned and publicly burned in Geneva on 18 June 1762; in Holland, where the privilege had been issued, the sale of *Emile* was banned on 29 June and that of *Du contrat social* on 20 July; in France, the condemnation of *Emile* would seem to have been possible because, although the title page named a publisher in Amsterdam, it was well known that the work had been clandestinely printed in Paris (see below, chap. 3). As for *Du contrat social*, which was printed in Amsterdam, the Parisian authorities were able only to prohibit its entry into the country. All of these measures, of course, only slowed somewhat the dissemination of both works. On these circumstances, see Marcel Françon, "La Condemnation de l'*Emile*," *Annales de la Société Jean-Jacques Rousseau* 31 (1946–49). For an account of censorship in France during the period, see Nicole Herrmann-Mascard, *La Censure des livres à Paris à la fin de l'Ancien Régime (1750–1789)* (Paris, 1968).

the general prosecutor and archbishop of Paris who had written the order condemning *Emile* and its author.)

> A citizen of Geneva gets a book printed in Holland, and by a decree of the Parliament of Paris, this book is burned without any respect shown to the sovereign whose privilege it had obtained. A Protestant proposes, in a Protestant country, certain objections against the Church of Rome, and he is condemned by the Parliament of Paris. A republican makes objections, in a republican state, against monarchy, and he is condemned by the Parliament of Paris. It seems the Parliament of Paris has strange notions of its jurisdiction, believing itself to be the legitimate judge of the whole human race.[16]

What is more, continues Rousseau, these measures were taken against him merely because his name appeared on the title page of the offending book.

> The same parliament, ever so remarkably circumspect in their proceedings when individuals of their own nation are concerned, neglect them all in passing sentence on a poor foreigner. Without knowing whether this foreigner was really the author of the book imputed to him, whether he acknowledged it, or caused it to be printed . . . they began their process by ordering him to be clapped in prison [on commence par le décréter de prise de corps]. . . . I know not how far such proceedings may be consistent with the law of nations [le droit des gens]; but I know very well that where they are carried on, a man's liberty, and perhaps his life, is at the mercy of the first printer who chooses to set that man's name to a book. (240; 4:930)

The point about verifying authorship might seem to be too fine.[17] Rousseau, however, is not just splitting hairs about the legal status of a signature. His argument against the procedures of those who decreed his arrest on the basis of a signature is amply motivated by two kinds of considerations.

[16]*The Miscellaneous Works of Mr. J. J. Rousseau*, vol. 3 (London, 1767; rpt. New York, 1972); the French text is in 4:929.

[17]In chapter 3 below, we discuss from a different angle this complaint that the Paris authorities neglected the formality of verifying whether Jean-Jacques Rousseau was indeed the author of the book titled *Emile*.

First, there is the status of a signed *fiction*. Beaumont and his colleagues took no account of the fact that the "Profession de foi du Vicaire savoyard," which was the principal target of their attack on *Emile*, was represented as the reported speech of an unnamed person.[18] In a fragment not included in the letter, Rousseau reflects on the implications of this confusion:

> What a large door one would be opening to violence and persecution if one could impute to the author in an equal fashion all the assertions he makes in his own name and all those he puts in the mouths of others. It would follow that every time he sets up contradictory discussions, one could impute both the pro and the con to him, especially when the question is not clear enough to allow for an irrefutable solution. One would be free to charge him with whichever of the two opinions would render him guilty and then, on the pretext that he did not combat the guilty opinion forcefully enough, maintain that it is the one he secretly favors.
> (4:1029)

He then cites examples of criticisms leveled at the author of *Julie*, a text that presents itself as a collection of private letters in which Rousseau would have had the role only of editor.[19] But the same point could be made about any text as soon as one recognizes that there can be no certainty about the relation between intention and text. An author may disavow the opinions he or she nevertheless represents, or intend them ironically or satirically, or be unable himself or herself to affirm one intention to the exclusion of another, which is clearly the most

---

[18]At one point, when Beaumont does notice the fictional device, he gets it wrong and attributes a passage to the Vicar which was not, in fact, spoken by him. Rousseau points out his error, severely rebuking such negligent reading habits; see 4:948–49.

[19]We perhaps read this attribution too quickly if we take it to be "merely a fiction." De Man radicalizes the doubt about the author's authorship of such a text when he writes: "Taken literally, Rousseau's assertion that he does not know whether he or his fictional characters wrote the letters that make up *Julie* makes little sense. The situation changes when we realize that R. is merely the metaphor for a textual property (readability). Further inferences then become apparent, for example that R. is similar to N. in his inability to read *Julie* and that it is impossible to distinguish between reader and author in terms of epistemological certainty" (*Allegories of Reading*, 203).

troubling possibility for a law that has to suppose an imma-
nence of intentionality to itself as represented by a signature.
The issue of censorship is always finally about the disjunction
of intentions and utterances, as Plato thoroughly understood
when in the *Phaedrus* he condemned writing for its inability to
answer any questions put to it about its meaning.[20]

Rousseau, it is clear, just as thoroughly grasped the implications of the absence of the author from the text.[21] He complains
repeatedly, both in the *Letter to Christophe de Beaumont* and
in his *Letters Written from the Mountains* (which addressed the
censoring agencies in Geneva), about the rampant assumptions
made as to the intentions of the author of *Emile* and *Du contrat
social*. That both the French and Genevan authorities moved
against the author and not just the works, censoring or banning
both *l'oeuvre et l'homme*, the work and the man, was possible
only because in each case an unrestrained *procès d'intention*
was under way. As one result, Rousseau would spend the remaining sixteen years of his life denying his authorship of any
crime and trying to explain (and first of all to understand) in
confessional or otherwise self-reflexive writings the meaning of
his signature on his published work—as if the autobiographical
signature were any less a mark of absent intention.[22]

On Literary Property

Authorial intentionality and the signature were (and remain)
matters that positive law must seek to determine in order to

[20]"It always needs its father to attend to it, being quite unable to define itself
or attend to its own needs" (275e).

[21]In another unused fragment of the letter, he even seems to imply an identification with Socrates' fate at the hands of the state censors: "Ils ont crucifié
mon maître et ils ont donné la ciguë à un homme qui valait mieux que moi"
(They crucified my master and gave hemlock to a man more worthy than I)
(1016).

[22]E. S. Burt, in her forthcoming book *Rousseau's Autobiographics*, argues
forcefully that this writing must always occupy an undecidable position between fiction and a truthful genre (history or philosophy) and that it has to
overturn any attempt to fix the writer's intention. I am particularly indebted
here to Burt's reading of Malesherbes's *Mémoires sur la librairie et la liberté de
la presse*, which uncovers the mechanisms of censorship's inability to end the
scandal of unassignable intentions.

give some semblance of regulating the reproduction and circulation of ideas. In France, these laws have been written with reference to the notion of "literary property." The notion is, of course, fraught with irresolvable contradiction, but at no time, perhaps, was that contradiction more acutely in evidence than between 1723 and 1778, the dates of two important revisions to French law governing the publishing trades. Before proceeding any further to survey the state of the signature on *Du contrat social*, let us pause to examine the properness of the concept of "property" which both attaches to a signature and also necessarily detaches it from its proper "owner."

The debate about *propriété littéraire* in France should be understood in a context of the censorship deemed necessary to an absolute ruling monarch.[23] The point may be obvious but still bears restating that censorship must aim to suppress not ideas "as such" but their reproduction and dissemination. This distinction was enacted under the ancien régime in the indirect regulation of an author's activity through the regulations directed at publishers. The system of *permissions* and *privilèges* which evolved in France between roughly 1507 (the date of the

[23]Historians of "literary property" do not always observe this condition; see, for example, Pierre Recht, *Le Droit d'auteur, une nouvelle forme de propriété: Histoire et théorie* (Gembloux, Belgium, 1969), 26–47. There is an enormous bibliography on the questions of literary property, copyright, *droit d'auteur*, etc. Francis J. Kase has selected and annotated part of it in *Copyright Thought in Continental Europe: Its Development, Legal Theories and Philosophy* (South Hackensack, N.J., 1967). In the introduction, he writes: "The history of the development of copyright thinking brought a variety of theories all of which attempted to explain the nature of copyright and determine its place in the legal system. These theories usually center around either the results of the author's activities, the personality of the author, or the nature of the author's activity. The elusive nature of copyright and the very fact that copyright legislation needed a long time to materialize [Kase was writing in 1967, soon after revisions to copyright law in most of Europe, England, and the United States] have resulted in widely differing schools" (4–6). He then identifies ten principal theories with which jurists have attempted to pin down this "elusive nature." For the particular period that concerns us, I have consulted Claude Colombet, *Propriété littéraire et artistique*, 2d ed. (Paris, 1980); Marie Claude Dock, *Etude sur le droit d'auteur* (Paris, 1963); Henri Falk, *Les Privilèges de librairie sous l'Ancien Régime: Etude historique du conflit des droits sur l'oeuvre littéraire* (Geneva, 1970); Herrmann-Mascard, *Censure des livres à Paris*.

first known *privilège*) and 1791 (the date at which the revolution abolished and revoked all *privilèges*) codified restrictions and responsibilities for the publisher and concerned itself less with the author. Most important, *privilèges* were issued to publishers and only very rarely to authors themselves. Even when a *privilège* was registered in an author's name, the author was expressly forbidden to print and publish his own manuscript. He was thus obliged to contract for publication with a duly recognized member of the publishing corporation, called the *Communauté*. It is at this point that the interests of censorship meet up with the corporate interests of publishers. The *privilège* was not in fact an instrument of censorship (that function was reserved to the *permission d'imprimer*) but a protection for the publisher against counterfeiting. It granted exclusive publication rights over a period varying between two and ten years, and could be renewed in most cases. Both the state and the corporation had an interest in controlling the unauthorized reproduction of works. The author did as well, of course, but for most of the period with which we are concerned the only legal avenue for his or her interest was through its identification with the rights of the *privilégié*, that is, the publisher. The author's rights and interests were in effect eclipsed by this identification. Between 1723 and 1778, the concept of "literary property" was debated as a means to correct this apparent oversight.

The debate concerned the transfer of an author's property—the work—to an agent, who bought the right to print and diffuse it. The problem was that this transfer and transformation left a residue that could not easily be disposed of—the residue that is marked, precisely, by the signature. Once it was sold to a publisher, the work did not fully become his property in the way that the transfer of a title to real estate abrogates all the former owner's rights over that land. Undeniably, something of an author's relation to his "property" remains even after its transfer, its reproduction, and its diffusion. Defining this relation and with it the rights that could or should be protected by positive law would be the affair of that debate which, while it may have reached certain conclusions in eighteenth-century

France, has hardly been ended in any definitive sense. That is, both current literary theory (or "antitheory") and the current state of positive law concerning such issues as pornography, video reproduction, computerized "creation," and so forth are evidence that no definition of the signature has yet resolved these questions.[24]

The analogy to property law suggests itself because the author is held to be, as one commentator has put it, "owner of the manuscript he has created, but *owner to the greatest degree possible*, to such an 'intense' degree . . . that one finds perhaps no other examples of such a reality of right, since this right originates in the very person who exercises it: the writer has created the work."[25] As this description makes plain, the analogy to property and property ownership tends to uncover the assumption that the only indisputable right to assert ownership lies in the relation expressed by a phrase such as "the writer has created the work." By comparison, the right over real estate would have to appear arbitrary, ungrounded as it is "in the very person who exercises it" and who in this case is dependent on a state to legitimize (or at least defend) ownership.[26] Yet it is

[24]As just one example, Senator Edward Kennedy has recently introduced in Congress proposed legislation (the Visual Artists Rights Act) that would "prevent the intentional mutilation or destruction of [an artist's] work and provide for resale royalties." Schuyler Chapin, chairman of the Independent Committee on Arts Policy, and Alberta Arthurs, the group's president, in endorsing this bill, describe it as maintaining the "connection between a visual artist and that artist's work," a connection that is severed by the market, which treats such works as "ownable pieces of property." "Art," write Chapin and Arthurs, "is more than a piece of property that some one or some institution owns. And, yes, it is even more than a valuable commodity with one of the highest rates of return on the market. Works of art are much more than that. In some real way they belong to no one because they belong to all of us. . . . The issue is something larger than marketplace friction. It has to do with that connection between artists and their work that we want to recognize. It has to do with knowing that *the artist is the indispensable element here"* (*New York Times*, 29 October 1987; italics added). The question is why, if this element is "indispensable," the "connection" to it can be severed in so spectacular a fashion. This is the problematic of the signature.

[25]Falk, 92; italics added.

[26]One is reminded here of chap. 9, "Du domaine réel," in *Du contrat social*, concerning the legitimation of property: "Each member of the community gives himself to it at the moment of its foundation, just as he is, with all the

precisely this understanding of the work as property in a seemingly proper, unalienated sense which would have to get lost in the necessary transfer between that sense and the ordinary sense of ownership of goods and commodities, which is the only sense in which a publisher can be said to own the work he purchases from an author.

Publishers, particularly those in Paris, sought to enforce the analogy with property. Their argument was that by selling a manuscript, the author sold as well all rights of ownership, including—most important for the publisher's interests—its perpetuity or inalienability. The *Communauté*, in effect, sought to obtain a guarantee of perpetual *privilège* for works that were not already in the public domain. In fact, the Paris community of publishers sought to enforce their virtual monopoly on new works and to limit the scope of the public domain over against the demand of provincial publishers for stricter limits on the length and renewals of *privilèges*. It was also argued, somewhat inconsistently, that only such a system of perpetual *privilège* could protect the author's interests.[27]

---

resources at his command, including the goods he possesses. This act does not make possession, in changing hands, change its nature, and become property in the hands of the Sovereign; but, as the forces of the city are incomparably greater than those of an individual, public possession is also, in fact, stronger and more irrevocable, without being any more legitimate, at any rate from the point of view of foreigners [sans être plus légitime, au moins pour les étrangers]" (178–79; 3:365). We will return below to this problem of the "point of view of foreigners," that is, to the state's external relations.

[27]Diderot made this argument in *Lettre sur le commerce de la librairie*, ed. Bernard Grasset (Paris, 1937), 87, where he writes as someone who has "more or less exercised the double profession of author and publisher." This text also returns repeatedly to the analogy with property; for example: "Does not a work belong to an author as much as his house or his field does? And can he not forever alienate their ownership? Should it be allowed, for whatever cause or pretext, that the one to whom the author has freely transferred his right be robbed of that right? Does not the substitute deserve all the protection of this right which the government grants owners against all other sorts of usurpers?" (63). This particular edition of the *Lettre* is interesting as well for the introduction and marginal notes by Bernard Grasset, the Paris publisher, who in 1936 wanted to enlist Diderot's testimony against proposed legislation by the Popular Front government which would have shortened the period of copyright protection. Grasset has little difficulty demonstrating that issues of *propriété littéraire* have evolved only superficially in two hundred years.

There was thus a recognition that, after alienating or selling all rights, an author retained some interest in the future of the work bearing his or her signature. The analogy to property here met one of its limits which even the most extreme partisans of the perpetuity argument could not get around except by insisting on the identity of the interests of author and publisher. As we shall see later, an opponent of *privilèges* and proponent of the free book market, Malesherbes, could be just as eager to understand the author's interests as identical with the publisher's.[28]

The argument over literary property points to a basic hesitation in the law between authorship of a work and ownership of a commodity. While in the matter of literary or artistic "property," the latter could not exist without the former, the two have strictly speaking nothing essential in common, nothing that could allow the one to replace or entirely subsume the other. The "elusive nature of copyright"[29] is tied to the elusive nature of a work that supports only with considerable difficulty the analogy to property. Nevertheless, even in its latest revisions, French law continues to use the classification *propriété littéraire et artistique* even as it concedes the insufficiency or inappropriateness of the term:

> While the idea of property seems sufficient to explain the nature of the author's patrimonial rights, while the term "incorporeal property" was indeed used by the framers of the 1957 law (art. I) [date of the last major revision of French copyright law], the notion does not seem to be able to account for a moral right insofar as it is inalienable and imprescriptible.
>
> The author's moral right is in reality a right of personality [droit de la personnalité]: because the work is the emanation of this personality, it generates not only a property but also an extra-

---

[28]In September 1761, less than a year before the condemnation of *Emile*, both positions suffered a setback when the *Conseil* granted the claim of La Fontaine's heirs to block publication of his works by unauthorized publishers. This decision was to serve as precedent for subsequent legislation recognizing a *droit d'auteur* that cannot be abrogated by publication contracts. The law of 1778 would specify, however, a term after which works entered the public domain.

[29]Kase, 6.

patrimonial right which has all the attributes of rights of personality. The juridical nature of the author's right is thus hybrid: a right of property as concerns patrimonial rights; a right of personality as concerns the moral right.[30]

This is what is known as the dualist conception of the author's rights. It consecrates the contradiction that fomented the eighteenth-century debate and remains essentially within that contradiction. The jurist's gloss on the two types of rights distinguishes between what is detachable and what remains attached. "As opposed to pecuniary rights which tend to become detached, the moral right is attached to the author just as the glow is to phosphorus."[31] The analogy here to a physical rather than a marketable property reinforces the idea of the inalienability of "the right of personality." Notice that the analogy attempts to naturalize the law and to reattach the necessary detachability of the symbolic relation. Yet it belies at the same time the elusiveness of the very quality of "attachment" that the analogy can name only metaphorically, in the form, that is, of a *detachment*. The legal theorist, in other words, must endeavor to explain how a "right of personality" offers protection according to a supposition of indetachability which continues to elude the very language that would name that right in its proper sense.

This consideration of *propriété littéraire* and *droit d'auteur* allows us to isolate several senses in which signature is functioning for the law. Under a censorship regime (and all states exercise censorship to some degree and in some form), the signature on a book or commodity is made to function as the proper name of the subject who can be held accountable for whatever effects the law deems dangerous to its own order. Under the liberal regime of the marketplace, the signature designates a property owner to whom certain benefits accrue. As part of a text, however, whose regime is precisely not that of property or ownership, the signature detaches from the function of proper name, or rather joins that function to the other

---

[30]Colombet, 16.
[31]Ibid., 136.

textual function of producing meaning without strictly determinable intentions. This textualization of names, which is precisely their detachability, is what the law disguises beneath the notion of an *inalienable* "droit de la personnalité." The problem for any law assigning the responsibility of signatures is that its application to the domain of property cannot depend simply on the seemingly untroubled functioning of the proper name. (If it could, then how would one explain the proliferation of laws protecting authors' rights?) Because names become textualized, however, signatures demand first to be *read* before any law can assign their meaning, whereas it is precisely the possibility of assigning a certain meaning or intention which reading puts in question.

This problem has its source in what might be called the *pseudoanonymous* regime of the text's signature. Between the law of the proper name and the space of reading, the author designated by the signature is "there as anonymous party." The author is positioned by a certain *effaceability* of his/her name with regard to the text it signs. The difference between the designated author and his/her effacement in the mode of an "as if" is the difference, once again, between the book as commodity or legal entity and the work as nonproperty. That is why Rousseau is able to expose the error that arises when this effaceability is forgotten by proposing to consider the intentions of a book's *publisher*. The passage occurs in the fragment on proceedings against writers from which we have already quoted:

> As regards the text, the author is there as anonymous party [l'auteur est là comme anonyme], even though the public may presume that this author is the author of the book; but if such presumption sufficed in court to condemn a man in a free country, then where would liberty and justice have gone?
>
> I am not saying that one may print with impunity any bad book provided that one is not the author; I am saying that while the publisher may be held responsible for the evil caused by the opinions he publishes, one cannot nevertheless impute those opinions to the publisher *himself* unless he has expressly adopted them. From this there follows an essential difference in procedure. (4:1029)

Clearly, the idea of imputing to the publisher *himself* the opinions he publishes is beyond the presumptions of even the archbishop of Paris. The point is that the author, like the publisher, is not author of everything published under his name, which must efface itself in order to permit the text's deployment. Rousseau's argument exploits the inadequacy in the legal definition of literary "property" which recognized a publisher's "ownership" with more consistency than an author's "authorship." Rousseau puts in question the very concept of literary "property" or ownership as empty of any meaning except that of the commodity when he draws a wholly unacceptable consequence from its premise: if the work is a "property," then it returns to its owner, that is, the publisher; and if it cannot return to its owner, it is because it returns properly to no one.[32]

Open Borders

Whatever tenuous order the notion of "literary property" managed to maintain within the debate that was ongoing in France, its pertinence was wholly beside the point with regard to the more or less unregulated book trade across national borders, a trade that resembled more often piracy. There were no international conventions governing the reprinting in one country of works originally published in another. "Counterfeit" French editions of books published, for example, in Am-

---

[32]In a letter dated 24 July 1762, Rousseau already makes many of the same points about authorship: "Is it certain that J. J. R. is its Author? Is it even certain that he is the author of the book that bears his name? Cannot the name of a man be falsely printed on the title page of a book that is not by him? . . . If this procedure were legitimate, then the freedom of every good man would be at the mercy of any printer. You will say that the voice of the public is unanimous, and that the one to whom the book is attributed does not disavow it: but, once again, before sullying the irreproachable honor of a good man, before attacking the freedom of a Citizen, one should have some positive proof . . . the book's Author does not claim to be the author of the profession of faith; he declares that it is a text he has transcribed in his book. . . . Thus, if one must punish he who is named on the title page of the book in which is found the profession of faith for having published it, it is as editor and not as author." *Correspondance complète*, ed. R. A. Leigh, (Madison, Wis., 1969), letter 2028, 12:96–97.

sterdam (where the press was accorded more freedom than in France) were common and their sale was uninhibited.

In 1754, Rousseau began dealing with Marc-Michel Rey, a Genevan publisher established in Amsterdam, for the publication of the *Discours sur l'inégalité*. The two were close collaborators by 1760, the year Rey undertook the considerable task and risk of publishing *Julie*. The risk was that a Parisian publisher would offer for sale a counterfeit reprint of the work before the original edition (or the part of it authorized to be imported into France) could be sold out. At the end of October 1760, the books were ready for shipment. Rousseau sent one of his advance copies to Malesherbes, who was *directeur de la librairie* (responsible for the issuance of *privilèges*, the administration of censorship, etc.), along with the not-so-subtle request that "this collection not leave your hands until it has been published. By then I am sure that its success will not tempt any one to counterfeit it and even more sure that you will not permit it."[33] Malesherbes understood the hint and replied that, on the contrary, he considered "counterfeit" editions entirely normal, and he replied to Rousseau to this effect:

> As for the counterfeiting that you seem to fear, I disagree with you over the principles that rule in this matter. No country prohibits the counterfeiting of a book printed in another country. There are two completely different interests [deux intérêts tout différents] to be considered: that of the publisher and that of the author. The publisher's interest cannot provide any reason to prohibit the reprinting in France of books printed in Holland unless it were also prohibited in Holland to print books that have already appeared in France. And for that to happen there would have to be some kind of treaty among nations [Il faudrait qu'il y eût pour cela une espèce de traité entre les puissances]. Not only is there no such treaty, but foreigners and specifically the Dutch reprint everything that appears in France; it would thus be absurd for France to have any scruples about using reprisals.

Notice that Malesherbes, a free-market liberal, first distinguishes "two completely different interests," the publisher's

[33]Ibid., letter 1126, 7:261.

and the author's, and then proceeds to deny that the publisher's interest can be taken into account given the state of generalized book piracy among nations. He next acknowledges the author's interest to be finally *indistinguishable* from the publisher's, thereby confirming inadvertently the contradiction we have already remarked:

> As for the author's interest, it is only right that in every country in the world an author receives every advantage possible from his work; and that is why he is given the privilege for his work, or, *what amounts to the same thing*, the privilege is given to the publisher [ou ce qui *paraît être la même chose*, on donne ce privilège au libraire] that he chooses and designates.[34] (Italics added)

This letter concludes with the advice that Rousseau should choose a publisher in Paris and sell him the rights to the "counterfeit" edition of *Julie*.

In his response to this letter, Rousseau protests that such an arrangement is unethical since he would be selling the same rights twice over and, in effect, stealing future revenue from Rey's pocket. No doubt such a protest would have been considered at best naïve, at worst disingenuous. And indeed, Rousseau finally did (with Rey's consent) resell the rights to *Julie* to the Parisian publisher Robin. The latter's edition was severely expurgated (of some hundred pages) by French censorship at Malesherbes's instigation and over Rousseau's objection.[35] The disfiguring of this text was one of Rousseau's bitterest experiences before the 1762 banning and public mutilation of *Emile*. It must be read as contributing to the context of the "mad" declaration made in 1774 disavowing reprints of his works. It is also echoed in the warning addressed to Christophe de Beaumont that where such procedures are permitted, "a man's liberty, and perhaps his life, is at the mercy of the first printer who chooses to set his name to a book."[36]

[34]Ibid., letter 1133, 7:269; italics added.

[35]See *Correspondance complète*, letters 1126, 1133, 1152, 1244, 1303, 1304, 1327, 1350.

[36]Rousseau's fantasy in *Les Dialogues* of the "faithful impression" carried out by a loyal *dépositaire* of his works has an obvious connection to this apprehension about misprints and forgeries; see below, chap. 4.

But Rousseau's reply to Malesherbes has a place in our discussion of the "state" of the signature for another reason. His letter inscribes authors' rights and publishers' rights in the context of international political economy. In so doing, he replies to Malesherbes's observation that "there would have to be some kind of treaty among nations" and to the blind assumption that, in the absence of such a treaty, a kind of unregulated parity was de facto the case. The letter nails Malesherbes's complacent acceptance of a state of affairs that, Rousseau argues, not only benefits the French book trade at the expense of its neighbors but shores up a system of arbitrary repression by allowing it to hide from its internal contradictions. Our lengthy quotations from this letter will allow us finally to return to *Du contrat social* and to a similar inscription within its borders of international affairs.

It is with the notion of *droit des gens* or law of nations[37] that Rousseau introduces his reflections:

> I will first remark that, on the subject of *le droit des gens*, there are many unrefuted maxims that nevertheless will always be vain and without effect in practice because they presume an equality between nations as well as between men. As concerns the first, this principle is wrong with regard to both their size and their form, and it is thus also wrong as concerns the relative right of the subjects that derive from one and the other . . . *le droit des gens*, which depends on the statutes of human institutions that have no absolute term, varies and must vary from nation to nation. Large nations impose on smaller ones and exact their respect; at the same time, they need the smaller states and need them more than the smaller states need the larger ones. They therefore must give up something equivalent to what they demand. Considered in detail, advantages are not equal, but they cancel each other out. This is the origin of the true *droit des gens*, established not in

---

[37]*Jus gentium* in Roman law. While juridical theorists debated whether there was a real difference between *droit des gens* and natural law, there was general agreement on its sense as the law applied to foreigners and to foreign states. It is in this latter sense that Rousseau consistently uses the term; see Robert Derathé, *Jean-Jacques Rousseau et la science politique de son temps* (Paris, 1970), 387–90.

books [non dans les livres] but among men. Some nations have
honor, rank, power; others have ignoble profit and petty utility.[38]

The "true *droit des gens*," the one that is not to be found in
books because it varies from one nation to the next, is an
unequal exchange of "advantages." As concerns book trade between two such unequal partners, Rousseau predicts that only
an *internal* change in one or the other system of government
could permit the establishment of a uniform policy regulating
their exchange:

> The freedom of the press established in Holland requires rules for
> the policing of the book trade which differ from those that apply
> in France, where such liberty does not and cannot occur. Even if
> one wished, by means of treaties between states, to establish
> uniform policing and the same regulations in this matter between
> the two states, either these treaties would soon be without effect
> or one of the two governments would change form, given that in
> every country the only laws that are observed are those that derive
> from the nature of the government.

Once again, the *droit des gens* is described as limited to useless
treaties, good on paper but without effect in practice. Rousseau
traces the impracticability of an international treaty in this
matter to the arbitrary power of a censorship policy that toler-
ates too easily its own contradiction when the result is to its
advantage.

> Book sales are enormous in France, almost as great as in the rest of
> Europe altogether. In Holland, the book trade is almost nil. On the
> other hand, proportionally more books are printed in Holland
> than in France. Thus one could say that, in a certain sense, con-
> sumption is in France, fabrication is in Holland . . . that where the

---

[38]*Correspondance complète*, letter 1152, 7:297; cf. the fragment "Du bonheur public," where Rousseau was also thinking in terms of dependence of
nations on each other: "that the happiest nation is the one that can most easily
dispense with all others, and that the most flourishing nation is the one that
others can least dispense with" (III:512). Paul de Man's reading of *Du contrat
social* sets out from a reading of this fragment (250 ff.).

Frenchman is a consumer, the Dutchman is but a factory hand [facteur]. . . . Such is the relative state of this part of commerce between the two powers; and this state, imposed by the two constitutions, will always recur no matter what one does. I well understand that the French Government would like to see fabrication occur in the same place as consumption: but this is not possible, and it is the government itself that prevents it by the rigors of censorship.

According to one of the French Government's maxims, there are many things that cannot be permitted but that it is all right to tolerate. From this it follows that one can and must tolerate the importation of a certain book whose printing must not be tolerated. . . . However, when a book is printed in Holland because it could not and should not be printed in France and then is reprinted in France, the Government goes against its own maxims and acts in contradiction with itself. I would add that the idea of parity that authorizes this contradiction [and here Rousseau is responding directly to Malesherbes's assumption that France and Holland steal equally from each other] is illusory, and the consequence it draws from that notion, although correct, is not equitable. Since both France and Holland print for consumption in France, and since counterfeit editions of French works are not permitted entry into the [French] Realm, the reprinting in Holland of a book printed in France does little harm to the French publisher, whereas the reprinting done in France of a book printed in Holland ruins the Dutch publisher.

Recall that this letter is dated 1760—before the crisis of *Emile* and the *prise de corps*. Rousseau thus had already acquired a clear understanding of the principal limitation on any constitution of political rights beyond national borders, given the fundamental inequality, or difference, between national entities. Indeed, Malesherbes even suggests in his reply that Rousseau should treat the subject at greater length: "the observation you make as to the reciprocal advantages of large and small states is the basis of a very profound work. . . . But this subject cannot be treated in letters. Moreover, I have only a glimpse of such great theories. It would be up to a man of your stature to look into them more deeply."[39] Instead, Rousseau

[39]*Correspondance complète*, letter 1161, 7:312–13.

writes *Du contrat social*, which, as we shall see, stops short of any contractual definition of international relations. In fact, it gets arrested at the border. Yet the exchange with Malesherbes on the question of international book trade already analyzes why the contract cannot be extended over the border. But that is not all: from that border, a contradiction can be glimpsed within the sovereign nation—the contradiction of a sovereignty that "by the simple fact that it is, is always all that it must be," a sovereignty that governs by the fiction of its totality, as if it had no borders with difference. This is the fiction as well, then, of *Du contrat social*. But it can seem to stand up and stand alone only until one reaches its farthest edge.

Concluding the Contract

The final chapter of the final book of *Du contrat social* bears the title "Conclusion." Here the text comes to an end, but whether it can be concluded that *Du contrat social* has been closed (as one says of a contract after both parties have signed) is not at all clear.

CONCLUSION

Après avoir posé les vrais principes du droit politique et tâché de fonder l'Etat sur sa base, il resterait à l'appuyer par ses relations externes; ce qui comprendrait le droit des gens, le commerce, le droit de la guerre et les conquêtes, le droit public, les ligues, les négociations, les traités etc. Mais tout cela forme un nouvel objet trop vaste pour ma courte vue; j'aurais dû la fixer toujours plus près de moi.

FIN

(Now that I have laid down the true principles of political right and tried to give the State a basis of its own to rest on, I ought next to strengthen it by its external relations, which would include the law of nations, commerce, the right of war and conquest, public right, leagues, negotiations, treaties, etc. But all this forms a new subject that is far too vast for my limited view. I ought throughout to have fixed it closer to me.)

Three closures converge in the end: the state, enclosed within the perimeter of its borders with other states; the "moi" whose view can be extended only as far as this perimeter; and the text at whose perimeter the coincidence of the other two comes to be remarked. State, self, text: all are here brought to the brink where some external relation would have to be posed if one were to go any farther; all withdraw back into an interior but only after it has been remarked that the rest remains. The border is drawn by this gesture of taking one step over the limit and then withdrawing. The border is not reached until it is breached. The conclusion is thus double-edged, so to speak: the last chapter of the work that has been put in place—the state grounded on its basis—would also be the first chapter of a work that can have no single ground, whose basis is not a positive ground (or a territory) but a relation of forces between, for example, smaller and larger powers. It is a border as well then between, on the one hand, that which can be thought of as having borders and as being contained or defined by them and, on the other hand, a relational field of differences where borders are crossed, transgressed, redivided.

This other fringe, at the other end of the text, extends beyond the work's fabric and repeats the pattern put in place by the phrase from the *avertissement*: "Le reste n'est déjà plus." The conclusion of *Du contrat social* is double-edged because in order to say it excludes external relations, it must overstep its own limits and include the exclusion it excludes, much as "there remain no remains" says more than it means to say. A note by the editor, Robert Derathé, suggests that the usual means of dealing with this troublesome ambiguity of the "Conclusion," its included exclusion, has been to redraw the text's borders—to exclude, in other words, its last chapter. "Historians have given so little attention to this concluding chapter that it is common to call the last chapter of the *Contrat social* the preceding one on civil religion" (1507, n. 1). This omission follows more or less the same logic that severs a particle from the title of the text so as to insert it in a referential syntax. Like the "Du" of the title, the last chapter is the mark of a textuality that a stable system of reference must ignore or leave out, just as the theory of a stable national government will have to ignore the extraterritorial grounds or "appuis" of the state's existence: its interstate commerce, its internationality, which is also to say its intertextuality.

The extra mark, however, may also be ignored if one resets the textual boundary on the far side of the "Conclusion," rather than on its near side. Derathé, in effect, proposes the latter solution as a corrective to the contrary tendency. "It is in this chapter, however, that Rousseau summarizes the second part of the *Institutions politiques*, in which the State would have been studied in its external relations, the first part having been consecrated to the State or the principles of political right" (3:1507, n. 1). Yet, whether one disregards a part of the text that is there or projects a part of the text that is not there, one is still in flight from the same ghostly presence. Its exorcism seems to require either a withdrawal inward or an expansion outward if one is to settle finally on some sense of the thing that keeps turning itself inside out.

Fixing attention on the "Conclusion," without looking elsewhere for a more resolute form in which to contain it, one finds that this ghostliness insists and insists all the more as one approaches the last word before the end, the word "moi." And thus it is finally, in the end, the most familiar that has become the most strange.

As in the *avertissement*, where a lack of strength or "forces" is said to cut short the work, the last lines of the "Conclusion" invoke a physical limit that has forced the text into a partial or incomplete form. Because all that would remain to be considered about the state's external relations "forms a new subject far too vast for my limited view," I can look no further and have had to stop here. This is the meaning that is implied, but it is not quite what is said in the final sentence: "J'aurais dû fixer [ma vue] toujours plus près de moi," not "I have had to," but rather I should have, I ought to have fixed my sights ever closer to myself. The past conditional inflection (the tense of regret or remorse) cannot altogether be made to fit the notion of a forced constriction because it says that I should have kept my sights fixed closer than I have done in fact. I have already gone beyond the limits I should have remained within, the limits of the "moi." The strangeness or ghostliness would reside in the inexplicable distance from which "je" looks back, regretfully, on the "plus près de moi" without being able to explain how it has been led so far away from itself. Rather than a restriction that would have been imposed by the "moi's" limitation, this final phrase intimates that "je" has been carried outside its own limits, the "près-de-moi" or the proper, into some faraway region that cannot be brought under the self's purview. It is as if, by its final words, "je" were admitting that at some point it had lost sight of itself, become a stranger.

At some point, but where? At what point did "je" step out of the circle "près de moi"? One possible answer is close at hand: at the immediately preceding point where the state's external relations are envisaged as the support—the *appui*—that remains to be put in place. "I should have kept my sights fixed closer to me" would thus mean: I should never have even glanced at "all this," I should never have opened the question in this "Conclusion." I should have drawn the line "plus près de moi" and observed the limit imposed by my myopia. This reading fits with what we have said about the "Conclusion's" double gesture of overstepping and then withdrawing from a border. It would also explain why readers have generally found it so easy to ignore this chapter, as if it were already half erased and partially withdrawn.

But such a reading also functions as a kind of protective railing because it supposes that the edge is overstepped only at the last by the final step, which it would suffice to withhold in order to remain within a safe radius close to home. What is being guarded against, perhaps, is the full realization here at the end, after the fact, that from its very first step, from the moment "je" opens its eyes and says "Je veux chercher . . . ," it has left "moi" behind and is already in the mode of an estrangement that could be *"toujours* plus près," *always* closer. The question of external relations which seems to arise only at the end would in fact have been deferred from the outset; its definitive adjournment would be but the culmination of an initial deferral. The break that occurs here, instead of closing the state at its border, projects back from the edge and reopens the question of relations to and within difference which has been put off until it can be abandoned. The whole fabric of *Du contrat social* thus unravels from its far edge, returning to this side of the first step into the shadowy region of external relations, political institutions, the back and forth movement of their texts. The first step, that is to say a certain desire, a certain "Je veux . . ."

Du contrat social would have taken place between the initial "je" and the final "moi," a contract passed, therefore, between "I" and "me." Unlike the Sovereign, however, which passes a contract with itself and therefore does not need to sign, there where the contract breaks off and breaks down along its raveled edge, Rousseau signs or attempts to sign. But how can "I" sign in estrangement from "myself"? Or rather is not the signature the first and thus the strangest mark of that estrangement—at once closest to me and yet already without any common measure, "so near and yet so far"? My signature is a ghostly trace of my absence, a reminder not only of the limits on "mes forces" or "ma vue" but of the finitude that is "me." I sign, therefore, by withdrawing the signature: "J'aurais dû la garder toujours plus près de moi."[40]

Postscript

There is, in effect, a postscript to the "Conclusion" of *Du contrat social*, a passage in the *Confessions* where Rousseau mentions his abandoned *Institutions politiques*.

> Of the different works which I had on the stocks, the one I had long had in my head, at which I worked with the greatest inclina-

---

[40]In "Des Tours de Babel" Derrida considers the trait of the proper name to be the translation, the contract in the transcendental sense: "The debt does not involve living subjects but names at the edge of the language or, more rigorously, the trait which contracts the relation of the aforementioned living subject to his name, insofar as the latter keeps to the edge of language. And this trait would be that of the to-be-translated from one language to the other, from this edge to the other of the proper name. . . . The topos of this contract is exceptional, unique, and practically impossible to think under the ordinary category of contract: in a classical code it would have been called transcendental, since in truth it renders possible every contract in general. . . . The translation contract, in this transcendental sense, would be the contract itself, the absolute contract, the contract form of the contract, that which allows a contract to be what it is" (185–86). In effect, Rousseau's *Contrat* breaks off at the point where its terms would have to be translated.

tion, to which I wished to devote myself all my life, and which, in my own opinion, was to set the seal upon my reputation [et qui devait selon moi mettre le sceau à ma réputation] was my *Institutions politiques*. . . . What kind of government is best adapted to produce the most virtuous, the most enlightened, the wisest, and, in short, the best people . . . I thought that I perceived that this question was very closely connected with another, very nearly although not quite the same. What is the government which, from its nature, always keeps closest to the law [toujours le plus près de la loi]? This leads to the question, What is the Law? and to a series of questions equally important. I saw that all this led me on to great truths conducive to the happiness of the human race, above all to that of my country, in which I had not found, in the journey I had just made thither, sufficiently clear or correct notions of liberty and laws to satisfy me; and I believed that this indirect method of communicating them was the best suited to spare the pride of those it concerned, and to secure my own forgiveness for having been able to see a little further than themselves [d'avoir pu voir là-dessus un peu plus loin qu'eux]. (417–18; 1:404–5)

There are several echoes—or ghostly reminders—of the final lines of *Du contrat social*: "toujours le plus près de la loi" echoes "toujours plus près de moi," but also a certain nearsightedness is contrasted with the farsightedness mentioned in the final lines. And that is not all. Rousseau refers to his unwritten *Institutions politiques* as the work "qui devait selon moi *mettre le sceau* à ma réputation"—which would, that is, authenticate and confirm his reputation: seal it and sign it. The work that could never be finished is the one whose extension beyond the limited part would have required leaving home, crossing the borders of a "moi," entering into an estrangement from oneself. There, from the place of strangeness, Rousseau could have sealed his name. Instead, there is the unsealed signature "Rousseau," which we must recognize in its fugitive trait as it withdraws from the border with the other.

CHAPTER THREE

Author of a Crime

… le parti que j'ai pris d'ecrire et de me cacher …
—*Confessions*

It is a matter of no small pride for Rousseau that between 10 and 12 June 1762 he managed to write most of a short prose text he titled *Le Lévite d'Ephraïm*. The condemnation of *Emile* and the decree of a *prise de corps* against its author had been issued by the Parlement de Paris on 9 June. The following afternoon he fled Montmorency in a borrowed coach, and *la fuite de Rousseau* began a new phase. Both the *Confessions* and two *Projets de préface* to a never-completed volume (which would have included *Le Lévite*) insist on the uncomfortable but finally ennobling situation of this minor text that is, in a somewhat unusual sense, a *texte de circonstance*. First, the *Confessions*: "*Le Lévite d'Ephraïm*, if it is not the best of my works, will always be my favorite. I have never read it again, I never shall read it again, without being sensible of the approval of a heart free from bitterness, which, far from being soured by misfortune, finds consolation for it with itself, and, in itself, the means of compensation for it" (608; 1:586–87). The first *Projet de préface*, probably sketched a year or so after the tale itself, is just as self-congratulatory but mentions as well a particular form of vengeance that would have been Rousseau's own in writing what he himself admits, in the *Confessions*, is an "abominable" story: "Here is how I occupied myself in the cruelest moments of my life, overwhelmed by misfortunes for which no man should have to prepare himself. Drowning in a

sea of misfortune, crushed beneath the evil deeds of my un-
grateful and barbarous contemporaries, the only one from
which I escape and which remains with them to avenge me is
that of hatred" (2:1205).

That Rousseau was occupied with writing such a text rather
than plotting some vengeance, or rather that he savored his
vengeance only in an asymmetry with his persecutors—they
are full of hate, he is not—makes of that text the proof of
difference between victim and persecutor.[1] The proof is syl-
logistic: "un homme qui s'occupe *ainsi* quand on le tourmente
n'est pas un ennemi bien dangereux" (a man *thus* occupied
when he is being tormented is not a very dangerous enemy)
(2:1207). The "ainsi" here bears the whole burden of the proof of
difference, yet it is anything but an unambiguous indicator of
what is meant by the occupation of the tormented man. Indeed,
at least three simultaneously occupied positions are invoked as
a series of frames.

　1. At the outermost frame and in the most encompassing
sense, Rousseau is occupied with fleeing arrest by the authorities. The meaning of that flight is already in dispute, not because according to official decree Rousseau was a criminal esca-
ping retribution rather than a victim fleeing persecution (he, of
course, will never doubt his right to have written and published
Emile and *Du contrat social*); rather, it is because of the distinct
possibility that the condemnation of *Emile* had been precipitated by Rousseau's "protectors" (particularly the maréchale de
Montmorency), who had arranged for the printing of *Emile* by a
Paris publisher, against the author's express wishes. Had the
book originally been printed in Holland, as Rousseau insisted it
should be and even as he believed for a while it was, it is at least
open to question whether the Paris authorities would have

---

[1]In the account of these events in the *Confessions*, Rousseau insists on his
nonspiteful character: "It is due to this happy frame of mind, I am convinced,
that I have never known that spiteful disposition which ferments in a revenge-
ful heart, which never forgets affronts received, and worries itself with all the
evil it would like to inflict upon its enemy by way of requital. Naturally hot-
tempered, I have felt angry, even enraged, in the impulse of the moment; but a
desire for vengeance has never taken root in my heart" (607; 1:585).

found the grounds to decree a *prise de corps*. Rousseau's decision on 10 June to flee was finally taken, at least in part, to protect the "protectors" who had implicated themselves in his "crime" and who may even have feared that he would justify himself at their expense.[2] As we shall see, these circumstances have been reinscribed in *Le Lévite d'Ephraïm*.

2. Innermost, Rousseau is occupied or preoccupied by the story in the final three chapters of the Book of Judges, the same chapters he had just finished reading on the eve of his sudden departure when he was summoned in the middle of the night by the maréchale. The *Confessions*: "This history greatly affected me, and I was pondering over it in a half-dreamy state [j'en étais occupé dans une espèce de rêve], from which I was roused by a noise and a light" (601; 1:580). It is a tale of terrible vengeance but one that, unmistakably and perhaps inevitably, miscalculates, backfires, or otherwise goes awry. Given this indirection or double direction of the vengeful impulse, which multiplies the possible points of identification within the story, it cannot be easy to identify exactly how or in what sense Rousseau might be said to be "occupied" by it.

3. Between the outer and inner versions of his occupation, there is the writing of the tale, an activity with which he oc-

---

[2]Rousseau's account of these events in book XI of the *Confessions* hesitates to accuse outright the maréchale of engineering his condemnation. One is left to read between the lines. But one should also hesitate to dismiss Rousseau's intimations or suspicions as having only a paranoid sense, even if unquestionably the events of June 1762 have to be understood as one of the matrices of subsequent persecutory fixations. A reenactment of the events by Marcel Françon (in "La Condamnation de *L'Emile*"), while it cannot establish anyone's motives, leaves little doubt that Rousseau was ill served by his powerful friends. Recently, Benoît Mély has written: "The interest that these reforming aristocrats took in the author and his work derived finally from their wish to find a remedy, not for the misery of the people, but the problems that their social group was having in collectively imposing its authority on the latter. Their benevolence toward Rousseau did not go so far as to cause them to run the risk of compromising themselves by taking his defense too openly in case things went wrong. As for Rousseau, he maintained many illusions as to the good intentions of his aristocratic 'friends,' as well as to their capacity to protect him from any attack." *Jean-Jacques Rousseau: Un intellectuel en rupture* (Paris, 1986), 147.

cupies himself during the days on the road. The second *Projet de préface* describes this occupation:

> These mournful ideas followed me despite myself and made my voyage unpleasant. . . . I thought of putting my reverie on a different track by occupying myself with some subject [donner le change à ma rêverie en m'occupant de quelque sujet]; this one came to mind; I found it fit rather well with my thinking. It offered me a kind of intermediary [une espèce d'intermédiaire] between the state in which I found myself and the one at which I wanted to arrive; I could give in from time to time to my dark mood, then substitute for it more pleasant objects. Each time my subject permitted me to do so, I imitated . . . the delicious images of M. Gessner. Thus I achieved more or less my purpose and ended my trip in a pleasant way. (2:1206)

Jacques Derrida has established the link between Rousseau's frequent use of the expression "donner le change" (to describe, for example, a masturbatory practice, "the pernicious habit of sidetracking my needs") and the practice of writing, which supplements or substitutes for the presence of some other.[3] In the above passage, this link needs hardly any restating, since it is the writing of *Le Lévite d'Ephraïm* that is said to "donner le change" to "these mournful ideas [that] followed me despite myself." The expression is being used here almost in its first technical sense (from venery) of putting the pack off the scent, sending it on a false trail. While any real pursuers had been left behind on the outskirts of Paris, it is their internalized version, "these mournful ideas," that Rousseau is eager to put off his trail. Writing is thus, as Derrida has shown, a switching device that both diverts the writer from one "reverie" by occupying him with another and supplies a symbolic satisfaction or a semblance of the dream's "immediate" gratification.[4] The text

[3]See Derrida, *Of Grammatology*, 154: "*Donner le change*: in whatever sense it is understood, this expression describes the recourse to the supplement admirably." While this expression has indeed several senses, one of them is definitely not, as the translator suggests, to "give money."

[4]"The restitution of presence by language, restitution at the same time symbolic and immediate. This contradiction must be thought. Immediate experi-

of this writing is called "intermediary," by which Rousseau seems to mean here a mixture of genres or modes, or better still the contrast of manner and substance: as he puts it in the *Confessions*, the "idyllic and simple style [his model is a translation of Salomon Gessner's *Idylles et poëmes champêtres*] appeared little suited for such an atrocious subject." This mélange, however, is also said to represent a transition between states: "the state in which I found myself and the one at which I wanted to arrive" (2:1206).

The intermediate writing of *Le Lévite d'Éphraïm* is carried forward by a conjunction of forces that are not all at Rousseau's command. It is as if the very *situation* of this activity—Rousseau's flight in the borrowed carriage, the conduct of his journey in the hands of others (he notes that even his drivers took him for a naïf making his first trip by the post: "[I] became the laughing-stock of the postillions. I ended up . . . going however it pleased them" [606; 1:585])—were being doubled by the writing that proceeds according to some surprising command: "No sooner had I begun than I was astonished at how quickly my ideas came, and the ease with which I expressed them" (608; 1:586).

Yet clearly the occupation of writing is *intermediary* as well in the sense that it inscribes a transition between the outer and inner frames of this preoccupied *rêverie*, between a flight from vengeance and a complete submission to its demand. The question thus becomes how such a mixed inscription can ever sustain or prove the difference of the one from the other. Between real events and fictional story, between life and literature: this is the place of the signature. The question is also therefore the following: How is one to read Rousseau's signature on and in this text? Or rather, what signs "Rousseau"?

---

ence of restitution because . . . *it dispenses with passage through the world.* . . . Experience of *immediate* restitution, also because it *does not wait.* . . . But what is no longer deferred is also absolutely deferred. The presence that is thus delivered to us in the present is a chimera. . . . The sign, the image, the representation, which come to supplement the absent presence are the illusions that sidetrack us [donnent le change]." Ibid., 154.

A Vengeful Story

In its *grandes lignes*, the story Rousseau dashes off is well known. In the days "when there was no king in Israel," a Levite took as a concubine a virgin from Bethlehem whom he carried back to his home in Ephraim. The young girl "became angry with him" (Judges 19:2) and returned to her father's house. After a while, the Levite went after her and persuaded her father to let her return with him to Ephraim. The father managed to delay their departure for several days, but finally they left and came to the end of their first day's journey in Gibeah, "which belongs to Benjamin." They sat down in the open square of the city, waiting to be given hospitality by some townspeople, but none offered to take them in. Finally, an old man, who was also from Ephraim, gave them shelter and feasted them. During the feast, an unruly band of Benjaminites attacked the old man's house and demanded that he turn over the Levite to them "that we may know him" (19:22). The old man pleaded with them not to do such a vile thing to a guest in his house and offered to give them instead his own virgin daughter and the Levite's concubine. "'Ravish them and do with them what seems good to you; but against this man do not do so vile a thing.'" (Rousseau revises the story at this point, the old man, according to him, offering only his own daughter to the ravishers: "he ran to fetch his daughter in order to ransom his guest at the price of his own blood" [2:1214]; we will return to this difference below.) The Levite then intervened and thrust his concubine into the hands of the gang. "And they knew her, and abused her all night until the morning" (19:25). The next day, the Levite found her dead on the doorstep. He carried her body back to Ephraim, where he cut it into twelve pieces and sent them throughout Israel. "And all who saw it said, 'Such a thing has never happened or been seen from the day that the people of Israel came up out of the land of Egypt until this day'" (19:30). A throng of Israelites then gathered in Ephraim and heard the story of rape and murder from the Levite, who demanded vengeance from Benjamin. The Benjaminites refused to turn over the guilty men, so all the other tribes declared war on them. Although God approved the war, it went badly at first for the avengers, who were routed in two battles by Benjamin. But in the third battle the tribe of Benjamin was reduced to a mere 600 men. Israel relented at this point when it realized that one of its tribes was now menaced with extinction. The threat was quite real, for all the other tribes had also sworn an oath never to give their daughters to Benjamin for wives. To resolve the dilemma, they decided to kill the inhabitants of Jabesh-gilead (because they had not taken part in the war against Benjamin or sworn the oath) and to ravish the virgins of the town and present them to Benjamin. The plan was carried out, but they returned with only four hundred ravished virgins, so that two hundred Benjaminites still had no wives. It was then decided that these two hundred would steal the virgins of Shiloh when the latter left the town to celebrate a holy festival. The elders agreed that if the fathers of these girls came to them to complain, they would plead with them to grant their daughters willingly to the ravishers so that "a tribe be not blotted out from Israel." And so it was done.

From this outline of the legend, it is easy to see the strange turn taken by this vengeance of brother against brother. When Israel stops short of annihilating Benjamin, when the extinction of one of its members by the whole is at last understood as a form of self-mutilation, it achieves resolution by twice *repeating* Benjamin's crime. In the first repetition, the Israelites act as Benjamin's agents, stealing the virgins of Jabesh-gilead;[5] in the second repetition, the Benjaminites are authorized to steal their wives for themselves and promised immunity from retribution. Israel thus averts the threat to its unity and continuity as a whole by prescribing the crime that it had to avenge in the first place, by legislating and enacting in an exceptional manner the contrary of the law *as* the law. The Levite's avengers, after punishing Benjamin, find themselves forced to identify with the criminals they have punished and to refuse any demand for vengeance (by the fathers of Shiloh) of the very sort they have

---

[5]Biblical commentary explains the absence of Jabesh-gilead from the war, and thus their exemption form the oath, by "an old marital bond between Machir (Gilead) and Benjamin" (1 Chron. 7:15). G. A. Buttrick et al., eds., *The Interpreter's Bible* (New York, 1952), 823.

just carried out. The solution requires, in other words, that the victim—or the victim's representatives—exchange places with the victimizer, and that the new "crimes" be exceptionally exempted from any right to vengeance.

But this is not the only repetition of a crime; it is merely the final one that recloses a breach opened in Israel's wholeness. And if one looks closer, it will be noticed that Israel's "crime" does not *exactly* repeat Benjamin's: among other differences, the latter had ravished another man's wife (or concubine), whereas the former steals men's daughters. In fact, the "crime" that closes the series—the Benjaminites' abduction of the daughters of Shiloh—is more nearly a repetition of the Levite's carrying off of his concubine from her father's home when clearly the latter did not wish her to leave. As for the central crime of rape and murder, it too is doubled—this time deliberately, to signify the Benjaminites' offense—by the Levite when he mutilates the dead woman's body.[6] The possibility that the Levite may have been, all along, the original criminal and that, like Oedipus, he demanded in effect his "own" punishment introduces a far more resistant twist in this already twisted story of crime and punishment. Victim and victimizer, avenger and offender would not only have exchanged roles over time and in the course of events; as well the one may have been serving all along as mask—or defense—for the other.

The writing Rousseau calls "intermediary" is situated, then, between the ambiguities and repetitious doublings of the bibli-

---

[6]In the opening chapter of the *Essay on the Origin of Languages*, when Rousseau is arguing the superior expressiveness of a language of gesture over that of either voice or writing, he cites the legend of the Levite in example: "When the Levite of Ephraim wanted to avenge the death of his wife, he wrote nothing to the tribes of Israel, but divided her body into twelve sections which he sent to them. At this horrible sight they rushed to arms, crying with one voice: *Never has such a thing happened in Israel, from the time of our fathers' going out of Egypt, down to the present day!* And the tribe of Benjamin was exterminated." (In a note: "There remained only 600 men, with no women or children.") "In our day, this affair, recounted in court pleadings and discussions, perhaps in jest, would be dragged out until this most horrible of crimes would in the end have remained unpunished." In *On the Origin of Language: Two Essays*, ed. and trans. John Moran and Alexander Gode (Chicago, 1966), 7; French edition, ed. Charles Porset (Paris, 1970), 33.

cal account, on the one hand, and, on the other, the uncertain or unclear meaning of his flight from Paris. How does the one side of this nonequation read and rewrite the other?

Voicing Revenge

From the first, Rousseau's *récit* engages both sides of the frame by a complex mode of address that implicates a narrating voice with a narrated one. In the initial two paragraphs, apostrophes follow each other in rapid succession, as if the principal voice were unable to decide whom to address.

> Hallowed rage of virtue, come animate my voice. I will tell of the crimes of Benjamin and the revenge of Israel; I will tell of unmatched infamy and of even more terrible punishments. Mortals, respect beauty, customs, hospitality; be just without cruelty, merciful without weakness, and know how to pardon the guilty rather than punish the innocent.
>
> O you, good-natured men, enemies of all inhumanity, you who, fearing to confront the crimes of your brothers, prefer to let them go unpunished: What picture am I going to set before your eyes? The body of a woman cut into pieces; her torn and throbbing members sent to the twelve Tribes; all the people, frozen with horror, raising a unanimous clamor to Heaven and crying out in concert: No, never has such a thing happened in Israel, from the time of our fathers' going out of Egypt, down to the present day. Blessed people, gather yourself; pronounce judgment on this horrible act, and mete out the price it deserves. He who diverts his eyes from such infamies is a coward, a deserter from justice; true humanity looks them in the face so as to know them, judge them and detest them. (2:1208)

First, a stylized apostrophe to the "hallowed rage of virtue," which is invited to "animate my voice," the voice that will tell of Benjamin's crimes and Israel's vengeance. Next, an apostrophe to "[you] mortals," who, among other things, are warned to "pardon the guilty rather than punish the innocent." This apostrophe is rather inconsistently followed by another to "you, good-natured men . . . who, fearing to confront the crimes of your brothers, prefer to let them go unpunished," a reproach that, on the surface at least, seems to contradict the previous warning. The voice then asks: "What picture am I going to set before your eyes?" and answers: "The body of a woman cut into pieces; her torn and throbbing members sent to the twelve Tribes." We may well ask at this point who is speaking, since the voice here comes very close to doubling the "voice" of the Levite, that is, his gesture of presenting Israel with the sight of the woman's mutilated body. The two situations of address—of the *récit* and of what is recounted in the *récit*, of a text addressed to a reader and of a divided body addressed to Israel—have very nearly become superimposed here. What is more (and we will have to come back to this point later), by introducing the *récit* with this prologue that presents already the "picture" (*tableau*) of the mutilated body, Rousseau in effect duplicates the structure of the Levite's message or *envoi* that will then be followed with the *récit* of the mutilation.

Out of the superimposition that shapes the narrating voice to the Levite's call for vengeance rises a figure of unanimity as the text continues: "all the people, frozen with horror, raising a unanimous clamor to Heaven and crying out in concert: No, never . . ." The redundant insistence here on "unanimous" and "in concert" (*de concert*)[7] seems to be working to negate the tension between different voices, or a division within the voice of address, which has so marked the text already to this point. Its tableau of division would be repaired by the voice of unanimity. Even so, even though the response to the spectacle of dismemberment is of the whole, the tension will not go away. The unanimous voice of the people addresses the command to "gather yourself [rassemble-toi]." Although the voice speaking here already represents the gathering or *rassemblement* of the whole, it still addresses to "the people" the command to gather itself together. The address, in other words, presupposes the very division it would remedy with the command "gather yourself," "rassemble-toi." As the voice—some voice—continues, it will once again become impossible to say who is speaking to

---

[7]In the *Essay*, the same phrase is spoken by the people "en criant tout d'une voix." See above, n. 6.

whom about what. Is it the narrator or still the voice of the people? Who accuses the coward who "diverts his eyes from such infamies"? This accusation recalls the terms of the narrator's earlier address to "you, good-natured men," who, it is said, are afraid "to confront the crimes of your brothers." But at this point in the raveled threads of the invocation, it is impossible to distinguish a narrating voice from the unanimous voice of the people represented in the narration.

Le Lévite d'Ephraïm would be, then, the *récit* of crimes from which none can look away—from the crimes, from the *récit*. The Levite tells his own story with a force that, precisely, *forces* the attention of the addressee—and first of all, it would seem, Rousseau's. If there is a compulsive identification at the source of this writing, however, it cannot be located in any one figure but gathers its strength from an overdetermination and a shifting of possible points of identification. Indeed, it would even seem that this story of multiple mutilations lays bare a fundamental obstacle to complete identification of some whole with itself and without contradiction. The situation of address at the outset of the *récit* speaks less of a fusion than of a confusion of voices, less of a single demand for justice than of a difference in the notion of justice (is it the forgiveness of sin or an eye for an eye?), and therefore less of an unequivocal right to vengeance than of a possible reversal at the heart of the relation between judge and judged, accuser and accused, and so forth. And, in fact, it is the possibility of this reversal that will be exploited to bring the *récit* of Israel's divisions to a close.

Multiple Fractures

But the *récit* also clearly turns around the mutilation as around its center. As we have already suggested, the Levite's act is doubly a repetition: it repeats the Benjaminites' crime in order to signify it, but also it repeats the Levite's "crime" of separating his concubine from her family. One of Rousseau's variations in "le style champêtre" on the biblical text is a *mise en tableau* of this latter moment which foregrounds its mutilating aspect:

How many regrets were the price of this ill-fated separation! How many touching farewells were said and begun again! How many tears the young woman's sisters let fall upon her face! How many times they took her again in their arms! How many times her tearful mother, holding her again in her arms, felt the pains of a new separation! But her father was not crying as he kissed her: his mute embraces were doleful and convulsive; great sighs wrenched his chest. (2:1211)

As we leave this pathetic scene, the narrator eulogizes the lost family unity in terms that anticipate the girl's murder but implicate as well the Levite's "barbarism" in tearing her away from her parents: "How happy is the family which in purest union spends its peaceful days in the bosom of friendship and seems to have but one heart for all its members. . . . What furious barbarism it must be that did not respect your joys" (2:1212).

This, then, is the first "mutilation" on which the others follow.[8] The sundering of the girl's body occurs, therefore, not twice but three times: first as required by exogamous law, second as the crime of rape, and third as a mutilation of her body which signifies the rape. And because the cycle of violence will end only when the original crime is repeated under the guise once again of the law, there is just as much reason to read in that end a new beginning. The "remedy that could reestablish in its entirety the mutilated race of Jacob" (2:1220) resembles too closely the injury that has been done to it or that it has done to itself: "But the victorious tribes . . . felt the wound that they had inflicted on themselves" (2:1219). There is a hole in the whole and no law can heal it over. On the contrary, the law institutes the very separation it also covers over beneath the appearance of retributive justice.

Victim Identification

If, as we are supposing, Rousseau writes *Le Lévite d'Ephraïm* out of an inchoate identification with the forceful writing of the

[8]With the image of the mother "who felt the pains of a new separation," there is as well the suggestion of the first partition—parturition—by which the family is born.

Levite, it is also of course because certain analogies link the biblical account to the events of 9–10 June. Like the Levite, Rousseau is the target of a perverse attack while a guest in another man's house. The attack on him is perverse, in Rousseau's estimation, because it takes aim not only at *Emile*, which was condemned to be lacerated and burned in public, but also at the person of its author. In fact, Rousseau was still confident several days before the rumored decree was handed down that everyone around him was uselessly alarmed for his safety, for he remained persuaded that the law would act illegally if it decreed his arrest:

> I knew that the Parliament was very careful about formalities and that it would be an infringement of them all if in this case they began by issuing a warrant for my arrest, before establishing judicially whether I acknowledged the book and was really its author [avant de savoir juridiquement si j'avouais le livre et si réellement j'en étais l'Auteur]. I said to Mme de Boufflers: "It is only in the case of those crimes which threaten public safety that accused parties may be arrested on the basis of circumstantial evidence for fear they may escape punishment. However, when one wants to punish a crime such as mine . . . the custom is to proceed against the book and to avoid attacking the author as much as possible."
> (600; 1:578–79)

Moreover, when the decree is issued and Rousseau decides to flee, he does so partly to protect his hosts. At least three key elements of this situation are then taken up, slightly rearranged, in *Le Lévite d'Ephraïm*: an attack on the "wrong" object; an implied substitution of the "right" object; an action to protect the host. Through this rewriting, a sense of Rousseau's flight—a flight into writing—is allowed to emerge which otherwise could not. At the same time, this text presents a displaced—allegorical—meditation on the signature that has been judged criminal. It prompts us to ask: How does an author become the author of a crime? And, a still more puzzling question: How can such an act justify or annul itself by another signature?

In the biblical account, the "wrongness" of the attack on the Levite is signaled by the offer, which is accepted, to substitute for him two women. *Le Lévite d'Ephraïm* adjusts the structure of this substitution so as, in effect, to substitute one kind of substitution for another. When the concubine is turned over to her ravishers, it is as a substitute for the daughter of the host, whom the latter had offered in place of his guest (whereas in the biblical version, which Rousseau generally follows, the concubine was first offered, along with his daughter, by the old man).[9] The revision introduced at this crucial moment has the effect of disguising somewhat the fact that the concubine's delivery into the hands of the Benjaminites saves not only the host's daughter but first of all the Levite, who was the initial object of the attack. The Levite, one could say, *donne le change* to his pursuers. But Rousseau's text interprets his gesture only as the generosity of the guest repaying his host:

> But the Levite, who had been frozen by terror until this moment, regains his senses at this deplorable prospect, forestalls the generous old man, runs ahead of him, forces him to go back in the house with his daughter, and taking himself his own beloved companion, without saying a word to her, without raising his eyes to her, drags her to the door and hands her over to the accursed ones. (2:1214)

This breathless sentence even tries to screen the sense of the Levite's gesture behind the protest of "his own beloved companion" ("sa compagne bien-aimée"), although it is precisely such an affective note that rings most false in the brutal scenario. Yet, having at the outset of the text adopted the idyllic tone of a shepherd's romance (which, needless to say, has no echo in the biblical version), Rousseau here may have simply got caught in an irresolvable contradiction of manner and matter. The contradiction is dissipated only when the Levite is pictured impassively cutting up the body of his "bien-aimée":

> From that moment, occupied with the sole project that filled his soul, he was oblivious to any other feeling: love, regret, pity,

[9]In his fine study of this text, Thomas M. Kavanagh orders his reading around the several revisions that Rousseau introduces into the biblical legend. He does not, however, mention this revision; see *Writing the Truth: Authority and Desire in Rousseau* (Berkeley, 1987).

everything became fury in him. Even the sight of this body, which ought to have reduced him to tears, calls forth from him no more cries. He contemplates it with a dry and dark look; he sees in it only an object of rage and depair . . . without hesitating or trembling, the barbarian dares to cut the body up into twelve pieces; with a steady hand, he strikes fearlessly, cutting flesh and bones, separating head and members, and . . . sends to the Tribes these frightful messages. (2:1215)

This frightful writing of the Levite also involves, of course, a structure of substitution. The *envois* are sent to "speak" for themselves in place of a living witness to the act that, precisely, has rendered the body speechless. As messages or messengers, therefore, the body parts can "speak" nothing but the redundant meaning of mutilation, which they "are" rather than represent. As writing, this literal spacing out of a body is undecipherable. Because everything remains to be said about the concubine's rape, murder, and mutilation, because the message or the *envoi* cannot *represent* these events, in the manner of a pantomime or even a pictogram, a necessary moment in both the biblical version and *Le Lévite d'Ephraïm* is the *récit* within the *récit* when the Levite must recount what happened to the tribes that have gathered to learn the meaning of the strange message: "Then the Elders . . . interrogated the Levite before the assembly about the murder of the young girl" (2:1216); "And the people of Israel said, 'Tell us, how was this wickedness brought to pass?'" (20:3). Like a newspaper that publishes sensationalist photographs on the front page and directs readers to an inside page for details, the Levite's publicity stunt works first of all to get everyone's attention.

Yet, in a narrative where each event is repeating or being repeated and reversing its meaning, the Levite's publication of the crime is, if not its representation, then in some way its repetition. Clearly, the mutilation he performs repeats in a calculated fashion the brutal, frenzied mutilation of the same body by the Benjaminites. But is there not as well a suggestion of another repetition in the very gesture of sending the body as one would send a delegate or envoy or representative? In this sense, the gesture repeats or recalls not the Benjaminites' crime—rape—but the Levite's delegation of his concubine in his stead, the crime, if you will, of representation. The Levite's publication thus takes the form of his crime and sends a self-accusatory message. The *récit* he will then offer is also necessary to correct—or conceal—this other message, as it does in both the biblical version ("'the men of Gibeah rose against me, and beset the house round about me by night; they meant to kill me, and they ravished my concubine, and she is dead'") and Rousseau's version. In the latter, however, the Levite adds a note of protest about his veracity, as if he anticipated some objection to the account: "the townspeople surrounded the house where I was lodged, seeking to dishonor and kill me. I was forced to deliver my wife over to their debauchery; she died as she left their hands. Then I took her body, divided it into pieces and I sent them to each of you. People of the Lord, I have spoken the truth [j'ai dit la vérité]" (2:1216). That final note tends to confirm what we have been suggesting: the Levite is not simply the crime's victim (and he is not, of course, its primary victim) but also in one sense its *author*, insofar as he "wrote" it and published it, yet, more significantly, insofar as his representation *of* it reworks and conceals his representation *in* it.

Recall that Rousseau considered the procedure of the Paris parliament against him to be an infraction of basic legal forms: "it would be an infringement of them all if in this case they began by issuing a warrant for my arrest, before establishing judicially whether I acknowledged the book and was really its author." The point clearly is not that, given the chance, Rousseau would have disavowed authorship of *Emile*. Rather, he implies that since the "crimes" he is accused of are crimes of representation (and not commission), they carry with them a constant risk of *mis*representation, which the parliament should avoid or at least reduce by confronting the alleged author in person instead of through the delegation of a signature. Representation is the medium of this *mis-*, the constant possibility of a reversing repetition. Rousseau, of course, conceived voice to be the only reliable signature and thus the only tribunal competent to present, rather than represent, a man's acts. In the years to come, he returns frequently to this theme of a condem-

nation without any hearing.[10] It is all the more striking, therefore, that *Le Lévite d'Ephraïm* stages just such a hearing of a
"writer." Notice, however, that the text does not bear out the
putative reliability of voice and the unreliability of writing
because there is a crime—a crime of representation—which the
writing points to and the hearing covers over. Only writing can
accuse the crime that it is, even as it repeats it. "The author of a
crime" would thus have functioned as the hidden, rejected, or
inaudible phrase linking the two frames of this text.

Plus de voix: *(No) More Voice(s)*

At a moment when Rousseau finds himself more than ever in
need of a language with which to demand justice for himself, it
is the Levite's gruesome act that imposes itself as an emblem of
a writing that will "speak" with one, unequivocal voice and
leave no space to doubt the just meaning of the "speaker."[11] But
a question also thereby imposes itself: what might it mean that
the need or desire for a living or animated writing—a writing
that speaks with one forceful voice—takes as its model the
mutilation and dispersion of a woman's dead body? In what way
does this dead letter offer a refuge from the vicissitudes of
conventional writing? Such a question is not posed merely to
this text, to its author, to its signature, and to the conditions of
its composition. These latter would be more like lenses through
which to focus an aspect of the general cultural text that continues to link us to the legend of the Levite and his concubine,
for example, and that makes much of that story seem still
readable. More specifically, the question is posed to the signature on that general text and asks whether it remains readable

[10]After the condemnation of *Emile*, Rousseau becomes increasingly obsessed
by the scenario of being tried and sentenced in absentia. All the autobiographical texts, and particularly the *Dialogues* (which evoke at several points the trial
of a dead man), can be read as given over in large measure to this scenario.

[11]He dreams, that is, of an animated writing that will present the presence of
his intention in his absence and in such a way that none can question its purity
or integrity. Once again, the reference is to Derrida, *Of Grammatology*, in
particular chaps. 2–4.

because, through all the *envois*, translations, adaptations, and revisions such as Rousseau's, it continues to find a support or an echo in dreams of an unequivocal writing that will allow men to speak with one voice, to sign with one name. But again: what does it mean that the "voice" which can still "speak" to us is precisely not a voice at all, but its violent suppression in and by representation?

Needless to say (but the whole issue is precisely the status of such a foregone conclusion), the girl from Bethlehem has no voice in the matter, no voice at all. More than that, in Rousseau's text, whenever she might have spoken up or whenever she is addressed, there is a detour taken around her voice. That is, either some other expression—smile or tears—or someone else's voice supplies the meaning of what she could have said but did not. Thus, on her first meeting with the Levite: "He said to her: Daughter of Judah . . . *she smiled at him*; they were united, then he led her off to his mountains" (2:1209); on their second meeting: "he raised his eyes to his young wife and said to her: Daughter of Israel, . . . The young girl *began to cry*" (2:1210). The Levite then addresses himself to the girl's father who can speak for her: "Then he said to the father, . . . The father looked at his daughter, and the girl's heart was touched by the return of her husband. *So the father said . . .*" Nor can we infer that the girl is mute by nature since, at a very significant moment in the *récit*, she is said to have *no longer any voice* (*plus de voix*) with which to cry out:

> Without saying a word to her . . . [he] dragged her to the door and handed her over to the accursed ones. Right away they surrounded the half-dead girl [la jeune fille à demi-morte], they grabbed her and fought over her mercilessly. . . . O miserable men, who destroy your species through the pleasures meant to reproduce it, how is it that your ferocious desires are not arrested by this dying beauty [cette beauté mourante]? Look at her eyes already closed to the light, her fading features, her darkened face; the pallor of death has covered her cheeks, livid violet has replaced the roses in them, she has no more voice in which to moan [elle n'a plus de voix pour gémir], her hands have not the strength to repulse your insults. Alas! she is already dead [elle est déjà morte]! (2:1214–15)

This "femme-déjà-morte" is also already a figure for the woman without a voice, *la femme sans voix*, not only the girl from Bethlehem but, by general extension, her whole sex. "Slave or tyrant, the sex that man oppresses or adores, and whose happiness, like his own, he will never know without letting the sexes be equal" (2:1221), exclaims the text when Israel turns over the captured virgins to Benjamin. Rousseau even invents an episode at the end of the story that repeats yet again the configuration of the "already-dead-woman" whose silence is the condition for the reunification of the whole. Axa, one of the virgins of Shiloh, is compelled by her father to accept a Benjaminite as husband and forget her fiancé, Elmacin. Her father implores her:

> The salvation of your people and your father's honor must take precedence over [Elmacin]. Do your duty, my daughter, and save me from shame among my brothers; for it was I who advised everything that has happened. Axa bowed her head and sighed without answering; but when she finally raised her eyes, she met those of her venerable father. They said more than his [or her] mouth [ils ont dit plus que sa bouche]: she made her choice. Her weak and trembling voice barely uttering, in a weak and last good-bye, the name of Elmacin, she immediately turned and fell, half-dead [demi-morte], into the arms of the Benjaminite. (2:1223)

The ambiguous possessive of "sa bouche" says it all here; the father speaks with eyes and mouth, while the girl's mouth is sealed before the other's speech.

The condition for the gathering and preservation of the Whole will have (always) been the eradication of this other voice, these other voices, their expulsion outside any general understanding or hearing where they are like the already dead. What emblem other than the body without a voice (because it is already dead, because it is dead and then killed before being mutilated) could gather up in a more economic fashion all the traits of this condition? The dispersed body of the girl without a voice is a written contract which all the brothers (but also all the fathers and all the sons) sign against one of their own, to be sure, but first of all finding their support on the forever silent body which serves as their means of writing. The gathering of the one, of everyone, and of the Whole is signed in the dispersed silence of the other. This is the signature on the social contract.

But, as we have observed, this gathering is also accomplished at the cost of a disturbing repetition, one that can only threaten the just law (and the just voice) of the assembly. The law is threatened with being *annulled* by a return of the self on itself that would render null every judged, avenged, or condemned difference. Man's law finds itself condemned to take up again in its own name and on its own account the crimes that it seeks to punish, risking otherwise the loss of the very name by which it is authorized to judge and sanction vengeance. Thus the guilty one will also be the avenger, the avenger will also be guilty; the victim will be made culpable and the criminal victimized. Everything is between brothers, in the circle of the same; everything passes by way of the voice of Israel which addresses a terrible message to itself from which there is no turning aside until it has found death over and over again. The other voice, the voice of those who are taken exclusively as speechless objects (oppressed or adored), is already no longer capable of making itself heard; it is taken (it does not give itself) as being since forever already dead. Without it, without this other voice, difference finds no space in which to be remarked except in the reversal of opposites which are never finally simply opposed.

A Body of Writing

This, at least, would be one way to read the text Rousseau writes during his days of flight. Yet perhaps one should say that it is just as much the text that writes "Rousseau," giving him back in some way the signature that has just been annulled, abolished and made an outlaw, restoring in a certain way a voice that has had to silence its protest. Yes, but precisely in what way? Is not that what one always seeks to determine or to judge? If "Rousseau" signs this text, if he even boasts of having signed it, can one all the same be certain of how to read this signature, which is to say: do we know where, on what part of the text's body, a proper name is inscribed? It seems that by appropriating the biblical tale, Rousseau would have wanted to slip his signature—and his demand for justice—beneath that of the Levite on the dispersed body (or rather, *in* the intervals of that dispersion). That gesture, however, has to end up denouncing itself when the only permitted, recognized signature, the only signature validated by men's law, is traced on the already dead body in such a way that to sign is to stifle the other's voice, to name oneself the author of a crime, to represent one's guilt.

What then of this body as sign or signature of the excluded, unheard, inadmissible voice? Is it not here that one should look for the proper name, hidden beneath that other law of the signature? No doubt. "Rousseau," the outlaw signature, would have affixed itself on this text with or by the excluded voice which is a woman's.

And yet, by seeking to fix this signature, one finally risks beginning to look like those who decreed the *prise de corps*. One has yet to end the flight from this grasp. The body of writing would be precisely the place of an unassignable difference within the signature, a vanishing point—*point de fuite*—that will never sign with its ungraspable voice. This would perhaps explain the cold fury of the Levite whose writing only succeeds in multiplying the sites of the ungraspable without ever managing to let the other be heard, the innocent one who, however, would alone have the right to sign.

If one always signs in the other, as other, then *Le Lévite d'Ephraïm* would be the fable of a signature that attempts to refuse partition, to deny repetition, and to remain on this side of its "own" dispersion. Instead of writing that only occurs in partition,[12] there would be the representation of men's voices by the already dead and partitioned body of women. Rousseau's choice "to write and be hidden" ("d'écrire et de se cacher") would find here, in the couple of the young girl and her Levite, a kind of allegoreme in which the act of representing oneself by the other—whose name may be Julie, Emile, or the social contract—puts in place a screen behind which to take refuge from partition.

[12]It is to the recent work of Jean-Luc Nancy that we refer in using the term "partition"; see *Le Partage des voix* (Paris, 1982), and *La Communauté désoeuvrée* (Paris, 1986).

CHAPTER FOUR

Seeing through Rousseau

To see, or rather to show sight in its proper light, is a fairly good description of what Rousseau says he is up to in the *Dialogues*.[1] Whereas in the *Confessions* he proposed to "show my fellow men a man in the full truth of nature" ("montrer à mes semblables un homme dans toute la vérité de la nature") (1:5), *Rousseau juge de Jean-Jaques* (the actual title of the *Dialogues*) takes this project either one step further or one step back, depending on how you look at it. In the preface to this text he writes: "It was necessary for me to say how, if I were another man, I would see a man like me" ("il fallait nécessairement que je dise de quel oeil, si j'étais un autre, je verrais un homme tel que je suis") (1:665). Between the seemingly straightforward "Here is the man I am" of the *Confessions* and this otherwise contorted demonstration of the *Dialogues*, there had intervened the general failure of Rousseau's contemporaries to *see* the man he had taken such pains to show them.[2] It is easy to

[1]An earlier version of this chapter was read at the 1986 Dartmouth Colloquium on Modern Literature and Theory. The theme chosen by the organizer, Virginia Swain, was "Lumières et vision."

[2]There is a general tendency to read the *Dialogues* as a reply to the failure of the *Confessions*; see, for example Michel Foucault's introduction to the text. However, to posit such a causal or otherwise narrative relation between the two texts is to propose a biographical fiction, a unity of the subject, which may very

suppose how, unable logically to conclude that the fault was his, that he had obstructed public view rather than set himself in plain sight, Rousseau had to diagnose an obstruction, malformation, or distortion within the very faculty of sight he had counted on to apprehend his true nature. After all, there is little point in showing someone *what* to see—"a man," for example—if that person does not even know *how* to use his own eyes. The experiment of the *Confessions* had shown that, with few exceptions, Rousseau was surrounded by unsighted creatures who persisted in "seeing" not the man who had placed himself squarely in the light but only dim figures in the shadows with which the light contrasted. The *Dialogues*, therefore, would undertake to show nothing more or less than *sight*, which is in itself *nothing*. The text is not a *Letter on the Blind* but a letter *to* the blind, and therein lies the considerable if not impossible dilemma it has posed for itself.

In a sense, one can say that Rousseau never resolved this dilemma; that is, he never figured out to whom he could show this letter once it was written. Addressing it first as he did to divine providence only confirmed the dilemma without resolving it. In another sense, however, the terms in which the dilemma is posed—the visual terms—are themselves made obsolete or at least irrelevant by the performance of the *Dialogues*.

Saying What You See

This performance requires, as we have seen, a division of the "je" among at least three positions: "il fallait nécessairement que je dise de quel oeil, si j'étais un autre, je verrais un homme tel que je suis." There is the "je" who says "What if I were another?"; there is then this other "je" who offers his judgment on the man he sees; and there is finally the man *like* me, "un homme tel que je suis." These are the three positions implicit in every so-called autobiographical writing—*The Confessions*,

---

well be what has been put at risk by the proliferation of autobiographical texts. E. S. Burt is particularly persuasive in questioning precisely this sort of narrativizing tendency.

for example—where writer, narrator, and principal character of the narration are presumed by the conventions of what Philippe Lejeune calls the autobiographical pact to be identifiable by the same name.[3] But the *Dialogues* depart from Lejeune's schema in a manner that is finally troubling for any effort to define the limits of the genre because, precisely, the text does *not* break with or abandon the convention; on the contrary, it remarks that convention and exploits it to the limit. In so doing, the *Dialogues* demonstrate the essentially fictional resource at the source of autobiography, the fiction of "si j'étais un autre" which is conventionally covered over and forgotten by convention.

The programming sentence of this text, however, remarks the fiction not only in a thematic mode but also in a grammatical one. Its syntax assigns not three but four positions to "je," although the second and third positions are logically identified with each other: "de quel oeil, si *j*'étais un autre, *je* verrais . . ." The fact that there is a surplus articulation of the "je" should not be overlooked because it is this surplus, precisely, of a *necessary* articulation ("il *fallait nécessairement* que je dise") over sheer imagination which will prevent the eventual judgment from closing off the difference in the "je" which has been opened up. In other words, "si j'étais un autre," because it must be enunciated and not merely imagined or thought, carries the "je" beyond the possibility of a logical reduction of its two posited versions. Forgetting the excess of articulation can only produce another, uncritical fiction that the autobiographical work disavows even though it lends itself to the masquerade: the fiction that the subject is *the same thing* as the words deployed to name experiences.

---

[3]"Autobiography (the story telling the life of the author) supposes that there is *an identical name* for the author (who figures, by his name, on the cover), the story's narrator, and the character in question. This is a very simple criterion." Lejeune, *Le Pacte autobiographique* (Paris, 1975), 23–24. As Paul de Man has already remarked in "Autobiography as De-Facement," in *The Rhetoric of Romanticism* (New York, 1984), 71, Lejeune's model ignores altogether any specificity of the signature, which is not simply the proper name of an author.

The work to which Rousseau gave the title *Rousseau juge de Jean-Jaques* prevents this kind of forgetting at every turn. Its formal conventions distinguish four discursive positions. The interlocutor named "Rousseau" manifestly cannot be confused with the subject of his long discourses, identified only by the initials "J. J." The writer who signals his activity at regular intervals with notes at the bottom of the page is also not to be confused with either one or the other. On the other hand, the name "Rousseau" and the initials "J. J." constantly provoke the sort of logical identification or reunification of Jean-Jacques with Rousseau which is held off or deferred by their formal and discursive differentiation. The fourth position, however, that of the other interlocutor identified only as "le Français," stands somewhat outside the circle of the other three, outside, at least, the circle of the proper name "J. J. Rousseau." It is this position of a certain remove that preserves, as we shall see, the only possibility of a continued articulation of "je's" stifled truth.

There is much at stake in this playing with the conventions of autobiography. To show sight, to show "de quel oeil je verrais un homme tel que je suis," the *Dialogues* must uncover the space of fiction. It uncovers, that is, the space conventionally forgotten in the autobiographical gesture of showing not sight but an object for sight—to wit, "a man." If, then, the *Dialogues* are to be read as a corrective supplement to the *Confessions*, it is because the latter would have hidden its fictional spacing behind the figure of "a man" which functions finally as a blind, screening from view the intervals spacing out a set of positions never rigorously identical with each other. "Man," in other words, is a totalizing figure. But it is also a figure that screens from sight the fictional operation of a narration that calls itself a "showing." The fiction that the *Dialogues* contrive finally to bring into the open by spacing out the "man" in question is the fiction of visual perception, sight or showing as a figure for reading. Which is to say that the *Dialogues* proposes to show that "showing," "seeing," and "sight" are all figures that blind one to the necessity of reading and that they do so all the more effectively because, taken literally, they promise the contrary of blindness.

J and J

The demonstration would proceed dialectically, that is, by means of a dialogue that gradually reduces the difference between the two interlocutors with regard to the subject of their conversation: J. J. Indeed, these double initials may be taken as an emblem of the difference that propels the dialogic machine—the difference between the man J. J. and the signature J. J.—and, most important, the relation of one to the other. The interlocutor named "Rousseau" has read and admired works signed "J. J." but has never seen their author. The interlocutor designated only as "le Français" has never read or seen "J. J.," but this has not prevented him from endorsing the negative opinion of his peers concerning both the man and his writings. By the end of the first dialogue, this experiential difference between the interlocutors has been reduced to the difference between seeing and reading. The end of the dialogue, spoken by le Français, proposes an exchange of these functions:

> Listen, I do not like J. J. but I hate injustice more, and still more betrayal. You have told me things that strike me [qui me frappent] and on which I want to reflect. You refused to see this unfortunate man and now you have decided to do so. I refused to read his books; I, like you, have changed my mind and for good reason. You go see the man, I will read the books; and then we will meet again. (1:772)

The second dialogue opens by recalling the terms of this contract:

> Le Français: Well, Sir, have you seen him?
> Rousseau: Well, Sir, have you read him? (1:773)

The floor is then given over to the interlocutor "Rousseau's" account of what he saw in his meetings with J. J., his conclusions as to the latter's character, and his renewed convictions that this character has been directly responsible for the works he has admired. He believes, in other words, J. J.'s signature to be genuine. Thus, it would seem that a fictional space between

"Rousseau" (the author) and "J. J." (the man) has been opened up only so as to collapse their difference in an identificatory illusion of perfect transparence and total visibility. And with this, the difference between showing a "man" and showing "sight," between seeing and reading, also tends to collapse.

But nothing is harder to show than the collapse of this difference, of fiction and of the space of reading, because the play with mirrors is playing constantly on two registers and every proposition advances on the back of its contradiction. On one side, "Rousseau's" encounter with J. J. is given as a model of man's capacity to *see* and therefore to judge his *semblable* ("comment je verrais un homme tel que je suis" in the programming sentence), to enter fully the interiority of an other and give it its due; on the other side, the same encounter serves as a demonstration of precisely how such interior vision remains impossible except as a phantasm of identification. This phantasm is allowed or put in place by what is given as the fiction of "Rousseau's" difference from J. J. (the "si j'étais un autre" of the text's program), but at the same time and with the same stroke, transparency is denounced as nothing but a fiction or phantasm. Likewise, behind the phantasm's presumption of transparent judgment is what we take to be the extratextual truth of Rousseau's identity with J. J. (which is why he can describe him from the inside as it were), but the extratextual reference also denounces the judgment as a false model of one man's encounter with another. "Seeing" these contradictions (and seeing no way out of them) defines and determines the experience of reading the *Dialogues*, whose dialectic cannot overcome the difference that drives it, the difference spacing the repetition of J. J.'s double name.

Two mutually exclusive meanings fight for control of the *Dialogues*: on the one hand, the text seems to have no purpose other than to get one to *see* J. J., as "Rousseau" does after the first dialogue; on the other hand, it urges one *to refuse to see* him, as "le Français" does until the very end, and to read instead the works one has avoided reading before. Because his final consent to see J. J. closes the last dialogue, the Frenchman's encounter with the author of the works he now admires is deferred beyond the end of the text and outside the space of reading—both his and ours. It is therefore impossible to decide whether such a text wants to precipitate its reader's identification with an imagined transparency, its author, or whether it wants to denounce precisely that phantasm as the blindness that prevents reading. To decide that question, one would have to have access to some notion of Rousseau's intent or aim or desire in a space that is not at all that of reading but of interior or immediate understanding. Which is to say, one would have to have recourse to the very identificatory mechanism, to the phantasm of transparent vision, that one has yet to determine is a valid description of the intent of a work like the *Dialogues*.

Although this dilemma no doubt always affects reading, it clearly absorbs the principal interest of the *Dialogues* where it is not just left to lurk in the margins. The acuteness of the dilemma (and the acuity with which it is formulated by this text in various ways) may be measured by the symptomatic discomfort that so often accompanies efforts (such as this one) to say anything whatsoever about the experience of reading it.[4] Besides silence, the most frequent response to the *Dialogues* is a diagnosis of Rousseau's persecutory delusions, of which the text would be a massive, inoperable symptom. But even this kind of dismissal of the work ends up confirming the seriousness of the dilemma that has been posed, since the judgment that the author is mad functions as a defense against the madness that may await the reader who takes the text too seriously. Nor would it seem that Rousseau held the key to the enigma of his text, that he, as its author, alone could escape the dilemma it posed. One need only recall some of the hesitations he recorded about the disposition of the thing once finished, his indecision about whether to abandon it (as he says he has done at the beginning of the *Rêveries*) or to hold on to it in the hope

---

[4]It is a measure, perhaps, of this discomfort that the *Dialogues* have, as far as I know, never been translated into any language. There are, however, notable exceptions to this general avoidance. Besides E. S. Burt's *Rousseau's Autobiographics*, see Christie McDonald's "The Model of Reading," in *The Dialogue of Writing: Essays in Eighteenth-Century French Literature* (Waterloo, Ont., 1984).

that he would finally figure out what to do with it. The fear that the *Dialogues* would never find an adequate reader, rather than giving proof of paranoia, could just as well be understood as a terrible lucidity about the fundamental unreadability of a work that destroys so effectively the conventional limits between fiction and autobiography. The alternative between lucidity and stupidity is perhaps not so easily decided.[5]

The Phantasm of the Writer

There is still a sense, however, in which it could be useful to speak of the *Dialogues* as a symptomatic work. It is the sense that Jean-Claude Bonnet has suggested in an article concerned largely with the Enlightenment's invention of a "public image" for its living writers.[6] Bonnet considers the *Dialogues* in the context of this invention and thereby shifts somewhat that text's symptomatic indications from a particular toward a general, social, or historical condition that he names "le fantasme de l'écrivain." The ambiguous genitive of that phrase nicely dislocates the situation of the phantasm because it places it between the writer and the reader, in the imaginary or fictional space of their face-to-face identification. But what interests Bonnet is how the phantasm can and has produced an institutionalization of "l'espace biographique"[7] in which such imaginary identifications are consecrated as a complement (even a

---

[5]Geoffrey Bennington states the dilemma for readers of *Du contrat social* who cannot know if the lawgiver is a "grande âme" or a charlatan. His reading also extends the dilemma to other works bearing that signature: "Rousseau's final reliance on posterity and providence to clear his name cannot escape this structure, and this explains the irony and the tragedy or—perhaps better— *stupidity* of the measures taken to ensure the survival of the *Dialogues*. The 'originary discrepancy' which gives rise to politics and history, writing and prejudice, also dictates that Rousseau . . . should 'end' in anguished concern over the survival of his texts, his signature and his *devise*. Rousseau's 'madness' could be read as an effect of the insistence of the charlatan in the legislator and this insistence can never be eradicated, insofar as texts cannot be guaranteed by legislation, *devise* or signature, but stand clear of authorial control" (171).

[6]Bonnet, "Le Fantasme de l'écrivain," *Poétique* 63 (September 1985).

[7]Ibid., 272.

necessary one) to "l'espace littéraire." He illustrates this process of institutionalization by reviewing several notorious instances of a reader become privileged witness to a writer's life: Boswell recording the life of Johnson, Eckermann recalling his conversations with Goethe. Seen in this light, the Age of Enlightenment would have issued in the Age of the Executive (or Executor) Secretary, the posthumous guardian of the great writer's public image.

The place that must be reserved for Rousseau's *Dialogues* in the history of this institution is at once central and in the margins, if not in a different orbit altogether. It is as if in that text Rousseau had spelled out all the rules others would have to follow but could do so only in the manner of an exception. Bonnet tends to explain this dissymmetry by distributing it between the system of the work or the "literary space," on the one hand, and the "biographical space" on the other, pointing out, for example, that "in real life" Rousseau shunned contact, broke off most of his relations, and thus never met up with his Boswell or his Maria van Rysselberghe, even though the system of the *Dialogues* is ordered around this very kind of encounter with the anonymous Frenchman which is announced at the end. There even comes a moment when, to sharpen this contrast, Bonnet has recourse to the biographical testimony of d'Escherny commenting on Rousseau's tendency to present himself as other than he, d'Escherny, knew him to be: "I saw him too often and at too close range to endorse the innocence of his judgments; yet I loved him and esteemed him no less for all that. He knew it and although he feared me somewhat because he saw that I saw through him [il voyait que je le pénétrais] and that his weaknesses did not escape me, he loved me nonetheless."[8] Bonnet signals no irony at this point in his procedure. This is remarkable because the quote from d'Escherny could clearly serve as an *example*—in fact a very good one—of the sort of identificatory phantasm part of whose history Bonnet is concerned to retrace. Rather than an example from *within* the institution of biographical space or of authorship, however, this

[8]Ibid., 286.

testimony is brought in, as it were, from the outside and applied like a tool that splits Rousseau's case into "l'homme" and "l'oeuvre"—in Bonnet's terms, "la vie réelle" and "le système de l'oeuvre." As a result of this gesture, no effective difference or distance remains between the first- and the second-degree biographical discourse, between the biographer and the biographer's historian. Bonnet's history, that is, becomes at this point an example of what it is describing. The point is not that the literary historian thereby falls into inconsistency; on the contrary, there can be no more persuasive demonstration of the consistency and continuity of the structures of phantasmatic identification which, Bonnet argues, we have in some measure inherited from the Enlightenment.[9] Notice, however, that this continuity or repetition inscribes the reference to *l'homme-l'oeuvre* Rousseau within a phantasmatic space that the literary historical discourse can no longer claim to describe from without. The question of whose "fantasme de l'écrivain" we are talking about is—if possible—more undecided than ever.

On the Dépositaire

The vanishing point of Bonnet's project to trace a history of "l'espace biographique" occurs somewhere in the margins of the *Dialogues*. This is probably more than a coincidence. But his history does manage to bring out an irreducible irony of that work: having invented the job of the writer's heir and literary

---

[9]Bonnet explicitly assumes this inheritance although he first acknowledges that "during the last twenty years, the questioning of the biographic method . . . inspired the most important advances of theoretical reflection" (259). The past tense of that acknowledgment signals that the historian's initial gesture is to establish a break with a recent past. He thus situates himself in a present, but one that turns out to be eternal: "However, it is useless to claim the end of the biographical theme and the author. It is not so much that they are back after having been banned for several years *but rather because they have never ceased to be there* in other forms and by means of new sorts of investigations" (260; italics added). Thus, the break that is initially signaled is not a break at all; but in that case, one can only wonder what function is being served by the fiction of a periodization of "theoretical reflection." One is tempted to read the gesture as a half-effaced wish that theoretical reflection were indeed a thing of the past, having been replaced by "biographical theme and the author."

executor, having provided in effect a step-by-step training manual for future Boswells[10] and Eckermanns, having shown the way to secure the future of a work, the *Dialogues* went wanting for a duly named and authorized *dépositaire*. This is the term with which Rousseau designates the safekeeper of his legacy—his-life-his-work—both within the fiction of the *Dialogues* but more insistently in its margins, in an epilogue that recounts the series of failed atttempts to dispose of that text, to identify its *dépositaire*. The temptation, as we have seen, is to explain that failure by contrasting life and work, biography and fiction. A closer look at the position reserved for the *dépositaire* suggests, however, why *bio*graphy, the story of a life, leaves almost everything still to say about the essential impossibility structuring that position. Almost everything is left to say, that is, about the *dépositaire* in relation to Rousseau's *death* as he lived and wrote it, but also in relation to the death of the author as the necessary condition for the survival of the work.

We can approach the way the *dépositaire* articulates this death in the work by remarking first that the *dépositaire* is not necessarily the *destinataire* of the *Dialogues*. This other figure, nevertheless, hovers ghostlike over the concluding pages of the epilogue, where Rousseau makes a final calculation of the best strategy for passing on his text:

> To multiply copies incessantly in order to place them here and there in the hands of people who approach me would be to tax my strength to no avail. It is not reasonable to hope that of all the copies thus dispersed, a single one of them will arrive intact at its destination [une seule parvint entière à sa destination]. I am thus going to limit myself to one copy, which I will pass among those acquaintances whom I believe to be the least unjust and the least prejudiced. . . . Experience warns me that none will listen to me, but it is not impossible that there will be one who does listen,

[10]Rousseau confided a copy of the first dialogue to a young Englishman who had come to see him and made a good impression. Rousseau later regretted his impetuousness, believing that he had been mistaken to trust him. By an ironic coincidence, the young man was James Boswell, who very soon after Rousseau's death arranged to publish the manuscript he had been given.

whereas it is impossible that men's eyes will of themselves open to the truth [que les yeux des hommes s'ouvrent d'eux-mêmes à la vérité]. This suffices to impose on me the duty of making this try, without expecting any success. If I do nothing but leave the text in my wake, this prey will not escape the rapacious hands [cette proie n'échappera pas aux mains de rapine] who are only waiting for my last hour so as to grab everything and burn it or falsify it. (1:987)

Destination functions here first in the sense of point of arrival on some trajectory, the destined purpose of a thing or the use for which it was intended. In this sense, the destination of the *Dialogues* is the event of the final revelation of the truth about Jean-Jacques: "que les yeux des hommes s'ouvrent à la vérité," that men see the truth in Jean-Jacques, or see Jean-Jacques in his truth. But it is impossible, writes Rousseau, that men's eyes will open *of themselves* to admit the truth, and this impossibility imposes on the *destinateur* an obligation to see, as far as possible, to the safe delivery of the intention of his message, to survey and verify its passage through a series of relays. In this sense, the destination of the *Dialogues* is the act of a will directing their transmission which in the passage just quoted is defined over against two versions of the absence of will: first, leaving things to chance by scattering copies of the manuscript here and there, and second, doing nothing, leaving the manuscript to be found and disposed of at the death of the author. The latter version, which incites the rhetoric of beastly brutality that has been a constant throughout the *Dialogues* ("cette proie n'échappera pas aux mains de rapine," etc.), situates most clearly the disaster threatening destination. Identifying a *dépositaire* is supposed to prevent this disaster.

> If, however, among those who will have read me, there is found a single manly heart or even just a sensible mind, my persecutors will have wasted their time and soon the truth will break upon the eyes of the public. The certainty that, if this unhoped-for good fortune comes my way [si ce bonheur inespéré m'arrive], I will not mistake it for an instant encourages me to try once again . . . if, against all expectation, there is one to be found who is struck by

my reasons [que mes raisons frappent] and who begins to suspect the truth, I will not have a moment's doubt as to this effect, and I have the sure sign [le signe assuré] for distinguishing him from the others even if he chooses not to confide in me. It is he whom I will make my *dépositaire* [De celui-là je ferai mon dépositaire]. (1:988)

In this anticipatory projection of a recognition scene with his *dépositaire*, one can but recognize a principal trait of Rousseauian *écriture* as Jacques Derrida has allowed us to understand it: writing as the transcription of a dream of the transparent and immediate sign, a system of *s'entendre-parler* (hearing/understanding oneself speak).[11] In this transcription of the dream, "le signe" that will identify the *dépositaire* can be said to be "sure" because it never leaves its originating orbit, but circulates back to its source unaltered. The destination of *s'entendre-parler* takes the form of a circle, leaving from and returning to the same point. The *dépositaire* who inspires the dream is himself featureless, a kind of blank surface waiting to be imprinted or struck by Jean-Jacques's seal: "if there is one to be found who is *struck*. . ." As a kind of nonresisting surface, the *dépositaire* would not oppose, conceal, distort, or otherwise cause to deviate the truthful sign impressed upon it. He—or it—would simply repeat it, reproduce it. The transmission of the *Dialogues* to the *dépositaire* could thus be said to resemble nothing so much as an author's control of printed copy against the original manuscript. Rousseau certainly knew that, among the relays of destination, the printing operation was always fraught with risk,[12] the reason, perhaps, this transfer is envisioned only "against all expectation" and as "this unhoped-for good fortune." Nevertheless, in the dream the good fortune

---

[11]Rousseau "*dreamed* of the simple exteriority of death to life, evil to good, representation to presence, signifier to signified, representer to represented, mask to face, writing to speech. . . . And what must dream or writing be if, as we know now, one may dream while writing? And if the scene of dream is always a scene of writing?" (Derrida, *Of Grammatology*, 315–16). The *Dialogues* quite explicitly put J. J.'s writing under the sign of the transparent sign by means of "Rousseau's" allegory of "le monde idéal" at the beginning of the first dialogue; see in particular p. 672.

[12]See above, chap. 2.

"m'arrive," it happens to me, it comes to me and comes back to me.

The Return on Deposit

But the dream does not end with the transfer to the *dépositaire*.

> It is he whom I will make my *dépositaire*, without even determining whether I can count on his probity. . . . If he has foresight and knows how to wait, his good reasoning ought to make him faithful to me. I would go further and say that even if the public persists in its same attitude toward me, still the natural order of events will sooner or later lead it to desire to know at least what J. J. would have said had he been given the liberty to speak. Let my *dépositaire* show himself at that point and say to them [Que mon dépositaire se montrant leur dise alors]: So you want to know what he would have said? well, here it is [et bien, le voilà]. Without taking my side, without trying to defend my cause or my memory, by being simply my reporter [en se faisant mon simple rapporteur] . . . he can cast a new light on the character of the judged man: it is always a trait added to his portrait to know in what terms such a man dared to speak of himself. (1:988)

Here it is, then, "le voilà": the destination of the *Dialogues*, its arrival at an unhoped-for good fortune. The scene is produced by a redoubled speculation: Rousseau speculates on the eventual speculation of his *dépositaire*. The return on all this speculative investment seems at first almost negligible: just another trait added to his portrait. But the apparently modest expectation of gain cannot entirely conceal the unheard-of coup or killing that Rousseau stands to make on this futures market. When the *dépositaire* shows himself, presents himself, and says "le voilà," the ambiguity of that demonstrative declaration suddenly lays bare the incalculable stakes of the game. A first ambiguity operates at a juncture with the identificatory phantasm that substitutes seeing an author for reading an author's text. Because "le voilà" is said in response to the desire to know "what J. J. would have said had he been given the liberty to speak," it may be heard either as "here it is" (i.e., what he would have said, the manuscript of the *Dialogues*) or as "here he is," J. J. himself, at last given the floor. This latter sense, of course, is at best a figuration and at worst a hallucination since it supposes the impossible return of a J. J. able to speak after his death. But might not the "le voilà" of the *dépositaire* find its most desired resonance in precisely such an impossible scene of return, against every expectation, of a ghostly or resurrected or never-dead J. J.? There is as well a second ambiguity concerning the address of the phrase. In the legal sense of the term, the *dépositaire* (who is not the *destinataire* but, as Rousseau is careful to point out, a "simple rapporteur,") is someone who says "here it is" to the depositor when he returns to claim his deposit.[13] The *dépositaire* is not the *destinataire* but rather a figure who can relay, *rapporter* J. J. across the space of his double destination of himself to himself as *l'homme-l'oeuvre*, reconciling the difference of the one in the other, doing the impossible of giving J. J. back in death what he could never claim in life.

The essential impossibility of this return and of the unification beyond duplication will have to leave the *Dialogues* forever in the hands of a *dépositaire*, will have to keep the circle of destination open. The restricted economy of that circle is overrun since J. J.—*l'homme*—cannot return to claim the full value (with interest) of Rousseau—*l'oeuvre*. There is no saving the text from the necessity of the other or the proxy, and no economic calculation can close the interval of their difference. The *dépositaire* bears finally no resemblance to the legal or economic figure of the same name. Indeed, there is no possible resemblance to anyone at all. We have already seen how Rousseau expects to have no trouble *recognizing* his *dépositaire* when he arrives, but we can now ask whether the impossible destination of the text must not also bar such a scene of recognition. This is to suggest that the two moments of the deposit— entrusting it and then recovering it—are structured by the

[13]For an excellent study of the depositor's contract in Rousseau's thought, see Felicity Baker, "Remarques sur la notion de dépôt," *Annales Jean-Jacques Rousseau* 37 (1966–68).

same impossibility of return. In other words, the first moment of recognition is already inhabited or haunted by the impossibility of the second moment of return. In the potential *dépositaire*, the sign by which Rousseau would recognize the vouchsafing of his truth is finally indistinguishable from an image of himself beyond death or in death, beyond, that is, all possibility of recognition. Given this inevitable association, we should not be surprised that Rousseau had far less difficulty recognizing in all those around him his own disfigured image and concluding that he was surrounded by mortal enemies who wished him dead. Because the appearance of the *dépositaire* must occur at the limit between the recognizable and the unrecognizable, between the identification of the same and the radical difference of the other, any figure it can assume is immediately menaced with disfiguration or else menaces to disfigure.[14]

The Promise of "le Français"

The *Dialogues* would seem to remain suspended before this limit, before the featureless and unrecognizable *dépositaire*. Within the text, he—or it—is called "le Français," at once Everyman and No Man, a mere surface that has taken the imprint of general opinion regarding J. J. "Le Français" is the pivoting term of the reconfiguration of J. J.'s image, the eventual *dépositaire* who will give face and voice to an absence no longer able to speak or appear. He—or it—is the place of the promise to keep safe J. J.'s deposit, to share with the interlocutor "Rousseau" the risks of guarding J. J.'s unpublished writings. The *partage* of their dialogue thus concludes with the agreement to *partager*, to share the deposit, but it is "le Français" who explicitly engages himself to keep the depositor's promise, who performs the speech act called a promise: "I offer to share with

---

[14]One could also take into account the double and contradictory senses of the verb *déposer* in French: to put in a safe place, but also to cause to fall, to bring down, especially in a political sense, to deprive of power. If we follow the second thread, a candidate for the *dépositaire* of Rousseau's opus might turn out to be the large dog who knocks him off his feet in the *Deuxième promenade* and precipitates the false rumors of his death.

you the risks of this deposit and I promise to spare no trouble to bring it one day before the eyes of the public just as I received it" ("je m'offre à partager avec vous les risques de ce dépôt, et je m'engage à n'épargner aucun soin pour qu'il paraisse un jour aux yeux du public tel que je l'aurai reçu") (1:975). Such a promise has every appearance of being a wishful fiction, offered as it is by no one really. But this is not necessarily to say that nothing happens when Rousseau makes his deposit with "le Français." Perhaps, on the contrary, the delusion is to imagine that a "real" *dépositaire* could rescue the charge of truth from the corrosive disfigurement of fiction. While that may well have been a delusion Rousseau shared, the text of the *Dialogues* nevertheless consigns itself to *le français*—not a man but a language. This is the fourth, irreducible position of articulation whose necessity, as we remarked at the outset, exceeds the circle of Rousseau's self-judgment, or of any judgment. In several senses of the phrase, *le Français* is a figure of speech; specifically, he—or it—is a prosopopeia, an animation of the language to which and in which the *Dialogues* have been deposited. It is this figure of animated language that promises, in turn, to give "voice" to the author beyond his grave. He promises, that is, to continue signing "J. J. Rousseau."

Le français is Rousseau's only—and only possible—*dépositaire*. Although it gives no one and nothing to see, it goes on promising "to show a man in the full truth of nature," it continues to repeat "le voilà." And we, of course, are still trying to see through that false promise of a signature.

Endpiece

The temptation now is to fit these pieces of "Jean-Jacques Rousseau" together or, as we tend to say, *back* together, as if they were the scattered remains of an originally intact whole. In its most familiar version, this temptation assumes the form of a biography of the famous writer and there are more than enough examples of the genre in Rousseau's case. Biographical narrative appears indeed to be the most economical means of gathering, with some semblance of coherence, the disparate marks left by the practice of writing. More than that, this narrative mode, with its virtually inevitable supposition of some form of psychological determinism, procures the benefit of appropriating to the subject a transcendent position in relation to the texts associated with it through the signature. The biographer or reader "reads" by identifying (with) this position. Rousseau's biographers have confirmed repeatedly that even the idea of a mad Jean-Jacques is preferable in the end to the alternative lurking around the edges of that idea: a "madness" of words or rather, since even that description relies on a psychological analogy, a functioning of language that remains radically other than the various uses to which it is put and which include reference to, among other things, psychological states. The condition of possibility for reference to a whole, a unity, an identity, or a totality—that is, some kind of intactness that the pieces would be pieces of—is the denial or exclusion of this otherness, the otherness of language as such. The untenability of this denial signals an exclusion concerning the otherness that can never come to be represented as part of some whole but whose exclusion permits the very concept of the whole to come together. This inexorable logic produces its most visible effects, to be sure, elsewhere in the general sociocultural text and tends to cover its traces within that part of the text called "language" in the strict sense. The problem, however, is precisely that language—in some form or other—is also a means by which one refers to all the rest of the fabric through a kind of folding over of one of its parts. To deny or disregard the difference between language and its referents is always, thus, to risk the suppression of all the different, nonlinguistic eruptions of otherness.

Resisting the temptation, then, to conclude, we leave the pieces of Rousseau's signature where they lie without assembling them in a story or a history. If the disposition we have given them nonetheless traces a pattern, to what does it correspond? Not, we have said, to the determinate and determining psychological configuration that would return to the historical subject Jean-Jacques Rousseau; or to the formal, discursive, and literary configuration of Rousseau's *oeuvre*. If there is a pattern, it takes shape precisely at the articulating limit between these two regimes of signification, between the historical/biographical regime of reference and the regime of formal linguistic/discursive structure. The pattern, in other words, is that of marks left by the one on the other, marks that at once limit and open up both orders of meaning. Rousseau's signatures are neither inimitable singularities nor formal generalities; in that way, they both *are* and *are not* exemplary of the functioning of signatures "in general," a notion that is prevented from coming together precisely by the singular eventuality of each "case" or "example" of signature. To put it in the paradoxical terms required by this double regime, we would have to say that "Rousseau" is exemplary of the limits, the necessary impossibility of its—or "his"—own exemplarity. The pattern traced by that signature is thus precisely not a pattern to be followed, at the same time as it illustrates with many of its traits the double limit on any event of signature.

What are these traits that have been accumulating in the preceding chapters?

First, the act of signing cannot authenticate itself because it depends necessarily on the possibility of its repeatability and thus on the possibility of an inauthentic double: copy, simulacrum, forgery, imitation, false attributions, distortions, and so forth. A signature, that is, cannot determine the limits on its own validity, and there is, theoretically at least, no first or final occurrence of a signature. This is to say that a signature never occurs as a pure event, without precedent and without copy. Its possibility arises only from this limitation on pure singularity. In the course of a work signed "Rousseau," it is possible to see how this limit imposes itself with an insistence more or less in proportion to the inauthentic or false doubles of that signature which accumulate around it and adhere to its surface, threatening always to displace it. Precisely insofar as that signature claims to sign only for the truth (Rousseau's motto: "Vitam impendere vero"), its impetus—the force that sets in motion the act of signing—will have to come more and more from the urgency to dissociate itself from its doubles. It is this necessity that can dictate "mad" declarations of the signature's effective termination which nonetheless remain as just one more proof of the ineffectiveness of such gestures, their essential incapacity to produce the event they describe.

Second, the signature, taken as a sign of property, disarticulates the very relation it appears to name. Laws concerning literary property or copyright, which must suppose a predictably stable functioning of signatures, construct themselves around an analogy with real property. This analogy, rather than stabilizing the notion of literary "property," tends to get overturned—de-limited, its borders opened up—when brought into contact with the work of writing, whose real "properties" must finally return to no one.

Third, as an element functioning within a censorship regime (which is always the flip side of property rights), the signature dissimulates a necessary anonymity. The "criminalization" of Rousseau's signature, by revoking its anonymity, not only precipitates it toward an endless attempt at self-naming, but, more obscurely, brings it to the very edge of the structure of exclusion in which the law takes shape. At that edge, the search for an "innocent" signature encounters its limit in the crime of representation, where vindication takes the form of repetition. The impossibility that arises here is that of signing from the place of the excluded other.

Finally, as that which survives the signatory, as depository of the name no one can claim, the signature is disseminated, the promised repair of its division deferred into an indefinite future and conferred into the hands of an anonymous *dépositaire* who is faceless, featureless, and therefore not necessarily recognizable as another man or intentional subject. Rousseau's signature, that is, will not take place until it is countersigned, while the spatio-temporal structure of its event remains that of an elsewhere that has both already and not yet occurred. It is this incalculable structure that we call its modernity, for it has left "us moderns" with the task of undoing the promise of its reconstitution, of countersigning "Rousseau" in his absence.

Repeatability, improperness, representation as exclusion, countersignature: all are traits or traces of an otherness that insists in the very place of identity's signature. If they do not form an as yet recognizable set of features, isn't that the way it has to be? For who can sign for the other?

PART II

NO ONE SIGNS
FOR THE OTHER

CHAPTER FIVE

Baudelaire au féminin

> Le sens, ce sens *en question*, est toujours *de l'autre*, dans tous les sens de cette expression.
>
> —Jean-Luc Nancy

A violence undeniably accompanies writing about signatures, an aggravation of the movement of expropriation which cannot be made more acceptable by noting the inevitable necessity of that movement. On the other hand, neglecting the signature's trace is hardly more benign. Only the unsigned work seems to provide a reprieve from the dilemma, as if the author had delivered his or her prior pardon for the erasure of signature that the reader will perform. This is largely wishful, of course, as the case of Rousseau can once again illustrate: his insistent fretting over the fate of his signature did not exempt, on the contrary, the fate of his "unsigned" novel, *La Nouvelle Héloise*. But what if one were to juxtapose this text with other "unsigned" works that it recalls or repeats? Would it not then appear that some kind of permission for this gesture has been sought in the conditional absence affecting the signature? Although I ask the question in view of a certain generalization about reading signatures, I offer it first autobiographically, having myself elsewhere assembled for study five texts, including *La Nouvelle Héloise*, which all disturbed in some fashion the simple attribution of authorship.[1]

---

[1]Peggy Kamuf, *Fictions of Feminine Desire: Disclosures of Heloise* (Lincoln, Nebr., 1982). The other four texts are the letters of Heloise and Abelard, *Les Lettres portugaises*, *La Princesse de Clèves*, and *Les Liaisons dangereuses*.

While I was interested by the circumstance that none of the texts was unequivocally signed, I did not then interrogate the coincidence of the five absent signatures which I had brought about. Since then and unexpectedly, I found myself confronted with this coincidence while puzzling over what seemed a particularly cryptic assertion in Paul de Man's essay "Autobiography as De-Facement." The assertion, I discovered, became more accessible only after it had turned the tables on me, so to speak, and given me some access to my own encrypted fascination with missing signatures. De Man writes: "Any book with a readable title page is, to some extent, autobiographical."[2] I cannot say what prompted me to read this sentence "autobiographically," but once I had done so I also noticed something that should have stood out from the first: the work is autobiographical, asserts de Man, to the extent that its title page, the place of the signature, is *readable*. That is, the minimum criterion for autobiography concerns the readability of proper names, more precisely of signatures. It therefore points to the necessary deviation of the name from what it properly signifies, necessary if the name is to become readable or iterable.

But what, then, is a readable autobiography? Or rather, *whose* autobiography does one read when reading signatures and the texts they sign? It now seems that what is problematic in the sentence "any book with a readable title page is autobiographical" is less the difficulty of consenting to such an all-inclusive assertion than the difficulty of facing up to the way it upsets a basic certainty about the autobiographical work and its signature. By making it a function of readability, de Man does not so much dissociate autobiography from writing and the writer as place it *between* writer and reader, writing and reading. Thus the same gesture *both* allows one to assert that any text is more or less autobiographical *and* prevents a certain attribution of autobiography to reader or writer. Autobiography is an all-inclusive genre precisely to the extent that it remains impossible to conclude whose life is being written—or read.

The implications of generalized autobiography would have to

[2]De Man, *Rhetoric of Romanticism*, 70.

be taken into account whenever a relation between signature and work is at issue; whenever, that is, *readable* title pages are considered part of the work to be read (and to a certain extent, as de Man would say, they always are). This, of course, is easier said than done, since what has to be taken into account by definition cannot be fully calculated or predicted by any *one* reading or writing subject.[3] Yet not ever fully knowing what is going on when one reads and writes does not mean that the complications, the co-implications of signature simply disappear when one's purpose is to construct some theory of its workings. This double bind leaves its mark whether one knows it or not. Such a setting aside or ignoring of co-implications would, however, be necessary to transfer any formal aspect of the signature to the text of the work it signs. If, for example, this move were to take one *from* the fact of a male or rather a male's signature on certain theoretical texts—those, for instance, that have so complicated thinking about signatures—*to* the notion of something called "male theory," then one would have effected the sort of transfer from form to meaning which de Man describes according to patterns of metaphor and metonymy. These are patterns whose epistemological reliability is not necessarily enhanced by being pressed into the service of political or other programs. On the contrary. Specifically, the move from the signature of a male to a "male signature," and from there to something called "male theory," transfers a formal, known attribute from one "thing" to the nonappearing, nonphenomenological "thing" that is the meaning of a text.[4] As in the psychoanalytic situation of transference, the interpreter is at

[3] A text such as Jacques Derrida's *Glas*, whose author obviously calculates to an entirely new power the autobiographical back and forth between readable signatures, is at the same time a persistent demonstration of the necessary failure of that calculation, the unsaturable context of any text that makes for its interest. "But you can take interest in what I am doing here only insofar as you would be right to believe that—*somewhere*—I do not know what I am doing" (64R).

[4] Alice Jardine, in *Gynesis: Configurations of Women and Modernity* (Ithaca, N.Y., 1985), refines somewhat each of these steps. Still she retains the positions in their integrity and speculates on what a "female signature" would look like (185).

high risk in this situation of plugging her or his own "content" into that space presumed to be full of meaning which is a text.

Yet, if we recall the aphorism about title pages, it would seem that this kind of "autobiographical" or transferential operation is also what allows a text to become readable. It is thus, to some extent, inevitable. Is this not, therefore, a circle of some sort— hermeneutic, vicious, or solipsistic? The answer to that question can never be a simple yes, precisely because *there is* auto- biography circulating through all the transfers of meaning. The circulation of readability, of iterability, is the circulation of a deviation and of autobiography as always already the auto- biography of the other.[5] Or, in still other terms, one could say that there is autobiography of a "we" given by the division, the deviation, and the sharing of voices. With these terms, I am trying to translate the title page of Jean-Luc Nancy's *Le Partage des voix* and especially the sense of the circle it traces, which, paradoxically, makes no sense unless it is open:

> *Hermeneuein* names that to which every hermeneutic circle, whether it wants to or not, is *paradoxically* opened insofar as it is a circle. Opened, that is, to that alterity or that alteration of meaning without which the identification of *a* meaning—the circle's return to the same—could not even take place.
>
> The opening of *hermeneuein* is in this sense the opening of sense and to sense as *other*. Not to some superior, transcendent or more original 'other' sense, but to sense itself as other, to an alterity defining sense.[6]

This somewhat roundabout introduction brings me to the circulation or sharing of voices in a work whose signature—

---

[5]On this notion of the "autobiography of the other," see Derrida, in McDon- ald, ed., *The Ear of the Other*, 50–51: "Nietzsche's signature does not take place when he writes. He says clearly that it will take place posthumously . . . when the other comes to sign with him, to join with him in alliance and, in order to do so, to hear and understand him. . . . In other words . . . it is the ear of the other that signs. The ear of the other says me to me and constitutes the *autos* of my autobiography. When, much later, the other will have perceived with a keen- enough ear what I will have addressed or destined to him or her, then my signature will have taken place."

[6]Nancy, *Partage des voix*, 39–40.

"Charles Baudelaire"—one should perhaps not rush to read as in any simple sense "male." When I say "*one* should not," you of course already understand that it is I who am in no rush to do so, in part for the principal reasons I have just outlined but also no doubt for more obscure, even autobiographical reasons that I would share if I could.

To hear the deviation in Baudelaire's voice, not so as to tax him (or anyone else) with it, or to pretend to heal it over, but rather to share in its address and perhaps to readdress it: this will require activating the silent pole of a dialogue, taking up a position that, at first and even second glance, will not appear very *promising*. But I promise at least to return to what is promising, even if the route may not be exactly circular.

In 1856, an observer of the Parisian literary scene who wanted to illustrate Baudelaire's eccentricity reported that the poet regularly insisted on reading his verses to "his young Creole mistress." "The lady," remarked the observer, "does not find this diet to her taste and from time to time revolts against her lover's tyranny. 'Just hold your tongue,' he answers, throwing five francs at her. 'I know you're a silly goose, but I need to read my verses aloud and I insist on their being heard.' "[7] In a note, Claude Pichois, editor of *Les Fleurs du mal*, refers this piece of gossip to one of the poems ("Sonnet d'automne"), at a point where, precisely, the poet directs an abrupt "Tais-toi!" (Shut up!) to an inquiring feminine figure. The point the editor seems to be making with his reference is that, regardless of the anecdote's authenticity, Baudelaire at least fueled his own legend when he staged this moment in the poem, the moment at which the poet tells a woman to shut up and listen.[8] What is more, Pichois also implies that the anecdote accurately reflects Baudelaire's contempt not only for Jeanne Duval, his illiterate

[7]Quoted by the editor in *Oeuvres complètes* (Paris, 1975), 1:948; all further references will be included in the text.

[8]If indeed this is Pichois's point, it is not particularly well taken about "Sonnet d'automne," where a question put to the poet is put off because it is too probing rather than too stupid. The remark would have been better placed as a note to the "Taisez-vous" of "Semper Eadem," which is discussed below.

companion of many years, but for women in general. The implication is clear when, without transition or comment, Pichois simply juxtaposes to the anecdote the following quote from *Mon Coeur mis à nu*, just one of many he might have chosen from that text to illustrate its author's categorical disdain: "I have always been amazed that women are allowed to enter churches. What conversation could they possibly have with God?" With that gesture, Pichois, inadvertently perhaps, invites every woman to put herself in the place of Jeanne Duval when confronted with Baudelaire's verses. That is, every woman should hear herself addressed by "Shut up, silly goose, and listen." *Taceat mulier in ecclesiam.*

It might seem that the place of such an addressee is the least promising position from which to hear or read this poetry. Yet if that is so, then it would be not so much because it is the place of nonreaders like Jeanne Duval (or any of the *Fleurs du mal*'s other mistresses) but rather because these addressees are curiously positioned by a kind of double gesture that the anecdote neatly brings out. What Jeanne Duval was ordered to listen to over her objections were poems that, very often, included a form of address to some feminine figure. That is, she had to sit still for the address *of* this address, for a doubled address that, on both levels, talks, so to speak, over her head.[9] However, one assumes perhaps too quickly that her impatience with this maneuver can only be a sign of her dull imperviousness to Baudelaire's verse. One assumes, that is, that no link is possible

[9]"Apostrophes are embarrassing," writes Jonathan Culler in "Reading Lyric," *Yale French Studies* 69 (1985), 99, an article that is very helpful in elucidating Paul de Man's reflections on Baudelaire's lyric in "Anthropomorphism and Trope in the Lyric," in *Rhetoric of Romanticism*. De Man also notes the embarrassment of apostrophe when he remarks about the opening stanza of "Obsession": "We are all frightened by windy woods but do not generally make a spectacle of ourselves talking to trees" (255). Culler, particularly, suggests that absurdity or embarrassment may help explain why apostrophe is so often neglected by readers, leaving relatively untouched its trope of anthropomorphism, whose workings de Man is concerned to lay out. The point, however, would be that anthropomorphism is better hidden but no less at work when apostrophe seems "reasonable," when, that is, it is another talking creature, rather than woods, that is being addressed. Indeed, the violence that may be implied or entailed is all the more effective by appearing more reasonable.

between her exasperation in this situation and an understanding of the poems which would be more than just a passive hearing of them. But what if Jeanne Duval's naïve petulance were also the sign that just such a link has and should be made between the address *in* the poems and their address *to* an unwilling listener? Who, in fact, can say that Jeanne Duval has *not* understood what she heard?[10]

Jeanne, of course, supplies raw material for a Baudelairean thematics of woman—woman in the raw. Yet, as Michel Deguy has pointed out, woman figures as a theme in Baudelaire only because she is first what he calls the poem's *milieu*, its medium, that by which it names and measures the appearance of whatever appears. In his article "Le Corps de Jeanne," Deguy writes:

> For Baudelaire, woman is the Pascalian body; or, in terms of poetics, she *is the oxymoron.* . . . She—or he/it = her body—is the *milieu* in the sense of the division between high and low, converter of high and low into one another. She can *operate* this distension and this exchange by being *herself* aggrandized or made smaller. But first one must pass by way of her in order to see: her microcosmic unfurling gives the measure, the scale of reference.[11]

To call Jeanne a *milieu* is to place her at the heart of the poetic operation. And indeed it is to the operation of the word *sein*—breast or bosom, but by metaphor or metonymy also heart—

---

[10]The initial reporter in the 1856 journal article, Raymond de Breilh, betrays what may itself be a kind of naïve understanding of Jeanne's naïve—or at least unformulated— understanding. When he writes that "la dame ne trouve pas le régime à son goût" (the lady does not find this diet to her taste), his language suggests that this situation of address is to be compared to a forced feeding. The metaphor may even have prompted the use of the epithet "goose," which, besides having connotations of silliness and femininity (is it because geese are monogamous?), is also regularly subjected in the French countryside to *gavage*, or forced feeding. In any case, the image of the violent or at least unwelcome address implies a kind of interiorization when it likens listening (or reading) to eating. Although it's too early to judge, the comparison to interiorization may be telling more than it means to say about the violence of address.

[11]Deguy, "Le Corps de Jeanne," *Poétique* 3 (1970), 338.

that Deguy turns his attention. This move is completely consistent with the poems' own working through of these rhetorical possibilities, which Deguy draws out subtly and surely. I
wonder, however, whether it is not almost *too* consistent, too
closely joined with the movement it is tracing or describing, to
be able to remark, rather than just repeat, all that may be at
work here, including certain resistances. Deguy's term *milieu*,
when taken in the sense of poetic medium, may also name a
point of resistance that has been assumed uncritically or un-
knowingly by the commentary. To call Jeanne or woman the
poetic medium is to implicate her with the poem's language or
speech. Yet the body with which Deguy finds Baudelaire concerned is often rendered speechless.

What I want to begin to explore is this silencing that gives
voice to the poem. Silencing and not simply silence. Indeed,
only the difference between an unequivocal absence of speech
and a silencing of speech can make it potentially interesting to
sit up and listen when feminine figures are made to speak in
Baudelaire's poems. Because they *are* made to speak all through
Les Fleurs du mal, as we shall see. The point, then, is not that
this medium is a speechless body but that its speaking in the
poem and by the poem is stamped by a kind of equivocation or
double gesture: both a giving and a taking away of voice.[12]

Les Fleurs du mal opens, in fact, with two women screeching
to the heavens their intentions to make the Poet suffer. Such an
opening scene sets up a kind of sounding board against which
many of the voices of *Les Fleurs du mal* resonate. First, even
before the Poet speaks for himself, "Bénédiction," the initial
poem, cites the speech of the Poet's mother. In a caricatural
parody of the Virgin Mother, her invective invokes God to call
down a curse and a blight on the son who is her punishment for
unnamed crimes.[13] Next, the opening poem invokes the Poet's

[12]Barbara Johnson has also noticed that "something strange soon happens"
when Baudelaire's verse addresses a feminine figure and gets her to talk. See
"Apostrophe, Animation, and Abortion," *Diacritics* 16 (Spring 1986), esp. 30–
31.

[13]This is the first and last time in *Les Fleurs du mal* that the word "mère" is
employed in its primary, biological sense. Sima Godfrey, however, has argued

woman—"Sa femme va criant sur les places publiques"[14]—who vows to usurp the place of divine honor in his heart, then to rip it from his chest and throw it to her dog. "Bénédiction" concludes with the Poet in his own voice humbly thanking God for the suffering he has endured at the hands of all humanity, represented principally by the speech of mother and mistress.

The figures of feminine voice or voice attributed to feminine figures are numerous and diverse enough to require a much longer study if one were to propose an exhaustive census of them all. Such a study, moreover, would have to set out a sure and decisive criterion for distinguishing among the poems' different voices, for establishing where one ends and another begins, in order to enumerate all those that the Poet attributes or lends to feminine figures. I suspect that such a criterion will always finally elude the most patient research, and, what is more, it may be precisely because the criterion allowing one to distinguish one voice from another is in default that conventional solutions risk being too easily welcomed to take its place.[15] Any procedure for separating out a feminine voice or voices in *Les Fleurs du mal* has to consider the possibility that there is a defensive component to its reaction in the face of a mixed voice, a middle voice, or even a doubled and undecidable voice, a voice that both is and is not the Poet's own, that both is and is not the voice of an addressee, *destinataire*, or interlocutor. It may be that unless one suspends as far as possible this

---

persuasively that the "mère des souvenirs" is a figure close to the source of Baudelaire's lyricism and should also be read literally; see "'Mère des souvenirs': Baudelaire, Memory, and Mother," *L'Esprit Créateur* 25(2).

[14]"His woman goes screeching through the public squares." All translations from *Les Fleurs du mal* are my own and are meant only to give a sense of the rhetorical patterns that are the focus of the readings proposed here. The specificity of these patterns tends to disappear in the published translations.

[15]This could explain why, for example, one could propose to speak of "dialogue" in these poems and then be forced to recognize that one of the dialogue's interlocutors is almost always silent. Russell S. King, in "Dialogue in Baudelaire's Poetic Universe," *L'Esprit Créateur* 13(2), writes: "Dialogue . . . is here defined as that portion of a poem contained between inverted commas, representing the conversational element. Usually only the addresser's speech is present, with the addressee remaining silent" (115).

defensive reaction, one has no chance to determine how it is working within the poetry itself, no chance to hear what sounds like a wound in a voice trying to heal itself by expelling or expressing the instrument of its injury. The question, however, is whether this impossible expression is not precisely what gives the Poet his voice. One thinks, for example, of these lines from "L'Héautontimorouménos" (The self-tormentor):

> Elle est dans ma voix, la criarde!
> C'est tout mon sang, ce poison noir!
> Je suis le sinistre miroir
> Où la mégère se regarde.
>
> Je suis la plaie et le couteau!
> Je suis le soufflet et la joue!
> Je suis les membres et la roue,
> Et la victime et le bourreau![16]

The shrill "elle" who is "dans ma voix" does not refer to the woman who presumably is addressed by the poem's first line, "Je te frapperai sans colère" (I will strike you without anger), but rather to voracious Irony, "la vorace Ironie," of the stanza preceding the ones cited. "Elle" is but an allegorization that takes advantage of grammatical gender to turn Irony into a shrew.[17] Likewise, all the images of ironic doubling in the final lines confront masculine- with feminine-gendered nouns. The voice of gender has thus been extended well beyond the apparent limits of woman's or man's speech. At the very least, these lines thematize the obstacle that would confront the attempt to separate different voice strands from each other along some dividing line between genders.

Still, there are poems in *Les Fleurs du mal*, indeed many of them, that represent some feminine or feminized speaker. If,

[16]She is in my voice, this screeching one! / All my blood is this black poison! / I am the sinister glass / In which the shrew looks at herself. / I am the wound and the knife! / I am the slap and the cheek! / I am the limbs and the wheel, / The victim and the executioner!

[17]"Elle est dans ma voix" might be called a parasitical or inverted prosopopoeia since, instead of lending voice to the figure of Irony, the poet's own voice is here infiltrated and taken over by "la criarde."

however, one insists on the strictest criteria for determining what constitutes represented speech, then such poems would have to be counted as rare.[18] And even where one encounters what seems to be a dialogue that puts in play a woman's speech or voice, one can never dismiss the possibility that a defensive dissimulation or projection of the ironic doubling featured in "L'Héautontimorouménos" may be at work. The opening of the sonnet "Semper Eadem," for example, which appears to be a question put to the Poet by his mistress, should perhaps be read as already a displacement out of the echo chamber of self-questioning. Yet the fact that the poem adopts at the outset the device of another, feminine speaker remains interesting if for no other reason than that this voice is invoked only to be silenced.

This sonnet opens with the citation of a question put to the Poet by a mistress in what we must imagine to be a light, perhaps even a mocking tone. The first six lines then articulate the pair question/answer with another pair: joy/pain.

"D'où vous vient, disiez-vous, cette tristesse étrange,
Qui monte comme la mer sur le roc noir et nu?"
—Quand notre coeur a fait une fois sa vendange,
Vivre est un mal. C'est un secret de tous connu,

Une douleur très simple et non mystérieuse,
Et, comme votre joie, éclatante pour tous.[19]

[18]Consider, for example, the poem "Confession," about which Jean Prévost remarks: "This is more or less the only time in Baudelaire's whole opus that the beloved woman is treated as a thinking being." *Baudelaire* (Paris, 1953), 205. The poem stages the scene of a courtesan (Mme Sabatier is usually taken to be the model) confessing to the Poet a despair that, as a woman of the world, she must keep hidden. The eleven lines of this confession are between inverted commas and are specifically attributed to her voice (rather than to her eyes, for example), more precisely, to a dissonant note in her voice. Yet the syntax of the quoted lines indicates indirect rather than direct discourse and thus effects a curious mixing of reporting and reported voices, of addresser and addressee: "Pauvre ange, elle chantait, votre note criarde: / 'Que rien ici-bas n'est certain, / Et que toujours . . .'" (Poor dear, your grating note sang: / "That nothing here below is certain, / And that always . . ."').

[19]"From where, you were saying, does this strange sadness come over you, / Rising like the sea onto the black and naked rock?" / —Once the heart has had its harvest, / Living is an evil. It's a secret that everyone knows, / A very simple and unmysterious pain, / And, like your joy, obvious to everyone.

That a pain is said to be *like* a joy because both are "éclatante pour tous" might seem to be an abuse of metaphor until one begins to suspect that the forced resemblance is a kind of cover thrown over what is actually a metonymic relation of cause and effect between the terms. That is, the questioner's joy does not resemble the Poet's pain; it inflicts that pain. The point of their exchange, the place where both of them burst out, is clearly named in the next stanza with another metonymy: the woman's mouth. It is her childishly laughing mouth, her "bouche au rire enfantin," that the poem twice commands to be silent with a repetition of "taisez-vous" on either side of the sonnet's principal division:

> Cessez donc de chercher, ô belle curieuse!
> Et, bien que votre voix soit douce, taisez-vous!
>
> Taisez-vous, ignorante! âme toujours ravie!
> Bouche au rire enfantin! Plus encor que la Vie,
> La Mort nous tient souvent par des liens subtils.
>
> Laissez, laissez mon coeur s'enivrer du *mensonge*,
> Plonger dans vos beaux yeux comme dans un songe,
> Et sommeiller longtemps à l'ombre de vos cils![20]

The imperative command "taisez-vous" makes way for the gentler imperative of the final stanza: "Laissez, laissez mon coeur," and so on, which brings the poem to a close with what is the most characteristic—not to say obsessive—of all attitudes in the face of the feminine figures mustered in the pages of *Les Fleurs du mal*: the Poet dreamily drinking in to the point of drunkenness the light (or shadow) of her eyes. "Semper Eadem" is interesting in this regard because it installs the dreamy attitude only after imposing silence on the woman's childlike

---

[20]So stop looking, o beautiful, curious one! / And, even though your voice is sweet, be quiet! / Be quiet, ignorant one! Always ecstatic soul! / Childishly laughing mouth! Even more than Life, / Death often has a subtle hold on us. / Let my heart get drunk on a *lie*, / Dive into your beautiful eyes as in a dream, / And sleep for a long time in the shadow of your lashes.

speech. Her question, in effect, betrays a forgetting, and as such it marks a return to the child's ignorance of the simplest truth: Death has a better hold on us than Life. This poem, therefore, not only situates the poet's dreaming in the woman's eyes but locates them as a displacement of her mouth "au rire enfantin," a displacement that is a forgetting or a repressing of *her forgetting*.

If, however, the movement traced from mouth to eyes and from speaking to dreaming is one that goes toward a forgetting, then what exactly is so painful about the woman's question, which, as I said, betrays a forgetting? One answer might be that, precisely, it *betrays* forgetfulness, that is, it is a reminder of what one wants to forget, whereas forgetting only works when one forgets that one is forgetting. But the poem perhaps gives another hint of what is so painful in this woman's happy or mocking question. Since it is said that the two states—pain and joy, but also remembering and forgetting—are linked by the fact of their being "éclatante *pour tous*," there may be a veiled reproach in this image of indiscriminate *jouissance* made available or promised to anyone.[21] These two motifs of reproach that fuel the repetition of "taisez-vous" can moreover be joined if one understands the woman's question as betraying her lack of memory and therefore the likelihood of her future infidelity.

The *mensonge* italicized in the last stanza would be a lie, then, about the woman's memory. Specifically, it covers over her forgetfulness, which always threatens to give the Poet a preview of his own death or an advance taste of his own disappearance for the other, in the eyes of the other. No sooner does she open her mouth than the poet is reminded of the world of others to which she belongs by her speech, almost as if she had spoken only in order to welcome a throng of partygoers into the privacy of their lovers' chamber. The intrusion, however, comes less from others than from the otherness of the woman

---

[21]Besides some thematic parallels with "Semper Eadem," the poem "A Celle qui est trop gaie" (To her who is too gay) suggests yet another displacement of the laughing, mocking mouth to "ces lèvres nouvelles / Plus éclatantes et plus belles" (these novel lips / More striking and more beautiful) which the Poet dreams of opening in the woman's flank.

that speaks a separation of their voices, their memories, their bodies, and their deaths.[22] It is this separation, this difference, and this otherness that the *lie* is called upon to dissimulate, although obviously it cannot do so very satisfactorily. The italics situate both an emphatic will to override or *faire taire* difference and, by a gesture that has to call attention to itself, a reminder of precisely the difference the Poet wants to forget.

If one were to plot further this conjunction of lying, memory, the Poet's death, and woman, a point adjacent to "Semper Eadem" would have to be the poem titled "L'Amour du mensonge," where all these terms are laid out in a similar way.[23] Since, however, it contains no explicit instance of a feminine figure made to speak and/or be silent, the latter poem risks diverting us from our primary concern. Still, two of this poem's metaphors can provide a brief but useful transition from the suppression of feminine speech in "Semper Eadem" to the un-silencing of feminine voice in Baudelaire at which we are trying to arrive.

The poem is a long question about a woman's memory and the reliability of its signs. Eyes, even the most melancholic eyes, may deceive one into thinking that they contain precious secrets when in fact they resemble lockets without relics, "médaillons sans reliques" (l. 19). This image makes explicit the two senses of memory which were already crossing and getting confused in "Semper Eadem." The souvenir locket meant to keep safe relics of the dead—a miniature portrait, a lock of hair—figures at once the *faculty* of memory and *that which* memory remembers or, as we tend to say, contains. It is *her* memory *of* him, *his* memory *in* her, a pocket of internalization but worn on the outside as a reminder of her memory of him, his memory in her—an external reminder to interiorize the other, to keep him alive in memory, to keep his memory

---

[22]See Deguy for a superb reading of "La Mort des amants," a poem that fantasizes the simultaneous death of the lovers.

[23]The fact that the two poems were first published together in the same issue of a journal (*Revue Contemporaine*, 15 May 1860) before they were both in-cluded in the second, 1861 edition of *Les Fleurs du mal* suggests a *renvoi* between the lie in the one and the other.

alive.[24] That the locket may be purely decorative, containing nothing of significance, that "médaillons" and "reliques" remain dissociable within the very metonymy that associates them, leads the poet once again to embrace rather unconvincingly the lie with which metaphor promises a more reassuring assimilation of one term by the other. As in "Semper Eadem," eyes as pure appearance, silent melancholic eyes, are thus preferred to any knowledge of what those eyes may or may not conceal. To attain this knowledge, to open the locket and gain access to the woman's memory, would require that she first open her mouth; it requires, that is, that she be desired to speak and desired *as* speaking rather than just appearing. But this poem, which concludes with the line "Masque ou décor, salut! J'adore ta beauté,"[25] has silenced even the silencing that installs the theater of feminine decoration.

Yet an earlier line in the poem will have warned the reader not to take this final cavalier dismissal of uncertainty too seriously. It occurs in the fourth stanza, which poses a series of metaphors for the woman's memory, the faculty of containing and holding the Poet's memory. One of these metaphors, more than the rest, brings out the container/contained topos of dissociable difference and, in effect, bars the flight into self-delusion which the Poet seems so eager to take. The line asks: "Es-tu vase funèbre attendant quelques pleurs" (l. 14),[26] a question that, because it asks about a future, promptly leaves the realm of truth or lying conceived as a system of correspondences or signs. It asks in effect: *Will* you hold my memory? and it is thus the sort of question that cannot be answered by a corresponding yes or no but only by a promise. This poem would thus suggest another understanding of the Baudelairean figure of the mourn-

[24]In "Getting Versed: Reading Hegel with Baudelaire," Cynthia Chase analyzes the poetic process with reference to memory in the two senses that Hegel distinguishes: *Erinnerung*, interiorizing remembrance, and *Gedächtnis*, thinking memory, but also the rote memorization of signs. *Decomposing Figures: Rhetorical Readings in the Romantic Tradition* (Baltimore, 1986), 113–38. It may be possible to read the poems concerned with the faculty of woman's memory as thematizing in effect an attempted suppression of *Gedächtnis* so as to preserve *Erinnerung* from potential erosion by exteriority, the other's speech.

[25]Mask or decoration, greetings! I adore your beauty.

[26]Are you a funeral urn waiting for some tears.

ing woman. She is a figure for the melancholic poet—a "soul-mate," as one critic puts it[27]—but the identification would be based less on resemblance than on a wished-for promise of remembrance. She is, in other words, a desired container or preserver of the Poet's memory.[28]

Both "Semper Eadem" and "L'Amour du mensonge" suppress, in different ways, the other voice that at the same time they call up or call for. Each concludes with an attempt to cover over or dismiss the difference that has been evoked, yet neither can do so satisfactorily. But "L'Amour du mensonge" at least leaves room in its margin for the feminine addressee to speak in a way—the promise—that may not fall back immediately onto the stage of emptied appearances. What of this other voice that is not to be heard even if the Poet's own voice can be heard calling for it?

If one looks elsewhere in *Les Fleurs du mal* for promising women's voices, the most insistent examples are negative either because they are threats rather than promises, such as the

---

[27]Richard Stamelman, "The Shroud of Allegory: Death, Mourning, and Melancholy in Baudelaire's Work," *Texas Studies of Literature and Language* 25(3), 395. Like other treatments of Baudelaire and mourning, Stamelman draws on Walter Benjamin's analysis of widowhood as an allegory for the condition of modern, urban life. *Charles Baudelaire: A Lyric Poet in the Age of High Capitalism*, trans. Harry Zohn (London, 1973).

[28]A more detailed reading of this poem would have to begin by correcting a frequent mistake concerning the lie that has to be sustained. This is not the lie of the woman's beauty *in spite of* her age. If anything, it is precisely the contrary that is asserted, since only the suggestions of her maturity can offer an apparent support for the desired illusion of a massive memory—"Le souvenir massif" (l. 10)—which is said to crown her. Baudelaire, in fact, may have been the first misreader of his poem, as the initial version carried an epigraph from *Athalie* (later deleted) which pointed to age as what had to be dissimulated: "Même elle avait encor cet éclat emprunté / Dont elle eut soin de peindre et d'orner son visage / Pour réparer des ans l'irréparable outrage" (She even had still that borrowed bloom / With which she was careful to paint and decorate her face / So as to repair the irreparable outrage of time). Sima Godfrey's reading, although it does not refer to this poem, enforces the link between the mourning woman and the container by placing the period of Mme Baudelaire's mourning at the matrix of the melancholic fantasy. Of this period, Baudelaire writes to his mother: "Mais j'étais toujours vivant en toi; tu étais uniquement à moi" (But I was still living in you; you were uniquely mine); cited by Godfrey, 35.

vows made by mother and mistress in "Bénédiction" to humili-
ate and destroy the Poet, or else because they are empty, false
promises. This latter category would be headed by the Siren-
like promises in "Les Métamorphoses du vampire" spoken by
the vampire woman, who, once she has had her fill of lovemak-
ing, appears first as a bag of pus and next as a pile of bones. It
may be, however, that it is not so much to a promise made *in*
the poem that one has to be attentive, but precisely to that
which no poem can represent of itself: the promise to keep the
poem's voice in memory and to keep giving it voice. Voices
represented, attributed, or assumed in the poem can, in the best
of cases, give one to hear or understand—in French, *elles
laisseraient entendre*—the absent voice, the absence in the
voice marking the place of the promise—and the place of the
other.

One late poem from *Les Epaves* puts a promise in its title:
"Les Promesses d'un visage" (The promises of a face). It is one of
the least noticed of any poem now figuring in the complete
works.[29] Most of its twenty lines are speech attributed to a
woman's eyes according to the familiar prosopopoeia. Although
this device seems to situate the poem steadfastly in the realm of
promising appearances that may always be deceiving, there is—
how to say it?—a ring of truth to these promises which moves
the composition closer to the edge of the visible stage and to
what might be called off-voice, to the other who has yet to enter
or has already left the theatrical realm of the visible.

> J'aime, ô pâle beauté, tes sourcils surbaissés,
>   D'où semblent couler des ténèbres;
> Tes yeux, quoique très noirs, m'inspirent des pensers
>   Qui ne sont pas du tout funèbres.
>
> Tes yeux, qui sont d'accord avec tes noirs cheveux,
>   Avec ta crinière élastique,
> Tes yeux, languissamment, me disent: "Si tu veux,
>   Amant de la muse plastique,

---

[29]As far as I have been able to determine, only Jean Prévost has given any
sustained attention to this poem and then only to dismiss it as *sournois* (shifty)
(285).

"Suivre l'espoir qu'en toi nous avons excité,
Et tous les goûts que tu professes,
Tu pourras constater notre véracité
Depuis le nombril jusqu'aux fesses;

"Tu trouveras au bout de deux beaux seins bien lourds,
Deux larges médailles de bronze,
Et sous un ventre uni, doux comme du velours,
Bistré comme la peau d'un bonze,

"Une riche toison qui, vraiment, est la soeur
De cette énorme chevelure,
Souple et frisée, et qui t'égale en épaisseur,
Nuit sans étoiles, Nuit obscure!"[30]

The composition, all in black, sets out from the shadows of
lowered eyebrows[31] and moves to the eyes, which, "quoique
très noirs, m'inspirent des pensers / Qui ne sont pas du tout
funèbres." This initial conjunction of shadowy eyebrows and
dark eyes states the nonfunereal principle that will be repeated
several times: an accord or agreement that is a repetition which
owes nothing either to metaphorical resemblance or to a metonymy of container/contained. These eyes are not windows
into some interiority, and thus they do not evoke a lost time or a
hidden place. They are rather nothing more (or less) than points

[30]I love, pale beauty, your lowered eyebrows, / From which shadows seem to
flow; / Your eyes, although very black, inspire me with thoughts / That are not
in the least funereal. / Your eyes, which agree with your black hair, / With your
elastic mane, / Your eyes, languidly, say to me: "If you wish, / O lover of the
plastic muse, / To pursue the hope that we have aroused in you, / And all the
tastes that you profess, / You can certify our veracity / Between the navel and
the thighs; / You will find at the end of two fine heavy breasts, / Two large
medals of bronze, / And beneath a smooth belly, soft as velvet, / Brown as the
skin of a bonze, / A rich fleece which, in truth, is the sister of that enormous
head of hair, / Supple and curly, and which is your equal for darkness, / Starless
night, obscure Night!"

[31]These "sourcils surbaissés" led George Heard Hamilton to wonder whether
Baudelaire's "pâle beauté" was not also Manet's "Chanteuse des rues," since,
when it was first exhibited in Paris in 1863, the painting drew hoots from one
critic for what he took to be eyebrows on either side of the bridge of the figure's
nose. See *Manet and His Critics* (New York, 1969), 40, n. 4.

of articulation on a differentiated surface that is not a surface covering or hiding something else. The principle of simple accord is stated directly in the second stanza, which also transfers voice to the other's eyes:

> Tes yeux, *qui sont d'accord* avec tes noirs cheveux,
>   Avec ta crinière élastique,
> Tes yeux, languissamment, me disent:

What these eyes will call their "véracité" is nothing other than the posing side by side—the *accord*—of different features without any claims made about their sense in some larger signifying whole. No relations of signification are claimed to exist between any of the parts: both the metaphoric and metonymic principles, resemblance and contiguity, have been emptied of their sense-making potential. These eyes promise, but they do not promise a future *meaning*. They promise, rather, only to go on promising.

The prosopopoeia, the eyes' speech, begins:

> . . . "Si tu veux,
> Amant de la muse plastique,
>
> "Suivre l'espoir qu'en toi nous avons excité,
>   Et tous les goûts que tu professes,
> Tu pourras constater notre véracité,
>   Depuis le nombril jusqu'aux fesses."

The relation between the eyes and the lower torso is articulated here like a sign: the one pointing to the other and arousing an expectation. The expectation is answered, however, in a markedly circular form: "Tu pourras constater notre véracité / Depuis le nombril jusqu'aux fesses." If the eyes can be said to point to—or promise—the lower torso, then it is because the lower torso points to the eyes' veracity in appearing to point to the torso and so forth. Each feature promises the other with a kind of redundancy that is perfectly stable because it keeps turning in a circle. Other features can be brought into the picture in the next stanza without substantial alteration to this pattern.

Only the final two lines seem to make a gesture off in another direction:

> "Tu trouveras . . .
> Une riche toison qui, vraiment, est la soeur
>   De cette énorme chevelure,
>   Souple et frisée, et qui t'égale en épaisseur,
>   Nuit sans étoiles, Nuit obscure!"

Do these last lines promise an equivalent or a substitute for the depth of night? If so, then the eyes' speech breaks with its own principle of veracity, its pattern of nonsubstitution and non-totalization. It would thereby come very close to echoing the sort of promise made by the vampire before she undergoes her metamorphoses. She says: "Je remplace, pour qui me voit nue et sans voiles, / La lune, le soleil, le ciel et les étoiles."[32] "Les Promesses d'un visage" may be hiding another face of the vampire.

One detail of these concluding lines we have yet to mention. At the same moment at which the eyes' discourse falls into promising the moon and the stars, it also turns to address the dark night: "et qui t'égale en épaisseur, / Nuit sans étoiles, Nuit obscure!" What difference, if any, does this detail of address make in the promising structure of the poem?

The answer lies in a deep fold along which the poem opens and closes like a mouth or an eye, its two lips or lids joining and parting. The final apostrophe to dark night is spoken by the dark eyes, which are themselves made to speak by apostrophe and prosopopoeia of darkness. Thus the final apostrophe restates the initial one: the poem's lower edge meets and joins its upper one in a circulation for which there is no end in sight and no promise of final meaning. Specifically, it cannot be said that the poem's initial voice, attributed to the poet, contains or encloses

---

[32]For whoever sees me naked and without my veils, I take the place of / The moon, the sun, the sky and the stars.

the other voice, atributed to a woman's eyes. Rather, the meeting or joining of the two voices makes of each the other's
container *and* contained. Each holds the memory of the other
and promises its return. This is its ring of truth.

One could ask, finally, why this poem has received so little
critical notice. I am tempted at least to wonder whether readers
have not always sensed something distinctly un-Baudelairean
in the voice which, once invoked, takes over the poem. I am
thinking of what could be called its flatness, the fact that it
remains on the surface and exposes the superficial relation not
only of the signs it speaks but of the very sign that it is assumed
to *be* by the Poet's address. This flatness is something quite
different from the depth of those eyes in "L'Amour du mensonge," which may be "plus vides, plus profonds que vous-
mêmes, ô Cieux."[33] In "Les Promesses d'un visage," the transcendent, celestial backdrop drops away and with it the promise
of metaphor's final revelation, its *corps mis à nu*. And this
despite the central topos of the striptease, which has been not
so much turned inside out as turned back on the spectator,
mocking the "amant de la muse plastique." The mocking tone
is to be heard in the distinctly prosaic line "Tu pourras constater notre véracité," as well as in the interjected "vraiment," a
mocking that aims at the Poet's predilection for the lie of metaphor, for women who are like decorative souvenir lockets or for
eyes whose dark depths seem to promise that of night. When
this very Baudelairean figure is invoked, therefore, in the last
lines, has it not been taken over and exposed in its turn as a lie
imposed by a willing blindness? And thus, is it even possible
still to hear it in Baudelaire's "own" voice?
One may want to make these questions go away and, along
with them, the noninteriorizable other who, I am suggesting,
has somehow managed to get out in this poem. One may, that
is, want to conclude that the mockery is simply self-inflicted or
calculated and thus recuperable to what is being mocked. To do
so, however, would be to seal off Baudelaire's signature, to

[33]Emptier, deeper than yourselves, O Heavens.

make it finally, for us, today, *unreadable*. If, on the other hand, it is precisely the recuperative or totalizing power of any *one* voice that has been given the lie in this poem, then an opening still remains and a chance for readdress, even— who knows?— for redress. In the end, this belying effect cannot be made in any simple sense internal to the lie's calculation. Some other voice will have had its say in "Les Promesses d'un visage." If this voice promises a return and lends to the poem its ring of truth, it is because of the deviation imposed or inflicted on the circular return of the same by the other. The only sense of this circle comes from the opening onto the sense of the other, the sharing, dividing of voice.

CHAPTER SIX

Penelope at Work

> . . . but always
> I waste away at the inward heart, longing for Odysseus.
> These men try to hasten the marriage. I weave my own wiles.
> —*The Odyssey*

As so often throughout our culture's poetic text, one encounters in *The Odyssey* moments of abyssal self-representation when the poem tries to occupy a place in two different and mutually exclusive spheres, when it slips between representing something and being the something represented. One such moment, in book I, happens to coincide with the first direct representation of Penelope. In fact, Penelope enters the scene of narration in order to interrupt it. In the passage to which I refer, Telemachos and the suitors are gathered in front of the palace, where they are listening to "the famous singer . . . [who] sang of the Achaians' bitter homecoming / from Troy."[1] Penelope, who "heeded the magical song from her upper chamber," is drawn down the stairs and, in tears, begs the singer to choose another song. At this point, Telemachos takes the floor, reproaches his mother for her intervention, and says to her:

"Go therefore back in the house, and take up your own work,
the loom and the distaff, and see to it that your handmaidens

A shortened form of this chapter appeared in *Novel: A Forum on Fiction*, vol. 16, no. 1 (Fall 1982). Copyright © 1982, Novel Corp. Reprinted by permission.
[1]Trans. Richmond Lattimore (New York, 1957), 325–27; other references are noted in parentheses.

ply their work also; but the men must see to discussion,
all men, but I most of all. For mine is the power in this household."
Penelope went back inside the house, in amazement.

(I, 356–60)

Much later in the poem, at a crucial moment that prepares
Odysseus' attack on the suitors, Telemachos again sends his
mother out of the room, using almost the same terms but with
one important difference. Instead of the poem or discussion, it
is an instrument of force—Odysseus' famous bow—that Telemachos orders his mother to leave in men's hands.

"Go therefore back into the house, and take up your own work,
the loom and the distaff, and see to it that your handmaidens
ply their work also. The men shall have the bow in their keeping,
all men, but I most of all. For mine is the power in this household."
Penelope went back inside the house, in amazement.

(XXI, 350–54)

By means of this repetition, the poem establishes a connection between the art of storytelling and the practice of force.
Both fall within a son's prerogative to exercise power in his
household, the power to send women out of the room. If, however, a distribution of power and the sexes occurs here, it turns
on the designation of woman's work as "the loom and the
distaff," the instruments of weaving and spinning. Both of these
tasks supply the poet with endless metaphoric possibilities in
this tale of men whose fate, for example, is "spun with the
thread at his birth" (VII, 198), where the storyteller can spin out
a well-made tale, and where cleverness weaves designs and
deceptions. Thus, in a way that we have been taught to recognize,[2] the exclusion of the distaff from manly discussion is
necessarily incomplete since Penelope's work is set out as a
kind of material support for the metaphorical field from which
the poem draws its crafty designs and deceptive stories. But
rhetorical repetition is not all that is working here to confound

[2]By, for example, J. Hillis Miller in "Ariachne's Broken Woof," *Georgia
Review* 30 (Spring 1977).

the distinction Telemachos would make. Power in the household is interrupted in quite another fashion by a woman's art

Pressed by her household to choose a new husband, Penelope does not want to decide. Instead, she has given herself the tedious task of unweaving by night what she has woven during the day. It is not a terribly clever trick, nothing like saying "No man" to the Cyclops Polyphemos, although perhaps that is what her unweaving means. In any case, it is a homelier remedy in a tight spot, which works even though her suitors, unlike Odysseus' Polyphemos, are perfectly able to see the tissue of her lies. Like a spider, she watches them fly into the web she has stretched across the entrance to the room in which she sits weaving. It is the same room she enters at night when others suppose her in bed. Here, then, is Penelope's great secret, what no man can see for no man imagines her anywhere but in bed. It is this secret passage out of the bedchamber that allows Penelope to promise her bed and yet always defer the terms of the promise. No clever play on words but rather a spatial and temporal shift between the two centers of her woman's life preserves Penelope's indecision. The suitors remain strangers to a woman's work which is never done, the tedium of the interior. As a result, their manly discussion is mystified by an obvious trick.

A Room of One's Own, the published text of lectures delivered at Newnham and Girton colleges in 1928, begins with the question of its own title: "But, you may say, we asked you to speak about women and fiction—what has that got to do with a room of own's own? I will try to explain."[3] Likewise, the title "Penelope at Work" needs some explanation. The title—that is, the right to claim attention to whatever Penelope might have to say about Virginia Woolf. Because authority here is a fiction, it can claim only the credit due the speculations of a common reader, in the sense that Woolf gives that notion in her two anthologies of critical essays, *The Common Reader*. I would

---

[3]Virginia Woolf, *A Room of One's Own* (New York, 1929), 3; future references are noted in parentheses in the text.

add as well the other sense taken by the narrator of *A Room of One's Own* when she sets aside a more systematic sounding of the depths, examining instead "only what chance has floated to [her] feet" (78).

I invoke Penelope in order to name what is at work in a text like *A Room of One's Own*, although the phrase "at work" already covers up in too purposeful a fashion the way such work entails as well its own undoing. I take Penelope as a shuttling figure in power's household, one whose movement between outside and inside, violence and poetry, the work of history and the unworking of fiction may allow us to frame one or two notions about the place of woman's art. This figure, moreover, may also serve to reformulate that other notion of woman's exclusion which always seems to arise whenever one takes up the question of power in stories and in histories. Finally, then, Penelope is the name I take in order to designate a conjunction of fiction in history in which a woman's text plots the place of its own undoing.

As already mentioned, *A Room of One's Own* opens with the question of its title. To provide an answer, the lecture's narrator introduces another fictional narrator (" 'I,' " she writes, "is only a convenient term for somebody who has no real being" [4]), who proceeds to recount a series of events interspersed with a chain of literary analyses. Asked to explain, in other words, the narrator promises an answer once she is through spinning out her story. But this narrative sets out from a doubling back or a crossing out in which a meaning, a sense of direction, gets lost.

Having finally fished up an idea for her promised lectures on women and fiction, the narrator has set off at a rapid pace across Cambridge's campus, little heeding where her feet are taking her. Where she might have been going, however, no one can tell because she is instantly called back to an order of distinctions that her thought had put aside in its unruly eagerness:

> Instantly a man's figure rose to intercept me. Nor did I at first understand that the gesticulations of a curious-looking object, in a cut-away coat and evening shirt, were aimed at me. His face expressed horror and indignation. Instinct rather than reason

came to my help; he was a Beadle; I was a woman. This was the turf; there was the path. Only the Fellows and Scholars are allowed here; the gravel is the place for me. As I regained the path the arms of the Beadle sank, his face assumed its usual repose, and though turf is better walking than gravel, no very great harm was done. . . . [However], what idea it had been that had sent me so audaciously trespassing I could not now remember. (6)

This setback, provoked by an interruption, is itself soon forgotten and the narrator is led, through a series of rapid associations, to set her course for a certain college library where one might consult the manuscript of Milton's *Lycidas*. Once again, she is carried forward unconsciously, her bodily movement forgotten as one text leads to another until it is a question no longer about Milton but about a Thackeray novel that brings her to the door of the library. Once again, her unruly associations have transgressed a fundamental order and the intertextual weaving is broken off when the narrator is recalled to the reality of her own unfitness in such a place:

But here I was actually at the door which leads into the library itself. I must have opened it, for instantly there issued, like a guardian angel barring the way with a flutter of black gown instead of with wings, a deprecating, silvery, kindly gentleman, who regretted in a low voice as he waved me back that ladies are only admitted to the library if accompanied by a Fellow of the College or furnished with a letter of introduction. (7–8)

In its initial movement, then, the text describes a zigzag, a series of interruptions and a repeated reversal of direction. From this angle, we may begin to see how *A Room of One's Own* frames the question of women and fiction within the field of an exclusion. What appears there is a contradiction like the one the narrator exposes in the following passage: "If women had no existence save in the fiction written by men, one would imagine her a person of utmost importance. . . . But this is woman in fiction. In fact, as Professor Treveylan points out [in his *History of England*], she was locked up, beaten and flung about the room" (44–45). The zigzag produced by a reversal of sense is here more clearly coordinated with the contradiction of fiction by history. And this zigzag intersects as well with the question of the title: Is "a room of one's own," in other words, an image, a metaphor with which to call up the immaterial, the timeless, and the imaginary defeat of power, or is it rather that which supports the metaphor, the denoted foundation on the basis of which figurative space is constructed? A place in history which exists therefore in social, political, and economic contexts, or a place that transcends these limits much in the way the narrator looks down on the street activity from her study window? How does *A Room of One's Own*, in other words, negotiate this angle of contradiction?

The narrator defers these questions by posing another in their place as if she had found another use for Penelope's trick of leaving one room for another, as if the promise she has made engages here to keep the passage open between these two spaces, to let them interfere with each other. Woolf's narrator, for example, cannot simply escape into the library from a ruder reality because once there she is drawn back into the rudest of scenes where young women are "locked up, beaten and flung about the room." Here, then, is another locked room within the first. The second enclosure takes shape in the fully loaded bookshelves lining the walls. Having locked women out of the library, history still rages at her from within. The narrator runs into this locked door repeatedly in the British Library, and even at home, in her own library, the violent encounters continue. Again and again, she is shown the door. Again and again, anger flares as it did when she was politely told she could not enter the college library. "Never will I wake those echoes, never will I ask for that hospitality again, I vowed as I descended the steps in anger" (8).

The narrator spins in the revolving door of the library. While anger pushes her out, something else pulls her back in. That something else has the force of forgetfulness—in its pull, one forgets one's place, one's self. In this back-and-forth motion, the narrator is strung out between an exclusion or negation of women and a forgetting of herself as woman. Here, then, may be as well one space of woman's writing, which always risks hardening into the negative outline of anger and thereby losing its chance for forgetfulness. This is the sense of the encounter with Professor von X., whom the narrator sketches as she reads his thesis *The Mental, Moral and Physical Inferiority of the Female Sex*.

> Whatever the reason, the professor was made to look very angry and ugly in my sketch, as he wrote his great book. . . . Drawing pictures was an idle way of finishing an unprofitable morning's work. Yet it is in our idleness, in our dreams, that the submerged truth sometimes comes to the top. A very elementary exercise in psychology, not to be dignified by the name of psychoanalysis, showed me on looking at my notebook, that the sketch of the angry professor had been made in anger. Anger had snatched my pencil while I dreamt. (31–32)

In this moment, the narrator has a view not only of the ugly face of the historian but also of her own distorted features: "My cheeks had burnt. I had flushed with anger." Yet these interceptions, which snatch the pencil from the hand and push thought off the path it was following, always set up the possibility of a new direction in which to proceed. When the negations of history are made to turn on themselves, the door of the library spins, setting the narrator in motion once again.

> All that I had retrieved from that morning's work had been the one fact of anger. The professors—I lumped them together thus—were angry. But why, I asked myself, having returned the books, why, I repeated, standing under the colonnade among the pigeons and the prehistoric canoes, why are they angry? And, asking myself this question, I strolled off. (33)

Through these deflections which turn a discourse back on itself, *A Room of One's Own* defines a novel position in relation to the locked room of history. That is, since women's history cannot be studied in the library, it will have to be read into the scene of its own exclusion. It has to be invented—both discovered and made up. As it spins around its promise to decide on the place of woman's writing, this text *ravels* the crossed threads of history and fiction. It ravels—which is to say it both *un*tangles, makes something plain or clear, and it *en*tangles or confuses something. An alternative definition of the transitive verb *to ravel* is (quoting from the decisive Oxford authority) "to unravel." Turning in the door of culture's most exclusive institution, Penelopean work blurs the line between historical prerogatives and fictional pretensions, always deferring the promised end of its labor, raveling/unraveling clear historical patterns at its fictional border.

In order to specify further this figure of the self-raveling text, one may turn to three different moments in *A Room of One's Own* where interruption marks the scene of writing. First, however, let us take a rather large detour whose only logic may be that of one text interrupting and unraveling another. The digression is proposed in order to step beyond a limited notion of interruption and thus a limited reading of Woolf's text. It passes through the work of Michel Foucault, most particularly his *Will to Knowledge* (*La Volonté de savoir*).[4] It might be useful to break into *A Room of One's Own* with Foucault's history of sexuality so as to point up the zigzagging fault lines in Woolf's speculations about woman's writing. Although the fault lines are quite plainly there, they can be too easily overlooked when this text is taken as a model authority for a critical practice content to go on making nasty caricatures of Professor von X., the nameless author and authority of masculine privilege and feminine subjection. The fault line beneath this sketch is the notion of sexual differentiation as a historical production which, if it has produced a privileged masculine subject, cannot also be understood as originating in the subject it only produces. To the extent, however, that one accepts to see "man" at the origin of his own privilege, then, one chooses paradoxically to believe the most manifest lie of "phallosophy": that of man giving birth to himself as an origin that transcends any difference from himself. It is with just such a notion of production that Professor Foucault's history, for example, may interrupt

[4]Foucault, *The History of Sexuality*, vol. 1, trans. Robert Hurley (New York, 1978).

whatever sketch we might make of privileged masculine subjectivity.

To resume very quickly, Foucault elaborates his history over
against a certain Freudian-Marxian tradition that has consistently distinguished sexuality from the power mechanisms that
repress it. According to this common notion, which Foucault
labels "the repressive hypothesis," power is structurally opposed to the anarchic energy of sexuality and functions to repress it, for example, by forcing conformity to the model of the
monogamous heterosexual couple. The corollary to this hypothesis, therefore, is the value placed on sexual liberation as
evidence of effective resistance to the bourgeois hegemony of
power. Foucault, on the other hand, proposes that the repressive
model of power is at best a limited and at worst a mystified one
insofar as it accounts only for negative relations and ignores the
far more pervasive evidence of power's production of *positive*—
that is, real— effects. He argues that, for at least two centuries
in the West, power has maintained just such positive relations
to sex and sexuality—sexuality, that is, is to a large extent
produced by power—and these have progressively assumed a
more important role as means for articulating power effects in
the individual and society. All of which is why the various
movements of sexual liberation need to be systematically re-
evaluated as instances also of the deployment of a will to
knowledge, of power's articulating itself in the first-person confessional mode that also constitutes sexual identity. In an earlier work on disciplinary institutions (*Discipline and Punish*),
Foucault gives an even clearer distinction of power in modern
Western society as articulated in the various sciences of the
subject, through the increasingly refined and differentiated
techniques of identifying and classifying the "I" of any discourse.

While one should hesitate to force Woolf's text into parallel
with this analysis, one may at least accept to see in it a background for a certain ambivalence. Woolf consistently sets the
apparent political and social gains of a new women's consciousness over against the disturbing signs of an intensification of
exclusive sexual identities, of sexually grounded subjectivity,

and of subjectively grounded sexuality. What can emerge perhaps from the excursus into Foucault's history is another context within which to read *A Room of One's Own* as turning away from this historical preoccupation with the subject, closing the book on the "I." The gesture which one can now read somewhat differently is that of the narrator when, near the end of her story and after leafing through the works of many women writers from Aphra Behn to her own contemporary Mary Carmichael, she takes one last book off the shelf. It is a novel by a certain Mr. A. (whose initial, like the Professor's X, seems to stand for the whole alphabet of possible proper names). Quickly, however, she replaces it on the shelf because

> after reading a chapter or two a shadow seemed to lie across the page. It was a straight dark bar, a shadow shaped something like the letter "I." One began dodging this way and that to catch a glimpse of the landscape behind it. Whether that was indeed a tree or a woman walking I was not quite sure. Back one was always hailed to the letter "I." One began to be tired of "I." (103)

What our detour through the Foucauldian critique should allow us to see is that the power of this "straight dark bar" to obliterate everything it approaches is not a power derived from the identity of a masculine subject to which the "I" simple refers. Rather, the identification of subjects is already an effect of power's articulating itself on bodies and "objects" in general, differentiating and ordering their intercourse, mapping the space of meaning.

Having noted this, however, we wonder what remains of Woolf's particular critique of the patriarchal subject's historical privilege. Have we not passed over this aspect in order better to assimilate Woolf's text into the broader critique of the humanistic subject which is Foucault's project? Is it simply insignificant that the latter's analysis never interrogates the hierarchical opposition of the sexes as an important link in the deployment of power, while that distinction repeatedly forces itself on Woolf's thought, interrupting it, causing it to lose direction? Is there not, in other words, a sense in which *The Will to Knowl-*

edge itself occupies a privileged space that knows no interruption?

Consider, for example, what one may call the narrator of *The Will to Knowledge*, the "I" that assumes direction of the discourse's argument. Like the narrator of *A Room of One's Own*, this "I" is "only a convenient term for somebody who has no existence," it marks only a relative position in a discursive or textual network. Nonetheless, it is in a clearly different position. As we have seen, *A Room of One's Own* proceeds on the model of an interruption that forces the narration to deviate in some fashion, that intrudes with an effective, forceful objection to the momentary forgetting of a woman's identity. In *The Will to Knowledge*, on the other hand, it is the narration that defines other discursive procedures as "deviations" and, compared to Woolf's narration, itself proceeds virtually free from distraction since no one ever gets in its way with anything but spurious objections.[5] To cite just one instance, it anticipates the particular obstacle to its progress which the Lacanian theory of desire might pose, the theory, that is, of desire as constituted in and by, rather than against, the law. That theory, then, has already carried out a critique of ego psychology's repressive hypothesis, but its implications for a history of sexuality are opposed to those drawn by Foucault. One need not enter here too far into the details of this debate in order to appreciate the discursive mode in which this objection is first formulated. Foucault writes:

> I can imagine that one would have the right to say to me: By referring constantly to the positive technologies of power, you are trying to pull off a bigger victory over both [Lacanian psychoanalysis and ego psychology]. You lump your adversaries together behind the figure of the weaker one, and by discussing only repres-

[5]One might argue that this difference is simply that of genres or modes of discourse, which indeed it appears to be. But if we were to adopt these terms, what genre or mode would we assign to *A Room of One's Own*? The fact that Woolf writes beyond genres of discourse, according to a rhythm of their interruption, and does so by necessity, cannot be accounted for in terms of generic difference alone.

sion, you want to make us believe incorrectly that you have gotten rid of the problem of the law [which is constitutive of desire].[6]

While the "I" will eventually respond to this objection, notice how in this moment (but there are many such moments)[7] the discourse imagines another position from which to address itself as "you." Is it any wonder the narrator is never at a loss for a reply? These interruptions of the narrator's pursuit of the analysis may be frequent, but they are never serious since no figure appears there who, like the Cambridge beadle, has the position and the power to wave the narrator off the turf or to demand to see his permit to enter the library.

It is in this sense, at least, that a discourse like Foucault's can still retain a place in the privileged domain of patriarchal thought, a train of thought which has been trained, precisely, to think without interruption. And, in a very important sense, the privileged space in question is The Room of One's Own. These capital letters will refer us back to the original room, the room properly named, the room of the Cartesian subject, where *Ego sum* is struck as an emblem bearing a proper name, taking up space whose limits can be delineated and, perhaps most important, where the subject becomes one—an individual and whole. Michel Foucault is among those who have forced entry into this room so as to see what is going on there. In an appendix to the second French edition of *Histoire de la folie* (*Madness and Civilization*), he writes that it is "a peaceful retreat" to which Descartes's philosopher retires in order to transcribe the exercise of radical doubt. In that exercise, the subject of the meditation encounters an early "point of resistance" in the form of the actuality of the moment and place of meditation: the fact that he is in a certain room, sitting by a fire, before a piece of paper. These conditions—a warm body next to a fire, writing

[6]Foucault, *History of Sexuality*, 108.

[7]Perhaps the most striking example of the technique is the final section of Foucault, *The Archaeology of Knowledge*, trans. Alan Sheridan (New York, 1972), where the discourse, in effect, interviews itself and answers all the questions it can think of.

instruments—are then taken by Foucault as synecdoches of the whole system of actuality which the subject cannot be thought to lack and still be posited as the subject of a reasonable discourse. In the appended essay to which I refer, "Mon corps, ce papier, ce feu" (My body, this paper, this fire), Foucault imagines that the meditating subject would have to reason as follows: "If I begin to doubt the place where I am, the attention I am giving to this piece of paper, and of the fire's warmth which marks my present moment, how could I remain convinced of the reasonable nature of my enterprise? Will I not, by putting this actuality in doubt, make any reasonable meditation impossible and rob of all value my resolve to discover finally the truth?"[8] For Foucault, Descartes's place in the history of the Western episteme is so important because it situates the juncture of an exclusion—of unreason, of madness—with the seizure of material reality by the Subject of Reason. By means of that exclusion and that seizure, reality can be a quiet place in which to meditate on oneself.[9] However, when Foucault takes up the synecdochic figure "My Body, This Paper, This Fire" as the title of his essay, he does so in order to reassert the abrogated claims of madness, to reassert, that is, the points of resistance to the elaboration of a reasonable subject. In a certain sense, these points provide leverage on the subject's discourse and give access to intrusion into it.[10]

It was as if someone had let fall a shade. . . . Something seemed lacking, something seemed different. And to answer that question, I had to think myself out of the room. (11)

---

[8]Foucault, "Mon Corps, ce papier, ce feu," in *L'Histoire de la folie*, 2d ed. (Paris, 1972), 595–96. For a critique of Foucault's reading of Descartes, see Jacques Derrida, "Cogito and History of Madness," in *Writing and Difference*, trans. Alan Bass (Chicago, 1978).

[9]See Susan Bordo, "The Cartesian Masculinization of Thought," *Signs* 11(3), for another, significantly different account of "masculinization" as an effect of separation.

[10]However, as Foucault writes in *La Volonté de savoir*, points of resistance "by definition . . . can only exist in the strategic field of power relations" (126). Jean Baudrillard has pointed out that resistance has a rather unexplained status in Foucault's discourse; see *Oublier Foucault* (Paris, 1977), 50ff.

Let us place this scene of a certain kind of intrusion into reason's discourse beside another that is imagined by Woolf's narrator. One will recognize a few reasons for doing so: the actuality of a scholar's meditation, a resistance, intrusion—all are in play here. The narrator in this passage is spinning out her image of the great man of letters, seen not as he labors in the overheated library of Cartesian discourse, but rather in an idle moment. In fact, he has left the actuality of the library for another room.

> He [e.g., Johnson, Goethe, Carlyle, Voltaire, or any other great man] would open the door of drawing-room or nursery, I thought, and find her among her children perhaps, or with a piece of embroidery on her knee—at any rate, the centre of some different order and system of life, and the contrast between this world and his own . . . would at once refresh and invigorate; and there would follow, even in the simplest talk, such a natural difference of opinion that the dried ideas in him would be fertilised anew; and the sight of her creating in a different medium from his own would so quicken his creative power that insensibly his sterile mind would begin to plot again, and he would find the phrase or the scene which was lacking when he put on his hat to visit her. (90)

A man of letters, a scholar, leaves his place by the fire in that quiet room and opens the door to a drawing room or nursery. There, the weary philosopher's work is supplemented by a "different medium," and he is given to see "the scene which was lacking" from the drama taking shape behind the other closed door. Notice that Woolf's narrator is both making up this scene and making up for its lack in the scene of history. It has no place, that is, in the history and the biographies of great men which one may consult. It is thus invented, but to take the place of what is missing in the scholar's medium. In other words, the encounter with a supplemental difference takes place as fiction in history. Or rather, it takes place in a mode that has as yet no proper name. Woolf writes:

> It would be ambitious beyond my daring, I thought, looking about the shelves for books that were not there, to suggest to the stu-

dents of those famous colleges that they should re-write history . . . but why should they not add a supplement to history?
calling it, of course, by some inconspicuous name so that women
might figure there without impropriety? (47)

When it acts to restore a missing scene in history's self-narra-
tive, the narrative of the great man, Woolf's text catches history
at a loss for words, interrupted in its train of thought. What is
restored here, then, is not simply some unrecorded moment in
the history of power but an interval, a hiatus where that discourse has been momentarily broken off.

In order to figure such an interval or interruption, Woolf's
text creates a passage out of the library and into another room.
Let us briefly compare this passage to the one located by Foucault in the Cartesian scene of meditation. The subject of that
meditation reappears in Foucault's essay just as he depicted
himself, sealed in his heated study. Now, we could say that
Foucault, unlike Woolf, simply finds no reason to imagine the
philosopher wandering about from room to room at a loss. No
doubt, one would have to acknowledge that such moments
occur, but it is reasonable for the historian of discourse to
exclude them. Indeed, if one did not exclude them but allowed
such idle fantasies to intrude, then it could hardly be called
history that one is writing. Notice how, when it is considered in
this manner, the reasonable omission reassembles the elements
of the Cartesian subject's exclusion of its own madness. In this
sense, at least, it constructs history by figuring only this com-
fortably situated position of power.

To return to the scene as it is imagined by Woolf's narrator:
surely the interruption figured there is too quickly, too easily
recuperated to the benefit of the suspended work. The great
man is just taking a little break. Woolf's text, however, also
figures two other sorts of interruption which are not so neatly
resumed within the continuous work of history. Both are described as eruptions into the space of woman's work.

The first frames the nineteenth-century middle-class woman
who, if she wrote, "would have to write in the common sitting-
room" (69) as Jane Austen did and where, of course, "she was
always interrupted" (70). The narrator quotes this passage from

James Austen-Leigh's memoir of his Aunt Jane: "How she was able to effect all this is surprising, for she had no separate study to repair to, and most of the work must have been done in the general sitting-room, subject to all kinds of casual interruptions. She was careful that her occupation should not be suspected by servants or any persons beyond her own family party." To this, the narrator adds: "Jane Austen hid her manuscripts or covered them with a piece of blotting-paper." Austen, in a recognizably Penelopean fashion, undoes her work repeatedly so that it might continue. Each interruption blots out evidence of a fictional work and replaces it with the cover of domestic tasks.[11] The homely fiction of domestic enclosure disguises the worldly fiction. That fiction is thus situated historically, materially. At the same time, however, a certain historical determination of woman's place is also seen to be conditioned by a fiction and based on a ruse which hides the contradictions of history.[12]

To understand some of the possible implications of this double-hinging effect of interruption, what I am calling Penelopian labor, one need only imagine that the weary scholar whom we earlier followed out of his study into a drawing room might have himself, without realizing it, walked in on someone like Miss Austen and found her "with a piece of embroidery on her knee—at any rate, the centre of *some different order* and system of life." The scholar's visit to this lady culminates in an inspiration which allows him to fill a gap in the discourse of reason, the discourse produced in a space of no difference, no interruption. By rewriting this familiar scene as we are suggesting, the phrase "some different order" comes to imply not only a difference from the order that governs the scholar's work but

[11]On how this "cover story" may be functioning thematically in Austen's novels, see Sandra Gilbert and Susan Gubar, *The Madwoman in the Attic* (New Haven, Conn., 1979), 153ff.

[12]Woolf's tampering with the distinction between fiction and history should also be read as an effect of their mutual implication in each other. For an excellent study of this question, see Suzanne Gearhart, *The Open Boundary of History and Fiction: A Critical Approach to the French Enlightenment* (Princeton, N.J., 1984).

as well a difference from itself insofar as that piece of embroidery just may hide the text unraveling the domestic scene. The inspiring vision of difference, that representation which always implies an identity, is acted out as a mask for this other difference from itself, the difference within identity. The scholar is able to draw inspiration for his task because he believes he has glimpsed a scene other than the scene of writing, caught sight of someone different, doing something else. Yet, because there may be a hidden text in the picture, it is perhaps someone much more like himself whom he has interrupted. The man of letters—historian, biographer, novelist, playwright, or literary critic—has failed to see himself as already represented in the room he has entered, and it is precisely a blindness to his own reflection that induces a credulous inspiration for his work. Is he not, like one of Penelope's suitors, fooled by his eagerness to find her keeping the promise of her embroidery? What the text may thus display beneath its embroidered cover is a self-delusion and in the very place, at the very moment that the scholar imagines for himself a way to fill a gap in the self's narrative. If history records the subject's delusion about its own identity, then fictions like Austen's and Woolf's restore to history the moments that precipitate such delusions, moments when difference can just be glimpsed before it disappears beneath a reassuring cover of familiar design.

All of this, of course, is quite fanciful speculation. Indeed, the little fiction about Jane Austen may be even more farfetched than it appears since at least one of Austen's recent biographers suspects that the whole description of the author hiding her manuscripts is apocryphal, at the very least an exaggeration. Despite her caution, however, this biographer cannot wholly avoid perpetuating the fiction for she writes: "I think this story . . . must be the happy later *embroidery* of Austen's nieces."[13]

Nevertheless, the caution is well placed. Let us try to conclude on more solid ground by returning to the language of Woolf's text and yet another scene of interruption. The passage

---

[13]Jane Aiken Hodge, *Only a Novel: The Double Life of Jane Austen* (New York, 1972), 133; italics added.

in question begins simply enough with the phrase: "One goes into the room," followed by a dash, a punctuated hesitation. This pause is just long enough to raise a question about the identity of the "one" in the opening sentence. Then, having hesitated, the narrator goes on: "but the resources of the English language would be much put to the stretch, and whole flights of words would need to wing their way illegitimately into existence before a woman could say what happens when she goes into a room" (91). This sentence marks the limit, or threshold, of any lecture on women and fiction. Unlike the ease with which one can imagine the scholar walking in on the drawing room or nursery, a woman enters the room in an unfamiliar, yet-to-be-written, even illegitimate mode. Clearly, for Woolf, such forced entry into the language will not simply substitute a feminine "one" for a masculine. This becomes clear when, as the passage continues, Woolf shifts, without transition, from the question of the identity of the subject entering the domain of language to that of the many rooms one may enter.

> One goes into the room—but the resources of the English language would be much put to the stretch, and whole flights of words would need to wing their way illegitimately into existence before a woman could say what happens when she goes into a room. The rooms differ so completely, they are calm or thunderous; open on to the sea, or, on the contrary, give on to a prison yard; are hung with washing; or alive with opals and silks; are hard as horsehair or soft as feathers—one has only to go into any room in any street for the whole of that extremely complex force of femininity *to fly in one's face.* How should it be otherwise? For women have sat indoors all these millions of years, so that by this time the very walls are permeated by their creative force. (Italics added)

In effect, Woolf displaces the issue of the "one" who enters the room by figuring in rapid succession a series of rooms to be entered, surveyed, plotted, described. But less obviously intervening here in the question of one's identity is the insistence of a form of self-interruption. By substituting the passive "a woman's room is entered" for the active "one goes into the room," this passage creates a disturbance on both sides of the threshold of subjectivity. And when the place of the feminine subject is abandoned in view of the multiple places of the "complex force of femininity," then, retroactively and with a certain delay, it has become possible to begin to say what happens when a woman enters the room: in a word, femininity, already there, already at work, *flies in one's face*. We must try to hear this phrase—a figure of self-interruption—in both of its possible senses at once: to become overwhelmingly obvious and to transgress flagrantly some law or rule. There is both a recognition and an infringement of the place of a creative subject which is no longer or not yet a "one." The feminine "subject" is here constituted through illegitimate intervention in the language: its "one-ness" resides already in the other's place(s), its unity derives retrospectively from an infraction that flies in the face of the grammatical order of subject and predicate. The "one" is at once predicated and divided.

Far more radically than first imagined, *A Room of One's Own* can offer refuge to no "one," for the history, no less than the fiction, accumulated there leaves the door open to intrusion. As we began by suggesting, Penelope's clever labor is figured by and reiterates the cleverness of Odysseus. The stories of their different exploits together assemble the elements for a meaningful reunion. In that fictional moment that closes the circle of the poem, when the ruse of power rejoins the ruse of no power, it has become impossible and thus irrelevant to know who is interrupting whom, whose task is suspended and whose continues, or which room is being entered and which left behind. Interpreted as a space of interruption, *A Room of One's Own* cannot give title to the room it names in its title. No "one" figures there who is not already many, and no ownership guarantees there an undivided property. Instead, the title promises a place of intermittent work, a book that, like a woman's thought, a woman's body, is frequently broken in on. And broken off. We can leave the last word to the narrator, who advises the audience at her lecture that "the book has somehow to be adapted to the body, and at a venture one would say that women's books should be shorter, more concentrated than those of men, and framed so that they do not need long hours of steady uninterrupted work. For interruptions there will always be" (81).

Epilogue: The Heterotext

The work (or play) of the Penelopean text implies a mutual interruption of fiction and history, feminine and masculine space. Its back and forth movement makes/unmakes, ravels/ unravels logical or "natural" oppositions—including the opposition that organizes the field of mutually exclusive contraries, that of logic or reason to unreason or madness. The writing of such a text is not attributable to any subject, whether singular or collective. On the contrary, it is the subject that is written into the text, and thus into the play of differences with itself.

We will look briefly here at fragments of a Woolfian heterotext—Virginia's and Leonard's—while retaining the notion of mutual interrupting instances.[14] The term *heterotext* is forged in view of better resisting the homology that urges itself all too easily on the attempt to read across sexual difference. The temptation is to apply a logic of sexual opposition, to impose its authority on the pattern of authorial instances and their signatures suspended in—or interrupted by—each other. The writing couple of the heterotext, however, has its "life" in the biographic and not in the biologic sense. Or rather, this difference is also being inscribed/effaced by the heterotext. Indeed, to read such a text, one must be ready to recognize the points at which the graphic of sexual difference—its inscription and erasure—already supplemented the logic of sexual difference—the exteriority of one to the other—even as this couple lived and wrote.

In January 1915, Virginia Woolf was at work on what was to become—after many turnings and returnings—the novel even-

[14]An earlier version of this epilogue was presented at an MLA special session titled "Writing Couples" organized by Naomi Schor.

tually published in 1919: *Night and Day*.[15] At about the same time, Leonard Woolf had begun work on a report for the Fabian Society which he describes in his autobiography as a study in view of "understanding the causes of the 1914 war and of war in general and of finding ways, if possible, of making war less likely in the future."[16] This report eventually found its way into "Leonard Woolf's influential book *International Government* (1916) used by the British government in its proposals for a League of Nations" (*Diary*, 22, n. 63). These two writing instances encounter each other on yet another writing stage, which is Virginia's diary, for in January 1915, Virginia Woolf resumed the diary she had kept for several short periods earlier. Although the return to the autobiographical habit continued almost without interruption through January, it was broken off at the entry for 15 February. The result, therefore, is something like a fragment diary, one that is situated, moreover, between what its editor terms "two fearful tempests of lunacy," between two phases of a manic depressive moon. The depressive phase had, in September 1913, taken the form of a suicidal compulsion by which Virginia had nearly succeeded in putting herself to sleep with no waking. The fragment, therefore, seems to introduce an autobiographical compulsion over against an auto-thanatological one. According to most accounts, the moon's manic phase began in mid-February 1915, about the time the diary breaks off.

With the four texts I have just referred to—Virginia's diary, Leonard's autobiography (based in large part on his own diary), the novel *Night and Day*, and the treatise *International Government*—we have the contiguous strands of this heterotextual fragment.

There has been a turn within Woolf scholarship toward a figuration of the oppressor of Virginia's writing and, beyond that, of women's writing in general. Leonard Woolf is one of the

[15]*The Diary of Virginia Woolf*, ed. Anne Olivier Bell (New York, 1979), 1:4, n. 6; referred to as *Diary* in page references included in the text.
[16]L. Woolf, *Beginning Again: An Autobiography of the Years 1911–1918* (London, 1964), 183; referred to as *BA* in page references included in the text.

names given to this figure. One need only cite a recent title—
*All That Summer She Was Mad: Virginia Woolf: Female Vic-
tim of Male Medicine*—to see how lines of division have hard-
ened into accusations.[17] The author of this study, Stephen
Trombley, argues that Leonard represented and relayed the
male-dominated psychological institution which diagnosed
and prescribed treatment for Virginia in her lunar phases. As
such he was complicitous in passing a judgment on her sanity
or insanity, which, as Trombley documents, constituted a
moral, ethical, and political judgment in England around 1915.
Trombley holds Leonard principally responsible for suppressing
the truth of Virginia's madness which was its reason, even its
reasonableness. The crucial period for his interpretation includes the dates of the diary fragment—the first six weeks of
1915. Actually, however, Trombley has little to say about
Woolf's diary from this period and refers only in passing to the
events of early 1915. He is far more concerned with reconstruct-
ing the details surrounding the suicide attempt of September
1913. It is here that Leonard is judged by Trombley with the
same force of ethical, moral conviction that is itself being
judged.[18] Thus this exercise has to end up repeating the presumption that one can reasonably distinguish reason from madness, and it does so because it takes Leonard and Virginia as
logical subjects that can be sorted out from the heterotextual
overlay. It is this presumption that we would test by considering how the heterotext graphically implicates these subjects in
each other in a fashion that has to overwhelm the use of logic.

[17]Trombley, *All That Summer She Was Mad* (New York, 1981). Trombley
quotes Quentin Bell, Virginia Woolf's "official" biographer, who writes: "In the
very large volume of literature devoted to the study of Virginia Woolf there is a
kind of lunatic fringe, and in this of late it has been possible to find authors who
are ready to denounce Leonard, to find in his rationalism an unsympathetic and
insensitive quality which, so the story goes, made him incapable of making his
wife happy. There is a distinct air of quackery about such writers, a rejection of
reason." Trombley then comments: "Thus the battle lines are drawn" (298).
The same battle lines have been redrawn in an acrimonious exchange between
Quentin Bell and Jane Marcus in "Critical Response I, II," *Critical Inquiry* 11
(March 1985).
[18]See, for example, Trombley, 163–67.

In his autobiography, Leonard Woolf says of the writing project he undertook in early 1915:

> My friends, and Maynard [Keynes] especially, were discouraging; they thought that I should find the whole thing very boring and a waste of time. It is significant that all these highly intelligent people . . . thought of the problem [of war] as simply and solely a question of arbitration. . . . The main reason for this was that in the happy, innocent golden age before 1914 intelligent people did not worry themselves about international relations and the problem of preventing war—they left all that to professional politicians and diplomatists. (*BA*, 184)

In effect, Leonard Woolf had to invent the very subject he was writing on. "You could not become an authority on international government in 1915 by reading books, because the books did not exist; you had to go to what are called original sources" (*BA*, 187). By immersing himself in a sea of data, Leonard became an authority in his own terms.

> I have often irritated people by saying that an intelligent person can become what is called an "authority" on most "questions" or "subjects" by intensive study for two or three months. They thought me arrogant for saying so, or, if not arrogant, not serious. But it is true. . . . In 1915 I worked like a fanatical or dedicated mole on the sources of my subject, international relations, foreign affairs, the history of war and peace. By 1916 I had a profound knowledge of my subject; I was an authority. (*BA*, 185)

This description of Leonard's work crosses over the heterotextual border between fact and fantasy, logical argument and graphic supplement, at several points. The first sign to follow is the question of Leonard's possible arrogance about claiming authority. A similar possibility has been raised when in his autobiography he discussed the events of Virginia's 1913 illness and suicide attempt. A reflection on "the state of knowledge with regard to nervous and mental diseases . . . in 1913" leads the autobiographer to confront his understanding as a "person . . . with experience of only one case of mental illness" (*BA*,

161) with that of the so-called authorities called in to consult, diagnose, and prescribe in Virginia's case: "It may sound arrogant on my part when I say that it seemed to me that what they knew amounted to practially nothing. They had not the slightest idea of the nature or the cause of Virginia's mental state . . . and they had no real or scientific knowledge of how to cure her. All they could say was that she was suffering from neurasthenia" (*BA*, 160). Woolf's "arrogance" led him to question the diagnosis of "neurasthenia," that catch-all term which designated many behavioral disorders. In particular, he sought to ascertain why this term rather than the (in 1913) new-fangled description "manic-depressive" applied in Virginia's case: "When I cross-examined Virginia's doctors, they said she was suffering from neurasthenia, not from manic-depressive insanity, which was entirely different. But as far as symptoms were concerned, Virginia *was* suffering from manic-depressive insanity" (*BA*, 161). Although Woolf does not claim to have become an authority on manic-depressive disorders, as far as "Virginia's case" was concerned, he "watched and studied it intensively for months" and thus can write: "I have very little doubt that some of my conclusions were right."

In one and the other case of study, Leonard Woolf had to invent his own authority. To understand madness on a global or an individual scale, to diagnose its causes and prescribe a regimen for the prevention of its recurrence, one has to face the possibility of one's own arrogance. This, it would seem, Leonard Woolf was doing on both fronts in early 1915. There is room to suppose that these fronts were projected on to each other in a crisscross pattern, the work on international government taking shape in the face of a constant threat of destruction closest to home—the succession of "happy, innocent days" and war supplying a background for the manic-depressive alternation. The speculation on a transcendent superrationalism (Woolf conceived of what he called a "Supernational Authority,")[19] maintains a link to the most fundamental gesture of reason,

[19]For a summary of *International Government*, see Duncan Wilson, *Leonard Woolf: A Political Biography* (London, 1978), 66ff.

necessary before reason can authorize or autograph itself: the definition or delimitation of madness. This gesture, however, may always be arrogant, which is to say that the delimitation of madness is never simply accomplished since reason's claim to its own authority may itself have transgressed the limit between reason and unreason, factual and fictional authority.

Because of the risk of one's own madness or arrogance, the biographer (and a fortiori the autobiographer) who would decide where to divide reason from unreason may have to encounter an illogic that betrays the finality of that decision. Leonard's autobiography exhibits a striking example of this disturbance within the determination of madness. It concerns the chronology of Virginia's illness which at one point is outlined as follows: "From the summer of 1913 to the *autumn* of 1915, Virginia's mental breakdown was not absolutely continuous. There were two insane stages, one lasting from the summer of 1913 to the summer of 1914 and the other from January 1915 to the *winter* of 1915; there was an interlude of sanity between the summer of 1914 and January 1915" (*BA*, 160; italics added). One can already begin to note an indecision here when the text gives both the autumn and the winter of 1915 as the end of the second insane stage.[20] Yet the term January 1915 is exactly repeated and, unlike the other dates, has the relative accuracy of a specific month rather than a season. Nevertheless, further along in the autobiographical narrative, when this outline chronology is filled in with some detailed events, January will be replaced by February 1915 as the month in which Virginia's manic phase began. We pick up the narrative at the end of 1914 when "it seemed as if things were going well. . . . Virginia's health seemed to have improved and she had begun to work and write again. I . . . had begun a book commissioned by the Fabian Society on international government. Then quite suddenly in the middle of February there was again catastrophe" (*BA*, 171–72). After describing some of the symptoms of the catastrophe,

---

[20]In the preceding chapter, Leonard Woolf rearranges these dates in yet another fashion, placing the beginning of Virginia's illness in 1914 and her suicide attempt in 1915; see *BA*, 76–77.

the text restates the chronology: "It was the beginning of the terrifying second stage of her mental breakdown." Putting this passage together with the preceding one, where January rather than February dates the beginning of the recurrence, one might conclude that the autobiography performs a retrospective diagnosis which detects latent symptoms behind or before the quite sudden outbreak of manifest symptoms in the middle of February. This alternative between the latent and the manifest appears to have occurred to Leonard because he writes, "it *seemed* as if things were going well" and "Virginia's health *seemed* to have improved." That a doubt persists on both counts might make it reasonable to date the beginning of the catastrophe in January before it openly declared itself. While this reasoning explains the chronological contradiction, it itself remains latent since at no point is it openly put forth as argument. It is precisely the status of Leonard's reasoning which cannot be decided, that is, whether it is reasonable or unreasonable to write that in January 1915 Virginia Woolf began to go mad again even though she "seemed to have improved and . . . had begun to work and write again."

No such doubts remain in Virginia Woolf's official biography by Quentin Bell or in the counterbiography by Stephen Trombley.[21] Indeed, the decision of this question opposes the two historical portraits and distills the opposition male/female that glosses Trombley's title. But to decide the question of Virginia's madness and Leonard's reason, both biographical stories have had to neglect the Woolfs' heterotext, the implications in each other of the author of fictions and the factual authority. The biological opposition of male to female may serve only to rationalize rather than analyze these implications. For another example, we can turn to a passage from Virginia's January 1915 diary which we have reason to place in the balance with Leonard's self-implicating indecision about his wife's mental state when she began keeping this diary.

[21]"By the end of the year Virginia was writing again—a novel or a story which has been lost; she also began to keep a diary. It is the record of a perfectly sane woman leading a quiet but normal life." Quentin Bell, *Virginia Woolf: A Biography* (London, 1973), 2:22.

We pick up the thread in the entry dated 18 January where an interruption by Leonard figures in the margins of the diary's composition:

> As I began this page, L[eonard] stated that he had determined to resign his commission to write a pamphlet about Arbitration—& now I shall stop this diary & discuss that piece of folly with him. It is partly due to my egoistical habit of always talking the argument of my book. I want to see what can be said *against* all forms of activity & thus dissuade L. from all his work, speaking really not in my own character but in Effie's. Of course it is absolutely essential that L. shd. do a work which may be superbly good. (*Diary*, 22)

Just two remarks for the moment: first, note the use of the term "Arbitration," the word with which Leonard specifically characterizes the misunderstanding that greeted his work on international relations among his "highly intelligent" friends. That Virginia was one of those "friends" who, like Maynard Keynes, was discouraging is not simply confirmed here, however. Instead, and this is the second remark, if Virginia wants to see if she can "dissuade L. from all his work," she speaks "not in [her] own character but in Effie's." Effie, it seems, was at this time the name of the central character in what would later become *Night and Day*.[22] Her intervention at this point signals that a graphic supplement is at work within the logical opposition of the project to "dissuade L. from all his work."

That Effie's supplementary "argument" may have produced an effect is suggested by the next diary entry for 19 January which begins:

> L's melancholy continues, so much so that he declared this morning he couldn't work. The consequence has been rather a melancholy day. Outside it is cold & grey too . . . the trees all black, & the sky heavy over London; but there is enough colour to make it even lovelier today than on bright days, I think. The deer exactly

[22]See Elizabeth Heine, "Postscript to *The Diary of Virginia Woolf*, Vol. I: 'Effie's Story' and *Night and Day*," *Virginia Woolf Miscellany* 9 (Winter 1977), 10.

match the bracken. But, Leonard was melancholy, as I say. (*Diary*, 22–23)

References to Leonard's inactive melancholy, which may or may not be an effect of Effie's activity, bracket this passage. Within that repetition, the passage traces a move from inside to outside, away from the subject of Leonard's inactivity toward an exterior object that both relays and relieves the inert melancholic weight. By following this excursion, we see that it inscribes a reversal of the subjective projection onto the seasonal landscape—gray days turn out to be "even lovelier" than bright days—and ends up with an image that effaces not only the subject in the landscape, but every distinction except color: "the deer exactly match the bracken." Because this movement is succeeded by recalling to mind Leonard's state of mind, it describes a pocket of forgetfulness within the self-absorption of that state which, as we shall see in a moment, the rest of the paragraph goes on to analyze as "sheer lack of self-confidence in his power of writing." As with Effie's intervention, there is here a detour created within logical exchange, a detour that is also the space given over to a written exchange of dark and light, night and day. Writing thereby contrives to defer the question of its truth or falsity by exercising its power to erase the subject in the landscape, shifting its depressive features.

But the time comes to say what one really means.

> But Leonard was melancholy, as I say. All I can do is to unsay all I have said; & to say what I really mean. Its a bad habit writing novels—it falsifies life, I think. However, after praising L's writing very sincerely for 5 minutes, he says "Stop"; whereupon I stop, & theres no more to be said. When I analyse his mood, I attribute much of it to sheer lack of self confidence in his power of writing; as if he mightn't be a writer, after all; & being a practical man, his melancholy sinks far deeper than the half assumed melancholy of self conscious people like Lytton [Strachey], & Sir Leslie [Stephen] & myself. There's no arguing with him. (*Diary*, 23)

With this passage we reach something like maximum density in any attempt to reason with and within a heterotext. The possibility of saying what one really means has been disturbed by Effie's supplementary/supplanting effect. Writing novels indeed falsifies life, but it also urges one to propose questions about authority, about the power of writing, about "fiction" in its effect on the "practical." These terms, that is, are knotted together in the form of questions to the dark future of the author's authority—his or her power to make light of that darkness. Whether, however, the question is posed by Virginia speaking in her own character or in Effie's, or by Leonard, and whether it is addressed to herself, to himself, or to the other, that's not to be said. The trace of Effie's intervention continues to throw a wild card into the exchange between authority and madness.

It is possible, of course, that when Leonard dated the return of madness as January 1915, his reason lay in episodes such as Effie's argument on 18 January. He may have confused the discussion with Effie and his other discussions with the "mad" Virginia, which he describes as follows:

> Her insanity was in her premises, her beliefs. . . . These beliefs were insane because they were in fact contradicted by reality. But given these beliefs as premises for conclusions and actions, all Virginia's actions and conclusions were logical and rational, and her power of arguing conclusively from false premises was terrific. It was therefore useless to attempt to argue with her. (*BA*, 164)

Note the echo from Virginia's diary, where the discussion with Leonard's melancholy breaks off at the phrase "There's no arguing with him." These would be but two instances where logical argument must break off in the face of the madness within logic, the implication of the one in the other.

If one approaches the heterotext in order to read women's writing as simply authored out of an opposition, then it is the implications of the subject's own doubleness which will have to be ignored. Precisely because Virginia Woolf is an exemplary woman writer, it is important not to conclude with a too-singular version of her authority, to preclude, in other words, the authority of otherness.

PART THREE

RESISTANCE THEORIES

CHAPTER SEVEN

Floating Authorship

> I hated to come to anything so uncongenial, so un-
> American, as a theoretical conclusion—to anything so
> theoretical and conclusive as a theoretical conclusion. I
> felt . . . that it is better to entertain an idea than to take it
> home to live with you for the rest of your life. But I sat
> surrounded by the results of doing the opposite: the light
> I read by, the furnace that kept turning itself on and off to
> warm me, the rockets that at that moment were being
> tested to attack me, all were the benefits of coming to
> theoretical conclusions; I was a living—still living—
> contradiction.
>
> —Randall Jarrell, *Pictures from an Institution*

Because Jarrell's academic novel was initially published in
1952, its first-person narrator, an English professor, would probably have retired long before his very American inhospitable-
ness to theory could assume an appropriate position in the
recent battles over literary study in this country. Like some
obtuse guest who has overstayed its grudging welcome, theory
has lately been the object of increasingly rude attempts to hus-
tle it out the door. There seems to be an assumption that, once
the intruder has been ousted, tranquil domesticity will be restored to the house of American literary studies, or at least that
there will be a return to a more congenial mode of disagree-
ment. Even if he were not an anachronism, however, one doubts
that Jarrell's English professor would have been able to take up
that fight in good faith. Theory, he realizes, long ago entered the
house. Indeed, it is he who is freeloading off "theoretical con-

clusions," living—still living—between the promise of continued light and warmth and the threat of final expulsion.

Where Jarrell's protagonist might have hesitated in the face of his own contradiction, others have declared themselves ready to close the door on theory and make do with a "new pragmatism." Several of the bluntest efforts in this direction are collected in *Against Theory: Literary Studies and the New Pragmatism.*[1] Someone who follows the ever-unfolding drama of literary theory on the North American stage might recall that this book began its career as an energetically polemical article, "Against Theory," coauthored by Steven Knapp and Walter Benn Michaels in a 1982 issue of *Critical Inquiry.* The authors' confident (some might say cheeky) dismissal of a handful of the most influential directions taken by literary theory in its more recent phase in this country, their summary decree that such theoretical efforts, having failed, should not be renewed in any direction new or old, their assurance that a streamlined version of "intentionalism" is just what we need to kick the theory habit—all of this in less than twenty pages—did not fail to achieve what was perhaps the main if not sole purpose of the exercise: an equally energetic response, in fact a barrage of "critical responses" from a variety of theorists who felt themselves directly or indirectly in the broadside's line of fire. *Critical Inquiry* found the whole episode "stimulating" enough to devote most of a 1983 issue to these responses (and to a response to the responses from Knapp and Michaels) as well as part of a 1985 issue to yet more responses from Stanley Fish and Richard Rorty (along with another reply from the initiators).

Almost without exception, Knapp and Michaels' respondents are led to comment in one way or another on a charming didactic fiction that "Against Theory" deploys at the outset. The fiction (which we cite in detail later) is supposed to demonstrate "how difficult it is to imagine a case of intentionless meaning" and therefore the general uselessness of theory which, according to Knapp and Michaels, always sets out from a "moment of

---

[1]W. J. T. Mitchell, ed., *Against Theory* (Chicago, 1985). References will be included in parentheses in the text.

imagining intentionless meaning" (16). A curious distraction, however, affects the several "readings" of this fiction collected by *Against Theory*. The sources, the motives, the shape and, perhaps finally, the inevitability of this distraction are the most interesting things about the debate over theory as staged by *Critical Inquiry*. One may be tempted to see there some large machine at work, or at least a rather dizzying perspective of revolving ironies.

It seems to turn on a single word out of place. The philosopher Alexander Nehamas, in a review of *Against Theory*, may have noticed the lapsus, but if he did, he calls no attention to it. Paraphrasing Knapp and Michaels' fiction, he makes an apt substitution of his term for theirs, which to some extent clears up the confusion. First his paraphrase: "Suppose you come upon some squiggles in the sand that seem to spell a stanza of a Wordsworth poem. And suppose that, for a variety of reasons, you find it impossible to believe that they were composed by *a conscious agent of any sort* [italics added]. Would this show that there was meaning without intention? Not at all, Knapp and Michaels think." Next, he quotes from their text: " 'To deprive the marks of an *author* [italics added] is to convert them into accidental likenesses of language. They are not, after all, an example of intentionless meaning; as soon as they become intentionless they become meaningless as well.' "[2] In his paraphrase, Nehamas has, inadvertently perhaps, corrected the word "author" by the phrase "a conscious agent of any sort," and he is right to do so since, in the context, the word "author" should be reserved for Wordsworth if one wants to avoid confusion. Perhaps this is a case of the philosopher giving the literary critic a subliminal lesson in more precise language use. Nehamas, in fact, goes on to do just that when he asks to know what exactly Knapp and Michaels mean by their word "meaningless," which, the philosopher knows, has many meanings. Yet he is no less confident than these authors themselves that he knows what they mean by their word "author": read "a conscious agent of any sort."

[2]Nehamas, "Untheory," *London Review of Books*, 22 May 1986, 17.

But how can one be sure that the authors *do* know what they mean by their word "author"? And, in the context of an argument about intentional meaning, does not this uncertainty hint at a nearly fathomless irony whirring in the background, its switch locked in the "on" position? Perhaps the reactive "critical response" from Knapp and Michaels' colleagues should be understood as a response to a crisis set off by a pair of tinkerers who were sure they knew what they were doing but made a terrible mess of things. Experts are called in to turn the damned thing off, but nothing, so far, seems to work. No "author" or "conscious agent of any sort" can get to the controls or get the last word.

Yet, as there is always something instructive in such critical flaps, one should also give Knapp and Michaels credit for setting it off. (Knapp *a*nd *M*ichaels, the authors: since this latter term will be more than ever of uncertain designation here, I propose—for the sake of brevity of expression and without intending the least disrespect—to abbreviate the names to the single acronym "KaM," to be used inconsistently in both the singular and plural.) It is a problem, of course, that they themselves do not seem to know what they have done. They think they have demonstrated why theory is a superfluous gadget that can be discarded without a second thought. But their performance of this gesture includes a neat demonstration of how the gadget keeps thrusting itself upon us with ever more insistent claims as to its usefulness. KaM misses the mechanical effect because he is playing with his gadget. He resembles an entrepreneur dreaming about the profits to be had within the institutional order once he markets his self-destructing theory-gadget. Perhaps KaM has done enough of a market survey to believe that the thing will sell briskly in the Peorias of the American literary academy. (And lest this sound like a geographic slur, I suggest we hear "Peoria" as merely a deformation or denegation of "aporia," a place, therefore, only on an imaginary map where an essential platitude seems to offer refuge from the pitfalls of a theory-machine that not only will not self-destruct but thrives on the good intentions of those who want to turn it off.)[3]

[3]"Nothing can overcome the resistance to theory since theory *is* itself this resistance." Paul de Man, "The Resistance to Theory," in *The Resistance to*

But KaM's mistaken use of the term "author" at a central juncture in their demonstration triggers the aporetic chain reaction and implodes their invention. Before reenacting the accident (if that is what it was) and in order to measure some of its longer-term effects, we need to recall where KaM intended to land if they had not gotten hung up on the shoals of authorship. The safe harbor is called "practice," by which is meant the practice of "interpreting particular texts." Theory, on the other hand, "is nothing else," writes KaM, "but the attempt to escape practice . . . the name for all the ways people have attempted to stand outside practice. . . . Our thesis has been that no one can reach a position outside practice" (30). It would not, I trust, be wrong to interpret this particular text as claiming quite forcefully that, if there is no position outside practice, then one is always *within* practice in some way, regardless of what may be one's own idea of where one is standing or what one is doing. Understood in these terms, KaM's point about the inescapability of practice (of interpreting or reading) seems inescapably correct. One would have wished, however, to know why, in KaM's opinion, so much effort is wasted trying to escape the inescapable. What, in other words, is so threatening about reading that readers should dream of acceding to an ideal "position outside practice"? Some attempt at an answer could have added considerable force to the conclusion that "the theoretical enterprise should therefore come to an end," even as it would also have explained why such a courageous recommendation was likely to go unheeded.

Although KaM is curiously unwilling to speak of the threat that may be driving the theoretical enterprise and the deluded wish to escape practice, the text of "Against Theory" is eloquent on just such a turning aside from reading. This eloquence, however, is not in the service of a discourse or an argument; indeed, its persuasive effect is won at considerable cost to the persuasiveness of an argument that proceeds, nevertheless, apparently unperturbed by the textual effects also being produced.

Theory (Minneapolis, 1986), 19–20. It is difficult to resist juxtaposing "Against Theory" with this essay that appeared almost at the same moment—especially since de Man is one of the theorists whose work Knapp and Michaels explicitly address. See below, chap. 8.

The scene of these countereffects is explicitly a scene of reading. It is also the only point at which "Against Theory" stages the kind of "practice" which it claims the literary theorist cannot escape.[4] Yet, the way KaM stages this encounter with a text to be read is so distracting that one may begin to wonder whether some vaguely sensed threat is at work urging the reader (KaM, KaM's reader, the reader "in" the text) to turn aside from something on the page.

To read such a text, then, it may be necessary to resist a certain seduction away from the page, to recall (oneself) at every step (to) the scene of reading: in a word, to *remark* the fictionality of a fiction. As it happens, the elaborately staged hypothetical narrative that KaM deploys in the interest of his intentionalist argument is a naïvely transparent one. And yet, by its very naïveté, the writing of this scene can expect to benefit from an understandable reluctance to subject the childlike pleasure of making up a story to any critical scrutiny. (This could explain why, for example, none of the critical respondents to "Against Theory," all of whom are eminent teachers of literature, has anything pertinent to say about its fictional procedures.) In this narrative, it is supposed that "you" come upon a poetic text in altogether singular, never-before-seen circumstances. Both the second person and the present tense of this narration function as constant reminders that the other scene being evoked—the fictional circumstance of a reading act as well as the surface and the means of an act of inscription—has no support in the real *other* than the scene of reading this "you" is then performing. Thus reminded, "you" will perhaps be less tempted to look away toward the fantastic events taking place somewhere else, on another surface (somewhere just off the shore of a Californian never-never land), to which KaM points with such delight and wonder.

---

[4]Knapp and Michaels, of course, are engaged in reading many texts throughout "Against Theory." By "practice," however, they seem to understand the interpretation not just of any written work but of literary or poetic texts that both demand and resist interpretation. This distinction is at the very least precarious but it is necessary to their other and principal distinction of theory from practice.

Three diegetical moments, three suppositions, compose KaM's fictional stage:

[I.] Suppose you're walking along a beach and you come upon a curious sequence of squiggles in the sand. You step back a few paces and notice that they spell out the following words:

> A slumber did my spirit seal;
>   I had no human fears:
> She seemed a thing that could not feel
>   The touch of earthly years.
>
>   .   .   .

[II.] But now suppose that, as you stand gazing at this pattern in the sand, a wave washes up and recedes, leaving in its wake (written below what you now realize was only the first stanza) the following words:

> No motion has she now, no force;
>   She neither hears nor sees;
> Rolled round in earth's diurnal course,
>   With rocks, and stones, and trees.
>
>   .   .   .

[III.] Suppose, having seen the second stanza wash up on the beach, you have decided that the "poem" is really an accidental effect of erosion, percolation, and so on and therefore not language at all. What would it now take to change your mind? No theoretical argument will make a difference. But suppose you notice, rising out of the sea some distance from the shore, a small submarine, out of which clamber a half dozen figures in white lab coats. One of them trains his binoculars on the beach and shouts triumphantly, "It worked! It worked! Let's go down and try it again." (Pp. 15–17)

The first of these propositions is followed by minimal commentary, while the radical suspension of the second proposition (which makes for all the interest of the tale) is accompanied by a list of some possible explanations of what the beach walker sees and an analysis of the presuppositions that would have allowed each explanation. KaM remarks that "all the explanations fall into two categories. You will either be ascribing these marks to some agent capable of intentions . . . or you will count them as nonintentional effects of mechanical processes." The third supposition—the sighting of the sub-marine and so forth—is followed by a comment which is also the moral of the fable: "You now have new evidence of an *author*. The question of *authorship* is and always was an empirical question; it has now received a new empirical answer. The theoretical temptation is to imagine that such empirical questions must, or should, have theoretical answers" (italics added).

Although this moral is meant to end the suspense and reassure the reader that intentional agents and mechanical processes remain distinguishable, one may not be so easily reassured if one notices that the "new evidence of an *author*" surfaces in the form of "a small submarine, out of which clamber a half dozen figures." Is this evidence of the author of the lyric poem which begins "A slumber did my spirit seal" or is it rather evidence (within a fiction) of a mechanical or technical process for inscribing marks on a distant surface? When KaM speaks of the "author" of what he calls the "wave poem," what does he mean? Does he mean that Wordsworth was a member of the submarine team and this was the event of the poem's composition? Doubtless no. But if it was not Wordsworth who "wrote" the poem on the beach, how can one speak of another "author" without controverting the force of the "empirical" evidence that is the point of the demonstration? Perhaps the demonstration can be saved by substituting for the incorrect term "author" (which KaM would have used by mistake or lack of precision) the correct term. But perhaps as well the mistake is a necessary one since a correct alternative would have to admit some resemblance and thus the possible confusion between intentional and mechanical agencies in the reproduction of marks. This is to suggest that only the term "author," despite its inappropriateness, can hold the line separating intentional, conscious agency from mechanical, nonconscious process. The choice of the word "author" would thus be no accident but itself produced by a *mechanical* defense of this distinction.

And, in effect, KaM repeatedly rejects any alternative to their use of the term "author" in the sense of a given text's actual, empirical composer. In "A Reply to Our Critics," for example, KaM refuses E. D. Hirsch's observation that "Against Theory" demonstrates only that "a text's meaning . . . must always be what *an* author intends it to mean" and not at all that it "must always be what *its* author intends it to mean." "What can the word 'author' mean," replies KaM, "if not the composer of the text? In our view, to 'postulate' an author is already to commit oneself to an account of the composer of the text, and there is nothing to choose between them because they are the same." In a later response, Richard Rorty returns to Hirsch's distinction and suggests that KaM has yet to come to terms with it, to which KaM again replies that there is no difference between "*an* author of a text" and "*its* author," that only the latter is implied in an intentionalist account of meaning and that "the only alternative to the intentionalism of 'Against Theory' is a formalism that imagines the possibility not of two different kinds of intended meaning but of meaning that is not intended at all" (142). KaM's all-or-nothing reasoning here (and we will return to this later) tends to confirm the suspicion that when they use the word "author" incorrectly according to their own definition—"What can the word 'author' mean if not the composer of the text?"—the mistake cannot be corrected without putting at risk the logic underpinning it and without admitting a significant gray area between KaM's empiricism and their bugbear: formalism.

The problem is far from being a superficial one of terminology because KaM's distracted use of the term "author" ends up pointing to a fundamental misunderstanding of the intentionality supposed by the fictional example with which they propose to cement their intentionalist argument. The fable of the wave poem is designed to illustrate that until and unless the beach walker can identify an "author's" intention to produce what is written in the sand, he or she will be forced to conclude that these marks are not at all the words of a familiar poem but only their accidental likeness. To read the marks at all, one must be able to assume that they were meant as words, as language; one must identify and identify with an intentionality. The problem with this basically sound proposition arises at the point identified by Hirsch and Rorty. When the lab-coated figure exclaims, "It worked! It worked!" this is presumably to be taken as empirical evidence of an intention to produce the marks on the beach, one that, moreover, has realized its aim. Now, what happens when we conjugate the premise of KaM's intentionalism which the fable is intended to support— "all meaning is always the author's meaning"—with the slip that designates the excited experimenter as the author? Is it this figure's particular, finite intention which is the "meaning" of the poem that can now be read on the beach? Clearly not, since "you" the beach walker and you KaM's reader are to understand that what you have just witnessed is a successful experiment in a method of telekinesis or telecommunication using previously untried media and for that purpose *any kind of iterable mark* could have served as well. The exclamation concerns strictly the iteration that has occurred and would have been fully as justified if, instead of a well-known poem, the underwater manipulations had managed to reproduce a series of geometrical figures or any other kind of "squiggle" whose form could be recognized when repeated. Thus, the intention of the figure whom KaM calls the author, the imagined empirical "fact" of this particular act of intentional inscription, would tend to empty the poem of all meaning beyond the sheer repetition of the appearance or form of the marks transferred onto a distant surface. KaM's exemplary "author" is a formalist of the purest sort, which obviously does not prevent in the least his assuming form as a high-tech empiricist.

As should be clear by now, KaM's mistake, which precipitates such profoundly unsettling effects on the intentionalist argument floated by the fable, can be traced to its source in the structure of *citationality* which has been covered over or forgotten (cited without acknowledgment) by KaM's commentary on the events on the beach. Whatever else the underwater experimenters may have been doing, a minimally correct description would have to include that they reiterate, repeat, reinscribe a set of hypercoded marks. To repeat: the fact that the experimenters cite a well-known poem (rather than some other set of coded marks) is or should be altogether irrelevant to the aim or intention of their experiment. By choosing to cite a poem, however, KaM in effect creates a situation in which a *citer*'s intention can seem to rejoin or reactivate an *author*'s intention, even though, in their finite senses, the two acts of inscription are apparently highly dissimilar. KaM's mistake can pass unnoticed because the citational act, whatever its particular, finite purpose, rejoins a general intentionality within which the poem cited finds its *original and continuing* horizon of readability. But it is no less a mistake and, in the context of "Against Theory" as well as the debate to which the article has given rise, a highly symptomatic one.

KaM's intentionalist argument forgets to allow for a general citationality or iteration. As one result, rather than showing "how difficult it is to imagine a case of intentionless meaning," their fable demonstrates most consistently (although it is unclear why this needs demonstrating) that the same words can be repeated with all sorts of different intentions or meanings. Because KaM neglects to make the distinction between a particular, finite (empirical) intention of some speech act and intentionality as an animating principle of language *in general*,[5] he has to end up misunderstanding his own demonstration and attributing to an agent of mechanical repetition the position of "author." When, therefore, KaM writes that "language has intention [rather than intentionality] already built into it," how not to read in that statement a denegation of the necessary

[5]On the Husserlian notion of intentional animation, see Jacques Derrida's "Introduction" to *The Origin of Geometry*, esp. pt. VII. KaM's wave poem resembles at moments that unreadable inscription which, writes Derrida, uncovers "the transcendental meaning of death": "But if the text does not announce its own pure dependence on a writer or reader in general, if it is not haunted by a virtual intentionality . . . then, in the vacancy of its soul, there is no more than a chaotic literalness or the sensible opacity of a defunct designation, a designation deprived of its transcendental function. The silence of prehistoric arcana and buried civilizations, the entombment of lost intentions and guarded secrets, and the illegibility of the lapidary inscription disclose the transcendental meaning of death in that which unites it to the absolute privilege of intentionality in the very instance of its essential failure." Trans. John P. Leavey, Jr. (Stony Brook, N.Y., 1978), 88; trans. modified.

detachability of words or marks from finite intentions illustrated and acted out by the fable? This denegation—the impulse to deny, in the face of a contrary certainty, the finitude of
intentions—is properly the stuff of fiction: the dream of an
impermeable, indivisible Authorship. Has KaM dreamed his
own intention and given it shape as the wonderful writing
machine that surfaces at the end of the fable? Like a vehicle
meant to navigate through a medium while remaining self-
enclosed, "Against Theory" takes one plunge after another,
apparently confident that its own notion of intention, and its
notion of its own intention, will prevent any confusion between its "inside" and its "outside."

But KaM would also be the first to admit that their polemical
engine is not of altogether original design:

> The claim that all meanings are intentional is not, of course, an
> unfamiliar one in contemporary philosophy of language. John
> Searle, for example, asserts that "there is no getting away from
> intentionality" ["Reiterating the Differences: A Reply to Der-
> rida," *Glyph* 1 (1977), 202] and he and others have advanced
> arguments to support this claim. Our purpose here is not to add
> another such argument. (15)

Does some responsibility for the design flaws of "Against Theory" have to go to John Searle and specifically to the form of his
"Reply to Derrida"? The answer is yes, *despite* a conspicuous
adjustment KaM must make so as to bridge a gap left in Searle's
argumentative vehicle, a gap through which conscious, finite,
selfsame intentions risk being detached from their meaning.
Searle, in effect, would have left a slight opening for different
meanings, for the meaning of difference, for a theory of the
other-than-the-one, the other-than-the-Author. KaM, however,
moves in to close things up:

> Even a philosopher as committed to the intentional status of
> language as Searle succumbs to this temptation to think that
> intention is a theoretical issue. After insisting, in the passage
> cited earlier, on the inescapability of intention, he goes on to say
> that "in serious literal speech the sentences are precisely the

realizations of the intentions" and that "there need be no *gulf* at all between illocutionary intention and its expression." The point, however, is not that there *need* be no gulf between intention and the meaning of its expression but that there *can* be no gulf. Not only in serious literal speech but in *all* speech what is intended and what is meant are identical. (17–18)

Despite this course correction, KaM has taken over in a wholesale and no-questions-asked manner Searle's procedure in replying to Derrida's "Signature Event Context." The proposed adjustment seeks to seal Searle's argument more effectively against his chosen opponent and to keep the notion of a single, selfsame intentionality out of reach of the otherness that necessarily inhabits and makes possible any intention. Having saved Searle from his own temptation to admit something like an originary gap in any intention, KaM can then proceed *as if* the "Reply to Derrida" were in every other respect an effective bulkhead against the fundamentally deconstructive law that an intention is always a priori "différante." This "as if" allows KaM to take a massive shortcut around all the questions about intention and intentionality that Derridean thought has scattered over the terrain of antitheory.[6] KaM, in other words,

[6]Since this essay first appeared, Knapp and Michaels have published "Against Theory 2: Hermeneutics and Deconstruction," *Critical Inquiry* 14 (Autumn 1987). There they belatedly take up the matter of iterability and attempt to measure their argument against those of Derrida in "Signature Event Context" and "Limited Inc abc . . ." That argument, which we will not attempt to reconstruct, does not anticipate or respond to any of the questions we are raising here and remains fundamentally impervious to the notion of a priori *différance* of intention. Nevertheless, one may remark two striking effects of this encounter with Derrida's texts: (1) Knapp and Michaels' antitheory is forced to betray more openly than in "Against Theory [I]" its essential investment in an understanding of meaning as self-contained, contained, that is, by the "self" who intends to mean. There is no other on this self's horizon; it is self-inventing and self-determining, and as such it is just another avatar of the idealist dream of a totalizable system of meaning that would have no *outside*, no other, no addressee, no difference from itself. All Knapp and Michaels are proposing is a very weak, because very worn-out, version of this wish to exclude otherness from the circle of a hearing/understanding-oneself-speak (*s'entendre parler*) which Derrida first described in *Speech and Phenomena*, trans. David P. Allison (Evanston, Ill., 1973). In this regard, it is no doubt significant that the

writes as if Searle had definitively replied to these questions, as if, therefore, antitheoretical empiricism and intentionalism could dispense with any direct engagement of Derrida's work.

But Searle, in KaM's reading, would have signed more than an excuse not to read. He has also provided them with their definition of what constitutes "the theoretical moment itself." "In debates about intention," asserts KaM, "the moment of imagining intentionless meaning constitutes the theoretical moment itself. From the standpoint of an argument against critical theory, then, the only important question about intention is whether there can in fact be intentionless meaning" (15). Searle provided the model for such an argument when he attributed to Derrida's "Signature Event Context" just such a "moment of imagining intentionless meaning" and then proceeded, without difficulty, to refute its possible occurrence. KaM has taken aim at the same imaginary target, accepting—apparently on simple faith—that Searle got things right in his "Reply to Derrida."

Regardless of how well this fiction or this let's-make-believe empiricism will sell in Peoria, it cannot controvert some stubborn facts. In fact, Searle's reply leaves almost everything unanswered, which is why it could become a pretext for Derrida to

---

example they give of a performative speech act, whose potential failure or infelicity, they want to argue, does not entail a failure of the intention to mean and thus of meaning itself, is the marriage ceremony. The failure to contract with the other, to receive one's meaning from the other, to affirm the meaning of the more-than-one, is not, they would claim, an *essential* failure of meaning because meaning is essentially *s'entendre-parler*. (2) When Knapp and Michaels do concede a notion of meaning in some relation to an other, that relation is just as thoroughly enclosed but now within the limits defined by convention. "But why should the claim that language is essentially conventional, even if it were true, undermine the possibility of saying what one means? Why should the need to follow the conventions compromise an intention if the intention is an intention to follow those conventions?" (62). Convention, for Knapp and Michaels, is essentially a general extension of *s'entendre parler*, which is why they can assert that "you can succeed in meaning when you don't follow any convention at all" (66). By means of these circular moves that attempt to enclose meaning and fend off its outside, Knapp and Michaels end up defending an empty solipsism and its generalized form: a marriage of intention and meaning solely within the limits prescribed by convention, there where an anonymous "I" speaks only to itself and can remain indifferent to whatever might interrupt its self-communion. That, at least, would be the dream.

reiterate at length, in "Limited Inc abc . . . ," the necessity of rethinking intentionality as a differential structure or stricture within a general iterability or citationality. Along the way, he repeatedly remarks Searle's habit of attributing a "moment of imagining intentionless meaning" to a text that *"at no time . . .* invoke[s] the *absence,* pure and simple, of intentionality. Nor is there any break, simple or radical, with intentionality."[7] What Searle (and later KaM) chooses to misunderstand as a simple or absolute absence of intentionality is in fact the not-so-simple yet undeniable absence which every written text supposes: the absence of its author. Derrida recalls and cites what he had already written in "Signature Event Context":

> "For a writing to be a writing it must continue to 'act' and to be readable even when what is called the author of the writing no longer answers for what he has written, for what he seems to have signed, be it because of a temporary absence, because he is dead or, *more generally, because he has not employed his absolutely actual and present intention or attention, the plenitude of his desire to say what he means,* in order to sustain what seems to be written *'in his name'."*

This general definition has the force, continues Derrida, of eidetic law (KaM's fabulous citation of Wordsworth's poem would be but a particularly fanciful illustration of the law's validity), which is "moreover . . . nothing but the consequence of iterability." An iterable intention is

> divided and deported in advance . . . towards others, removed [*écartée*] in advance from itself. This re-move makes its movement possible. Which is another way of saying that if this remove is its condition of possibility, it is not an eventuality, something that befalls it here and there, by accident. Intention is a priori (at once) *différante.* (193–94)

---

[7]Derrida, "Limited Inc abc . . . ," trans. Samuel Weber, *Glyph* 2 (1977), 193. Further references are included in parentheses in the text. There have been numerous commentaries on the exchange between Searle and Derrida. One of the most balanced is Ian Maclean's "Un Dialogue de sourds? Some Implications of the Austin-Searle-Derrida Debate," *Paragraph* 5 (March 1985).

KaM's denegation of the gap or gulf—the *écart*—within intention which is "its very possibility" relies on an oppositional logic of all or nothing which assigns an exclusively *negative* determination to the difference that sets it in motion. Because all-or-nothing logic (for example, "If all meaning is always the author's meaning, the alternative is an empty one") refuses or suppresses the movement toward the other-than-the-Author, it is powerless to account for the double determination or double movement of iterability as *both* the limitation *and* the possibility of any intention. Following Searle, KaM employs a kind of scare tactic, a repeated, intimidating assertion that *there is no alternative to oppositional thinking.*[8] It is no doubt for this reason that they are so eager to believe Searle's version of a text like "Signature Event Context," a text that explicitly indicates the horizon of a theoretical program based on a nonoppositional differentiation in which "the category of intention would not disappear:"

> *Rather than oppose* [italics added] citation or iteration to the non-iteration of an event, one ought to construct a differential typology of forms of iteration, assuming that such a project is tenable and can result in an exhaustive program. . . . In such a typology, *the category of intention will not disappear; it will have its place,* but from that place it will no longer be able to govern the entire scene and system of utterance. Above all, at that point, we will be dealing with different kinds of marks or chains of iterable marks and *not with an opposition* [italics added] between citational

[8]These intimidations are scattered throughout "Against Theory"; for example: "Our purpose here is . . . to show how radically counterintuitive the alternative would be" (15); or "It makes theory possible because it creates the illusion of a choice between alternative methods of interpreting" (20). KaM relies on a similar pattern of intimidating assertion in presenting the central thesis of "Against Theory," which equates meaning with authorial intention. Although eventually claiming to have *argued* this thesis (19), KaM repeatedly seems content simply to assert insistently (e.g., 12, 13, 21), without argument or explanation, that this identity must be *seen* or *recognized.* The problem is that if an alternative to such a perception or intuition seems "radically counterintuitive," that "counterintuitive" quality no more serves to make it false than mere assertion of a given alternative would serve to make it true. (My thanks to Philip Lewis for these remarks.)

utterances, on the one hand, and singular and original event-utterances, on the other. (197)

What "Limited Inc" will also call "something like a law of undecidable contamination" baffles the logic that offers thinking a choice only between *pure* intention (an ideal fiction constructed through the denegation of a priori iterability) and *no* intention. It is, for example, this nonoppositional "law of undecidable contamination" which alone can allow one to describe with some precision the situation of the cited poem in the text of "Against Theory." That is, only by acknowledging that the distinction between cited and citing text is a priori *not assured* to be rigorous or uncontaminated can one give any account of certain iteration effects that are, as we shall see, scrambling the relation between the poem and its narrative-discursive frame.

Before rereading the hypothetical narrative sequence, we should note that KaM does not simply and altogether overlook the fact of citation. They acknowledge that their citational activity is to be read as a *re-citation* not just of Wordsworth's lyric but of other instances of its quotation. A note to the first stanza supplies a source for the choice of the poem: "Wordsworth's lyric has been a standard example in theoretical arguments since its adoption by Hirsch; see *Validity in Interpretation*, pp. 227–30 and 238–40." Thus KaM's citation of "A Slumber Did My Spirit Seal" passes at least by way of Hirsch's citation of the same poem, but in fact (since the latter would have been only the first instance of a theoretical argument like KaM's which takes the poem as an example)[9] the note inscribes a site of multiple citings which is both cited and added to by "Against Theory." The purpose of this note, however, would

---

[9]In fact, Hirsch is already responding to other critical treatments of the poem; see below, n. 13. KaM actually owes more to P. D. Juhl's revision or refinement of Hirsch's use of this example. See *Interpretation: An Essay in the Philosophy of Literary Criticism* (Princeton, N.J., 1980), 71–72. KaM notes that "Juhl employs the same poem we do . . . in his own treatment of accidental 'language.' . . . The device of contrasting intentional speech acts with marks produced by chance is a familiar one in speech-act theory" (19, n. 9).

seem to be less to acknowledge this minor tradition in theoretical arguments about intentionality than to assert the indifference or exteriority of the "example" to the demonstration in which it serves. KaM is saying, in effect, that the same demonstration could be made with any linguistically coded material. To repeat: this indifference or arbitrariness of the cited marks is key to understanding the specific, limited intention of the submarine crew in the fable. And like those other fictional inventors *in* the fable, KaM, the inventor of the fable, is to be understood as practicing an empty or voided citation for the sole purpose of demonstrating experimentally the limits on the possibility of readable inscription. The fable is thereby constructed out of the coincidence of an "external" logic of indifferent quotation with an "internal" one. What is more, this coincidence can itself be described as a form of quotation: the submarine experimenters cite KaM's empty citation, or, put the other way, KaM cites the experimenters' citation of the poem. Either way, one can rightly say that the fable does little more than inscribe a supplementary set of quotation marks around the poem, placing any consideration of its meaning for a virtual reader ("you") at yet a further remove from the logic of a demonstration concerned exclusively (and regardless of what KaM says about what he is doing) with the iterability of marks as a necessary condition of meaning in general. The proliferating quotation marks would thus serve merely to underscore the exteriority of any particular example to such a general demonstration.

What if, however, all this empty activity were also an attempt to void or efface or simply *forget* a meaning that insists in the poem and that keeps returning with each citing and each sighting? What if, that is, the poem's supposed *exteriority* from the demonstration should be seen as functioning as an alibi for a relation that implicates otherwise the example in the argument, the quoted poem in the discursive/narrative fiction, according to the law of undecidable contamination?

To pursue these questions, however, one must read, at least in a minimal fashion, the two cited stanzas and traverse all the quotation marks voiding the place of the example. But then very quickly the poem begins to overflow the containing argument. While it is true that examples can almost always be shown to exceed (or fall short of) whatever they are cited to be examples of, the citation of "A Slumber Did My Spirit Seal" here exceeds its frame in a manner that reverses the exemplary relation. By means of this contaminating reversal, KaM's framing fable itself becomes an example of the mistake exposed by the poem.

This mistake is that of a spirit lulled by slumber into forgetting "human fears." To the poet, sealed in forgetfulness, "She seemed a thing that could not feel / The touch of earthly years." The first lines introduce the dream image of an eternal present, one that, however, only "seemed." The unsealing of the poet's spirit, by the event of her death which reveals his mistake, occurs in the space between the two stanzas. The shift in the second stanza to the present tense is underlined by the "now" of "No motion has she now, no force." A negation of things human continues in the next line: "She neither hears nor sees." Finally, the last lines refer back to the "thing" she seemed to be in the past: "Rolled round in earth's diurnal course, / With rocks, and stones, and trees." The eternal present returns in the final lines, but there is nothing in the least dreamy about these things left untouched by earthly years. Instead, the sleeper's vision has been replaced by the sight of an inexorable repetition that even invades the diction of sheer addition: "rocks, *and* stones, *and* . . ."

This rendering might approximate the sort of reading "you" could muster in the circumstances KaM imagines.[10] These circumstances even work to dramatize the poem up to a point, underscoring its temporal structure. The "now" in the first line

---

[10]In fact, the profile of KaM's beach walker hesitates between someone who does and does not recognize the poem inscribed on the beach. In the first moment, "you recognize the writing as writing, you understand what the words mean, you may even identify them as constituting a rhymed poetic stanza— and all this without knowing anything about the author." In the second moment, you are pictured wondering whether "Wordsworth, since his death, [has] become a sort of genius of the shore who inhabits the waves and periodically inscribes on the sand his elegiac sentiments."

of the second stanza, for example, would have to take on special resonance as "you" watched these lines being written on the beach. The fable's narration of the second episode even insists on the "now":

> But *now* suppose that, as you stand gazing at this pattern in the sand, a wave washes up and recedes, leaving in its wake (written below what you *now* realize was only the first stanza) the following words:
>
> > No motion has she now, no force.
> >
> > . . .
>
> You will *now*, we suspect, feel compelled to explain what you have just seen.

This succession of "nows" seems to be but the bare, almost mechanical punctuation of narrative, and as such it remarks the fundamentally successive structure of the poem. In the poem, "now" signals that a past, deluded version of eternal human presence has given way to a present version that places human "thingness" on a plane with "rocks, and stones, and trees." What is more, according to the framing narrative, this "now" arrives on the force of a wave, having been rolled round and deposited (somehow) on the beach. This alignment of the stanza as *énoncé* and *énonciation*, as an utterance that performs what it says, is really quite remarkable. Indeed, it is curious enough to give "you," the beach walker—provided you're awake and halfway lucid—an uncanny shock, as if you had just seen your own ghost. (And, in fact, KaM's fable could be understood as trying to exorcise the ghost it has so recklessly called forth.) The fable at this point conforms to a near-perfect allegory of the "truth" of the poem, or one could also say it performs the "truth" of the poem's allegory: the death of the other, "she," is also "my" death, the death of the speaker.[11] The speaker in the

---

[11]Paul de Man has written of this poem: "Wordsworth is one of the few poets who can write proleptically about their own death and speak, as it were, from beyond their own graves. The 'she' in the poem is in fact large enough to encompass Wordsworth as well." "The Rhetoric of Temporality," in *Blindness*

poem cannot speak his death in the present, whence the recourse to allegorical narrative. KaM's fable makes this allegory
readable by inventing the optimal condition for "hearing"/
seeing the absence in the voice that speaks the poem. It turns
out that the fabulous writing submarine is really a wonderful
reading machine.

This overlapping or coincidence, the tendency of the poem's
sequence to double itself in the surrounding narration, raises
the question: Who signs the fable of the "wave poem"? Has not
Wordsworth, the dead author, dictated at least in part the shape
of KaM's didactic narrative? Does the beach walker do anything
more than repeat—or quote—the sequence of illusion/disillu-
sion attributed to the poem's first person? Notice how the
signature of the dead poet, KaM's ghostwriter, can be restored if
the account of the events on the beach is rephrased only slightly: In an initial moment, the encounter with the first stanza
unfolds in a state of slumber, the beach walker or sleepwalker
remaining unaware of the blind assumption made concerning
the durable presence of a human intention. In a second moment
and with the arrival of the second stanza, this sleepwalker is
rudely jolted into wakefulness when the assumption of human
presence is unsealed, admitting in the present what was bliss-
fully forgotten in the past: the death of the "present" speaker.
KaM's discursive commentary on this narrative sequence[12] de-
parts very little from these terms and is thus unable to block
Wordsworth's ghost, a certain "she," from taking over the text.
Indeed, KaM himself seems to be sleepwalking though the
whole experience, unaware of what—or who—is showing up
on the page.

---

and Insight, 2d ed. (Minneapolis, 1983), 225. And is "she" not also large enough
to encompass KaM, and "you" and "me"?

[12]"As long as you thought the marks were poetry, you were assuming their
intentional character. You had no idea who the author was, and this may have
tricked you into thinking that positing an author was irrelevant to your ability
to read the stanza. But in fact you had, without realizing it, already posited an
author. It was only with the mysterious arrival of the second stanza that your
tacit assumption (e.g., someone writing with a stick) was challenged and you
realized that you had made one. Only now, when positing an author seems
impossible, do you genuinely imagine the marks as authorless" (16).

Even the uncertainty of signature, its implication beyond the fully conscious present of the signing author, may have been already inscribed and anticipated by the poem. The first line, which for lack of a title serves to name the poem, gives a version of the speaker's error in terms of an undecidable *seal* or, perhaps, signature. The emphatic verb "did . . . seal" allows for a grammatical interchangeability of subject and object, slumber and spirit: either a slumber sealed my spirit or my spirit sealed a slumber. So the question is: Did slumber turn my wakefulness into forgetful sleep, close me off from the light? or did my spirit put its seal on slumber, sign sleep for its own, recognize the end of wakefulness with its own mark? The first reading permits a certain exteriority of slumber and spirit, the former acting against or in opposition to the latter. The second reading empties out the opposition of lucidity to a sealing off from the light; instead, it marries them or seals them together. Either way, however, the line points to an eclipse of spirit in the act of sealing or signing. Perhaps the poem should be read in a circular manner, "rolled round" the eclipsing signature that unseals its error only to return to the position of signing the slumber which precipitated its fall. At the very least, the undecidable signing of "A Slumber Did My Spirit Seal" could explain why this lyric has repeatedly attracted intentionalist arguments like KaM's: that argument finds itself already cited—and challenged—there.[13]

But if, as we are suggesting, KaM's fable is a displacement of

[13]More recently, the same short lyric has also served as stage for a "representative" deconstructive reading and a dissenting counterreading of the deconstructor's moves: see Morris Eaves and Michael Fischer, eds., *Romanticism and Contemporary Criticism* (Ithaca, N.Y., 1986), for the essays by J. Hillis Miller ("On Edge: The Crossways of Contemporary Criticism") and M. H. Abrams ("Construing and Deconstructing"). Abrams' objections often turn on "intentionalist" points. His article also embeds a reference to Hirsch's previous use of the poem (145, n. 27), which, he recalls, was already an attempt to adjudicate the conflicting readings of still earlier readers: Cleanth Brooks and F. W. Bateson. At this point we might wonder if it is still possible to count the number of quotation marks enclosing the poem or rather detaching it from its "original" intention.

the text it cites, it is also a denegation of what it makes readable, a denegation that is marked by an important deviation that swerves the fable away from Wordsworth's lesson. The addition of the third episode (the sighting of the submarine and so forth) moves the fable beyond the two-beat sequence of the poem. With this turn or return, KaM attempts to recuperate the example back within the frame and to show us that it was all along merely the material of an experiment. Yet this third moment, when the fable seems to step outside the poem in order to manipulate its example from a safe distance,[14] resembles nothing so much as a return to the illusion characterized by the first stanza and discovered by the second. That is, it returns to, repeats, or reintroduces the illusion of a continuing presence (of intention) untouched by earthly years when it mistakes a (living) agent for a (dead) author. This, then, is how the fable becomes an example of the mistake exposed by the poem. The mistake occurs through a movement that denies the eclipse of a wakeful intention. Whereas in the second moment, the fable had allegorized a reading of the undecidable subject of the lyric, in the third moment it forgets everything it has read by fantasizing an "author" who rises out of the sea, resuscitated, not dead, still able to speak and to sign. One need have no human fears. The question is closed. "The question of authorship is and always was an empirical question; it has now received an empirical answer. The theoretical temptation is to imagine that such empirical questions must, or should, have theoretical answers."

If there is another moral to this story, we would have to look for it in the delusive figure of a fiction that distracts attention from its incoherencies and contradictions even as it preaches the inescapability of the practice of reading fictions, and thus the superfluity of any theory. That "Against Theory" cannot practice what it preaches is the sort of dilemma theory teaches

---

[14]Miller writes in "On Edge": "The poem leaves the reader with no possibility of moving through or beyond or standing outside in sovereign control" (108). Maybe this is what "you" come to realize after reading KaM's fable.

us to look out for. It becomes a moral dilemma, however, when that inability is declared to be of no theoretical interest. Yet one is left to understand such an assertion as a statement of fear—fear of the tool, reading, which alone can expose the mystifying, even demagogic argument in favor of closing the book on theory.

CHAPTER EIGHT

Pieces of Resistance

Teaching Resistance

A text such as the *Profession de foi* can literally be called "unreadable" in that it leads to a set of assertions that radically exclude each other. Nor are these assertions mere neutral constations; they are exhortative performatives that require the passage from sheer enunciation to action. They compel us to choose while destroying the foundations of any choice. They tell the allegory of a judicial decision that can be neither judicious nor just. . . . One sees from this that the impossibility of reading should not be taken too lightly.[1]

These sentences conclude chapter 10 of Paul de Man's *Allegories of Reading*, a chapter that is itself titled "Allegory of Reading." The repetition of the title suggests that the *Profession de foi* is exemplary of the allegorization of reading as both a necessary and impossible task—necessary because it is impossible. It would be reassuring to think that "unreadability" affected only the rare occurrence of a "text such as the *Profession de foi*," or that it could be isolated within the limits of particular authors' works—Rousseau's, for example. It would be reas-

---

[1]De Man, *Allegories of Reading*, 245; further references are included in the text.

suring but, like whistling in the dark, perhaps a benighted attempt to keep the shadows at bay. It would be better not to take
the impossiblity of reading "too lightly," warns de Man in the
last sentence.

But just how lightly is too lightly? While the question may be
unavoidable, the answer is bound to fall short, leaving readers
with a puzzle not unlike the one that confronts them on the
page displaying, in an epigraph to *Allegories of Reading*, this
phrase from Pascal: "Quand on lit trop vite ou trop doucement
on n'entend rien" (When one reads too quickly or too slowly,
one understands nothing). The phrase suggests that whoever
would understand what she reads must find the "juste mesure"
of reading: neither too fast nor too slow but, in the self-satisfied
words of Goldilocks, just right. Such a reading of the phrase,
however, may itself have gone too fast, neglecting to notice that
this rule does not set the speed for its own reading and thus
carries over the possibilities for error or misunderstanding it is
designed to warn against. Likewise, how lightly is one to take
de Man's warning that "the impossibility of reading should not
be taken too lightly," given that any reading—including the
one just completed of the *Profession de foi*—will at some point
have to cast off the burden of its own impossibility and leap out,
no doubt too heavily, over the abyss of understanding? Is there
not, as in Pascal's rule, a double error that has here been abbreviated into the more commonly occurring of the two: reading
too fast, taking the impossibility of reading too lightly?

The fact that reading, as de Man teaches it, always negotiates
with a doubled possibility of error is confirmed by some lines
we elided above from the concluding paragraph of "Allegory of
Reading":

> If after reading the *Profession de foi*, we are tempted to convert
> ourselves to "theism," we stand convicted of foolishness in the
> court of the intellect. But if we decide that belief, in the most
> extensive use of the term (which must include all possible forms
> of idolatry and ideology) can once and forever be overcome by the
> enlightened mind, then this twilight of the idols will be all the
> more foolish in not recognizing itself as the first victim of its
> occurrence.

The second error identified here is "all the more foolish," which could be taken to mean that it is more foolish than the first error, more foolish than the blind conversion to belief in an ordered meaning of the world. It is not more or less in error but rather more foolish to *believe* that belief can be overcome. In either case, reading, it would seem, leads to foolish behavior. While serious readers might understandably be expected to dismiss such an intimation, their reaction cannot disguise how the study of literary language installs a critical relation to the *institution* of all serious values—that is, to their interiority to themselves, to their self-evidence. It is this critical relation that institutions, naturally enough perhaps, resist, and, to the extent that literary study has come to identify itself with the stability or even the growth of institutions (particularly the teaching institution), one should not be surprised to find so many literary scholars reproving with one hand the critical enterprise that, with the other hand—the hand guided by a text's demand for reading—they endeavor to carry out.

The uneasy relationship between literary study and pedagogical institutions is one that interests de Man repeatedly, but nowhere, perhaps, so distinctly as in his essay "The Resistance to Theory."

One of the starting points of the essay (for there are several) is an empirical knowledge enunciated by a certain "we":

> We know that there has been, over the last fifteen to twenty years, a strong interest in something called literary theory and that, in the United States, this interest has at times coincided with the importation and reception of foreign, mostly but not always continental influences. We also know that this wave of interest now seems to be receding as some satiation or disappointment sets in after the initial enthusiasm.[2]

This general address, this "we know that there has been," is, we know, meant for scholars in modern languages and literatures in North American universities. We know this from the essay's

---

[2]De Man, "The Resistance to Theory," in *Resistance to Theory*, 5; further references are included in the text.

contextual introduction, which will be taken up later. For the moment, we need only remark an address that institutes a knowledge or a ground on which to let stand or fall a theoretical movement of thought beyond what it thinks it already knows. This ground, however, displays at its edges "an ebb and flow," a differentiated movement of forces. The passage continues: "Such an ebb and flow is natural enough, but it remains interesting, *in this case*, because it makes the depth of the resistance to theory so manifest" (italics added). In this ebb-and-flow movement of overturning, there appears a figure that has title to theory's interest and is here titled the resistance to theory. Having started out from the terra firma of what we know, we have come upon something that remains to be read and that interests whoever would speak of literary theory as a critical relation to institutions, the relation that has been made manifest in a figure. Resistance to theory thus engages an act of reading that oversteps whatever established formal limits usually or by convention contain that activity. This because the ebb and flow of the figure concerns precisely the movement of inscription and erasure that underlies ("the *depth* of the resistance to theory") any formalization of limits: those of an institution or those of "something called literary theory."

But reading the figure of resistance encounters at the outset an ambiguity of reference. What is interesting "in this case" is filed under the name—the resistance to theory—which is also the title of the essay. The deictic "this" of "in this case" points in two directions at once: to this essay and to the apparent phenomenon to which the essay refers. Thus, when the phrase "the resistance to theory" occurs in the body of the essay, one cannot be sure whether it appears there as a citation of the title or whether one should read the title as already itself a citation of the phrase from the essay.[3] This undecidability keeps the figure from closing off too quickly in an illusion of reference since the gesture of pointing to some reference cannot exclude its own

[3]This is but one of the possible complications in the relation between title and text. Derrida complicates it still further in "Title (to be specified)," trans. Tom Conley, *Sub-stance* 3 (1981).

act of pointing with which it exceeds the whole to be pointed to. Such is, of course, the case of any text,[4] but the traces of a supplementary resistance to which the essay or its title cannot be said simply to refer have been reinscribed in this case.

Its case, that is to say its falling or befalling like an accident, the occasion of its falling and the coincidence between the falling that befalls it and the falling it describes. All of these terms—case, accident, occasion, coincidence—draw on the same Latin root: *cadere*, to fall. As does the word "chance,"[5] so we will not be surprised to find that the essay's chances of success—its chances of being read and understood—are bound up with a certain failure or falling before its occasion.

The rising and falling of "The Resistance to Theory" is briefly recounted in some prefatory paragraphs. This account seems to fit easily enough into the genre of the preface or introduction and thus to require little more than the minimal attention of any reader who is only passing through on the way to the essay "itself." Yet to read these paragraphs as preface—standing before and outside the essay they point to—is perhaps to miss a point. Not just because one could justifiably speak here of a postscript rather than a preface but, more important, because these paragraphs, set off by a blank from the main body of the essay, allow one to question what are usually thought of as the limits of a textual body. Where exactly the text of the essay begins and ends, where it starts or stops falling are questions that the initial paragraphs render unavoidable.

That is, one cannot avoid noticing how the essay is made to double back on itself in these initial lines as the result of a resistance to "The Resistance to Theory." Here is the story, an allegory of reading the resistance to reading, as de Man tells it:

[4]"The surplus mark re-marks the whole series of the double marks of the text by illustrating what always exceeds a possible closure of the text folded, reflected upon itself. In excess to the text *as a whole* is the text 'itself.' " Rodolphe Gasché, "Joining the Text," in *The Yale Critics: Deconstruction in America*, ed. Jonathan Arac, Wlad Godzich, and Wallace Martin (Minneapolis, 1983), 69.

[5]On these words, see as well Jacques Derrida, "My Chances/*Mes Chances*: A Rendezvous with Some Epicurean Stereophonies," in *Taking Chances: Derrida, Psychoanalysis and Literature*, ed. Joseph H. Smith and William Kerrigan (Baltimore, 1984), 5.

This essay was not originally intended to address the question of teaching directly,[6] although it was supposed to have a didactic and an educational function—which it failed to achieve. It was written at the request of the Committee on the Research Activities of the Modern Language Association as a contribution to a collective volume entitled *Introduction to Scholarship in Modern Languages and Literatures.* I was asked to write the section on literary theory. Such essays are expected to follow a clearly determined program: they are supposed to provide the reader with a select but comprehensive list of the main trends and publications in the field, to synthesize and classify the main problematic areas and to lay out a critical and programmatic projection of the solutions which can be expected in the foreseeable future. All this with a keen awareness that, ten years later, someone will be asked to repeat the same exercise.[7]

I found it difficult to live up, in minimal good faith, to the requirements of this program and could only try to explain, as concisely as possible, why the main theoretical interest of literary theory consists in the impossibility of its definition. The Committee rightly judged that this was an inauspicious way to achieve the pedagogical objectives of the volume and commissioned another article.[8] I thought their decision altogether justified, as well as interesting in its implications for the teaching of literature.

These paragraphs recount a pedagogical failure, but one that "remains interesting in its implications for the study of litera-

[6]This is a reference to the *Yale French Studies* issue, no. 63, ed. Barbara Johnson, titled "The Pedagogical Imperative: Teaching as a Literary Genre," in which the essay was first published.

[7]This predictable obsolescence is confirmed by Joseph Gibaldi, editor of the collection in question, whose preface recalls the success of the two previous volumes in the series (published in 1952 and 1970) and then comments: "By the end of [the 1970s], however, the time was right once again for a new collection of essays by a new group of authors." *Introduction to Scholarship in Modern Languages and Literatures* (New York, 1979).

[8]This article, "Literary Theory" by Paul Hernadi, in Gibaldi, *Introduction to Scholarship,* follows the "determined program" in the first two of the three requirements de Man discerns, wisely stopping short of the third, the "programmatic projection of the solutions which can be expected in the foreseeable future." Despite its recognition that "quite a few critics even doubt the feasibility of defining literature on any grounds whatsoever" (100), the essay does not attempt to account for the resistance to theory, which may be a sign that its planned obsolescence is accelerating.

ture." It is therefore not, strictly speaking or exclusively, a pedagogical failure because in falling short it keeps an interest for the theory of teaching literature or the teaching of literary theory. The interest may be seen to reside in a resistance that rejects an *inauspicious* reading of theory's chances for producing a positive discipline of reading. This resistance is interesting because it implies that, according to a widely endorsed program, the teaching of literature would measure its success by the capacity to turn a student reader's attention *away* from signs that cannot be made to submit to reassuring definition and that are therefore, by definition, programmatically, judged to be "inauspicious." As de Man remarks toward the end of the essay, this interesting problem "quickly becomes the more baffling one of having to account for the shared reluctance to acknowledge the obvious" (18).[9]

The turning aside or turning away in an avoidance of reading the sign's rhetorical component is itself a trope to which de Man gives form in the words "resistance to theory." As we have seen, the figure points both to an obvious, albeit slippery, referent (what "we know there has been," the ebb and flow of interest in literary theory, the depth of resistance to theory made manifest) and to itself in a turning aside of reference, citing its title as the name of a figure. The turning of the figure is not arrested when it turns back on itself. Rather, it names "itself" as the error inherent in all proper names (and a title is also a proper name), their improper or rhetorical relation to a particular referent. Neither does the text "The Resistance to Theory" close itself off as a proper name having a known, historical referent. The empirical, referential meaning of "resistance to theory" is perforce turned aside when the phrase is used as title of the essay and when, in referring, it also refers to itself.

The essay proceeds, then, as a deconstructive reading of its title, just one more reason one cannot bypass reading it by way of paraphrase. One cannot bypass reading, but of course neither

[9]To be sure, the MLA Committee on Research Activities is but one locus of this shared reluctance; yet, by virtue of its representative function and structure, this locus also serves to represent what *should* be the interest of literary theory to modern language and literature scholars in the United States.

can one overlook the fact that immense institutional programs function, precisely, to turn away from reading, to turn away what turns away itself, of itself, or in itself. Each of these two imperatives, which seem to exclude each other, is in fact leaving or inscribing its mark on the other in such a way that neither can emerge in its pure form or in a purely formal way. On the one hand, that the "main theoretical interest [of literary theory] consists in the impossibility of its definition" will continue to manifest itself in institutional resistance to this undefined object. And, on the other hand, because the institutionalization of literary theory in this country has tended to follow the way in which it can be made into a method at the service of a pedagogical program[10] and because literary theory, when it pursues its main theoretical interest, has to question the defining limits of any such program applied to literary language, institutionalization can be made to appear in its effects—the marks it has left—on the movement of theoretical thought. "The Resistance to Theory" inauspiciously resists this program and thus bears the mark of a certain institutional closure.

Self-resistance

Given the deconstructed exteriority implicit in its title, such questions as What is it that resists or threatens? or, in the passive voice, What is it that is being resisted or threatened? are bound to encounter the complication or the coimplication of the supplemental mark of resistance from which de Man's essay proceeds. Because they are so bound, the essay comes to speak of "the displaced symptoms of a resistance inherent in the theoretical enterprise itself" (12) and finally of the language of theory as "the language of self-resistance" (19). In the course of an analysis of this self-resisting movement, what will have

---

[10]This point is made in de Man's review of Michael Riffaterre's poetic theory, "Hypogram and Inscription: Michael Riffaterre's Poetics of Reading," in *Resistance to Theory*, 28ff., and again in "Aesthetic Formalization in Kleist's *Über das Marionettentheater*," in *Rhetoric of Romanticism*, 272–73.

become apparent is a limit on the validity of the subject/object, active/passive mode of positioning any truth about resistance.

Yet, when de Man speaks of "displaced symptoms" of resistance, this choice of words seems designed to remind one of the key use of the term in psychoanalysis. Such echoes (for there are many in this essay) might even be heard as early as the title, since "The Resistance to Theory" does not specify what theory is at issue.[11] The title, in other words, can be read as citing some relation to psychoanalytic theory which the text of the essay hints at but never makes explicit. One may be sure, however, that the supplemental resistance complicating rhetorical theory's relation to itself will also divide and render complex whatever relation could be installed with a theory that is itself constructed or that constructs itself around the concept of resistance. As we shall see when we try to discern at least an outline of this complexity, it is once again through the institutional effect that one may be able to read a supplemental line of resistance dividing theory from its own constructions.

But first, it may be useful to recall that the concept of resistance has traditionally taken shape along the line of contact between the conceptual faculty and some exteriority. The concept, in other words, shows a double face, turned inward and outward, along the line presumed to divide consciousness from its outside or its other. The *Vocabulaire technique et critique de la philosophie*, for example, defines resistance as a "primary quality of bodies":

> Resistance: the quality of sensible matter by which it is perceptible to touch and muscular activity. "The sensation of resistance, in particular, would have a real privilege over all others for proving that matter exists in itself; for, as the partisans of this doctrine argue, *we observe directly* the existence of that which resists us and whatever resists us is necessarily outside of us since it knocks up against us and stops us. This reasoning, as one may easily see, comes down to saying that resistance is a primary quality of

[11]In this regard, it is interesting that the bibliography of de Man's work in *The Yale Critics* lists this article under the erroneous title "The Resistance to Literary Theory."

bodies" (Dunan, *Essais de philosophie générale*, 532; italics added)[12]

The definition situates resistance in the "outside of us" ("that which resists us is necessarily outside of us"), that is, outside a consciousness that has a direct or unresisted knowledge of material existence in itself and not only in consciousness. But this direct awareness depends on an ambivalent intervention of a body through "touch and muscular activity," ambivalent because it can be neither wholly assimilated nor rejected by consciousness. The notion of direct observation bypasses the necessity of this ambivalence (represented by the double sense—touching/touched—of the sense of touch) and thereby a body of resistance, the resistant body within the body of knowledge. What is on the line here, in other words, is the conditions of certainty for Descartes's subject of knowledge, the subject presumed to be sure of at least one thing: the difference between the thing it touches and the thing it only dreams of touching. Without this construction of difference, the subject simply will not stand up to its own rigorous scrutiny. It is not, however, just that the subject risks falling if it sees its construction dismantled, but that the fall takes down with it the distinction between standing and falling on the basis of which one could speak of a fall in the first place. The fall into uncertainty cannot even be certain that it is a fall. Such a formulation will return us to the final lines of "Resistance to Theory," where, as so often, de Man speaks of falling:[13] "Yet literary theory is not in danger of going under; it cannot help but flourish, and the more it is resisted, the more it flourishes, since the language it speaks is the language of self-resistance. What re-

[12]André Lalande, ed., *Vocabulaire technique et critique de la philosophie*, 9th ed. (Paris, 1962), 925.

[13]Earlier in the essay, a brief reading of Keats's two titles *Hyperion* and *Fall of Hyperion* elicits the question: "Are we telling the story of why all texts, as texts, can always be said to be falling?" (16); see as well De Man, "Rhetoric of Temporality," where Baudelaire's example of a fall in "L'Essence du rire" provides the key text for the discussion of irony (*Blindness and Insight*, 213–14).

mains impossible to decide is whether this flourishing is a triumph or a fall" (19–20).

Insisting on the undecidability of the theoretical enterprise, de Man seems to neglect altogether the anxiety induced by not knowing what, above all, one needs to know: whether one is falling or standing. If, as we have suggested, there is a subtext in this essay whose title would be something like "Resistance to Psychoanalysis," then the bracketing of anxiety as a source of "displaced symptoms of resistance" would constitute one of its essential gestures. This subtext resembles most closely another brief text of de Man's, his review of Harold Bloom's *Anxiety of Influence.*

There, the errors of an anxious selfhood or subjectivity are set over against the necessity of a "truly epistemological moment" that alone can make a literary theory possible. Resistance to theory, in other words, is seen here to occur in the form of self or subject and its intentions. Although to be sure *The Anxiety of Influence* does not propose a theory of poetry based on naïve intentionality (for Bloom, as de Man notes, "influence can emanate from texts a poet has never read"), it nevertheless fails, according to its reviewer, "to free poetic language from the constraints of natural reference" and instead returns us to a scheme that "is still clearly a relapse into psychological naturalism."[14] De Man even traces a regression from Bloom's earlier work to *Anxiety,* where Bloom "becomes more dependent than before on a pathos which is more literal than hyperbolic." This regression displaces theoretical concerns from poetic language to self or subject, a displacement that puts at risk the "truly epistemological moment" of poetic theory:

> From a relationship between words and things, or words and words, we return to a relationship between subjects. Hence the agonistic language of anxiety, power, rivalry, and bad faith. . . . [Bloom's] argument is stated in oedipal terms and the story of influence told in the naturalistic language of desire. . . . His theoretical concerns are now displaced into a symbolic narrative re-

[14]De Man, *Blindness and Insight,* 271; further references will be included in the text.

centered in a subject. *But no theory of poetry is possible without a truly epistemological moment when the literary text is considered from the perspective of its truth or falsehood rather than from a love-hate point of view.* The presence of such a moment offers no guarantee of truth but it serves to alert our understanding to distortions brought about by desire. It may reveal in their stead patterns of error that are perhaps more disturbing, but rooted in language rather than in the self. (271–72; italics added)

The "truly epistemological moment" cannot occur, de Man suggests, between subjects who are, inevitably, subjects of desire. The identification of the poetic text as a subject constitutes, in Bloom's case, a relapse or a regression. In another context, de Man has given a specifically historical sense to this regressive turn when, in the opening paragraph of "The Rhetoric of Temporality," he implies a continuity between "the advent, in the course of the nineteenth century, of a subjectivistic critical vocabulary" and "the romantic eclipse of all other rhetorical distinctions behind the single, totalizing term 'symbol'" (187–88). If, however, subjectivistic criticism like Bloom's is to be understood in its continuity with romantic theories of poetic imagination (and this historical/rhetorical scheme will be more or less sustained through the latest essays collected in *The Rhetoric of Romanticism*), then in what sense can this continuity also be termed a relapse or a regression?

Referring to Bloom's subjectivism or romanticism, de Man writes that the "regression can be traced in various ways." The example he chooses concerns the use of Freud:

> It is apparent, for example, in the way Freud is used in the earlier as compared to the later essay. Bloom, who at that time seems to have held a rather conventional view of Freud as a rationalistic humanist, respectfully dismisses him in *The Ringers in the Tower* as the prisoner of a reality principle the romantics had left behind. In *The Anxiety of Influence* Bloom's reading of Freud has gained in complexity, yet he is still, in principle, discarded as "not severe enough," his wisdom outranked by "the wisdom of the strong poets." Still, his argument is stated in oedipal terms. (272)

The regression traced here in relation to Freud shows a contradictory logic since, in the later work, Freud is dismissed, but as

a weak son who cannot stand up to his stronger poet/fathers—
he is dismissed, that is, in the oedipal terms of Freudian theory.
This move is regressive (and not merely contradictory) because
the dismissal of Freud ends up repeating the weak or later poet's
oedipal impasse. And thus, notes de Man, "Bloom has become
the subject of his own desire for clarification."

But it would seem that de Man is also pointing to a regressive
reading of Freud, one that remains governed by the anxious
desire for clarification in the face of precisely that impossibility
as concerns unconscious desire. That is, the regressive or anxious resistance to reading may be understood to include a resistance to the psychoanalytic theory of the unconscious and thus
as a defense of the ideological fiction of an unobstructed, unresisted self.[15] Clearly, however, this resistance can itself be overcome only in a regressive direction whenever literary theory
leaps over its object and heads for the cover of the oedipal
narratives with which Freud enriched the supply of psychological naturalism. By the same token, no literary theory that
would be "progressive" can avoid the evidence that "progress"
also remains almost wholly to be read as a fictional narrative
with a large network of roots feeding the same ideological functions as are fed by psychological naturalism. If it thus remains
"impossible to decide whether this flourishing [of literary the-
ory] is a triumph or a fall," then the question of whether one is
progressing or regressing, falling or triumphing in the sight, on
the site of theory will have to become, instead, the question of
how to keep one's anxiety about an answer to the first question
from precipitating a decisive fall into interpretive readings
based on defensive ego identifications.

[15]This is not to ignore de Man's more or less systematic replacement of
psychological terms with rhetorical ones but to recognize that the necessity of
this replacement can be traced in part to the break within traditional epistemol-
ogy effected by Freudian models of the unconscious. Nothing in de Man's work
prohibits the making of such a connection, while a number of moments, such as
the one examined here, encourage it. Geoffrey Hartman has remarked that
"despite the anti-psychologistic bent of de Man's practice," one may observe
certain "alliances" between that practice and psychoanalysis ("Paul de Man's
Proverbs of Hell," *London Review of Books*, 15 March–4 April, 1984, 4). For
another assessment of de Manian deconstruction in its relation to psychoanalysis, see Richard Klein, "The Blindness of Hyperboles: The Ellipses of
Insight," *Diacritics*, Summer 1973.

Overwhelming Resistance

"The Resistance to Theory" manages to remind one of the important use psychoanalysis has made of the term *resistance*, without all the same taking up an explicit discussion of it. One effect of this gesture is to propose a reading *en blanc* or between the lines of Freud's essay with the echoing title "The Resistances to Psychoanalysis" ("Die Widerstände die Psychoanalyse"). Without presuming to fill in this blank, I turn now to several details from the end of Freud's essay where one may recognize in Freud's rhetoric a scene of confrontation that de Man has analyzed elsewhere quite explicity and, indeed, more than once.

These details, which are rhetorical figures, are also what allow that text to narrate an end to the self-resistance installed by the confrontation with the truth of resistance to some truth. When, toward the end of the essay, Freud recapitulates his account of the resistance encountered by psychoanalysis, he shifts to the past tense, which, in the context, can only be read as a hopeful anticipation of the future defeat of that resistance.

> The strongest resistances to psycho-analysis were not of an intellectual kind but arose from emotional sources. This explained their passionate character as well as their poverty in logic. The situation obeyed a simple formula: men in the mass behaved to psycho-analysis in precisely the same way as individual neurotics under treatment for their disorders. It is possible, however, by patient work to convince these latter individuals that everything happened as we maintained it did: we had not invented it but had arrived at it from a study of other neurotics covering a period of twenty or thirty years.[16]

We will come back to the two complementary terms that supply the "simple formula" of the central analogy here—a totalizing figure ("men in the mass") and a figure of sheer repetition

---

[16]Freud, "Resistances to Psychoanalysis," in *Standard Edition of the Complete Works of Sigmund Freud*, trans. James Strachey et al., ed. James Stratchey (London, 1961), 19:221; further references are included in the text.

("in precisely the same way")—when they recur in another arrangement in the text. As for the emotional source that over-powers logic, Freud has earlier identified it as fear (*Angst*), in a passage that again sounds a hopeful, but perhaps not a fearless, note: "Psychoanalysis is regarded as 'inimical to culture' and put under a ban as a 'social danger.' This resistance cannot last forever. No human institution can in the long run escape the influence of fair criticism; but men's attitude to psycho-analysis is still dominated by this fear, which gives rein to their passions and diminishes their power of logical argument" (220). Freud's conviction that "resistance cannot last forever" may be read as a submission to that greater truth according to which nothing lasts forever. But, in that case, what of psychoanalysis itself as an institution? This question is not posed explicitly by Freud; however, because the essay concludes by pointing to the recent founding of the Berlin and Vienna psychoanalytic in-stitutes, the question may be heard all the same as adding an anxious note to this account of the defeat of resistances to psychoanalysis.

This defeat follows a certain narrative order—"everything happened as we maintained it did"—the order that psycho-analysis has uncovered through years of patient observation. Overwhelming evidence, however, may also show a tendency to overwhelm in an alarming way. Thus, having set out the simple, analogical formula ("men in the mass behaved to psycho-analysis in precisely the same way as individual neu-rotics"), Freud then comments: "The position was at once alarming and consoling [etwas Schreckhaftes und etwas Tröst-liches]: alarming because it was no small thing to have the whole human race as one's patient [das ganze Menschengesch-lecht zum Patienten zu haben], and consoling because after all everything was taking place as the hypotheses of psycho-analysis declared it was bound to" (221). This note of alarm is sounded in the presence of a figure—"the whole human race as one's patient"—a synecdoche that, more dramatically than the preceding figure of "men in the mass," identifies a collective entity of staggering proportions. This same figure, however, is given another face that consoles rather than alarms. It consoles by confirming and consolidating a certain narrative and a certain narration: "everything was taking place as the hypotheses of psycho-analysis declared that it was bound to." The figure has the effect of consolidating psychoanalysis with itself, joining it as a narrative whose end is already present in its beginning. Thus "the whole human race" lends consistency to that other whole called psychoanalysis, the latter realizing itself or completing itself in the fulfillment of a narrative. The analogical formula that leads to the alarming/consoling figure also tends to reduce the plural resistance of Freud's title to a same resistance, but one that has been distributed between the inside and outside of the practice of psychoanalysis. "The whole human race as one's patient" would serve, then, to erase even this topological distinction by uniting all resistance behind the representative guise of a single patient whose treatment can be made wholly internal to the analytic process, where it can be overcome. No doubt, the idea is not meant to be taken seriously or literally; nevertheless, the text as it continues seems to struggle to make good on its spontaneous figure, to comprehend the sum total of resistances to psychoanalysis, and thus to take in the totality of its outside. Or, to put this another way, the sentence that both alarms and consoles from the position of psychoanalysis can be likened to a moment of gagging on the enormity of the thing. How does Freud swallow this huge morsel in order to bring his essay to some conclusion?

He first weighs what he calls "purely external difficulties" that "have also contributed to strengthen the resistance to psychoanalysis." Freud enumerates them beginning with the difficulty of an independent judgment regarding psychoanalysis: "It is not easy to arrive at an independent [selbständiges] judgment upon matters to do with analysis without having experienced it oneself or practiced it on someone else" (222). The difficulty these sentences would point to referentially, in some pure exterior, remains caught within a syntax that illustrates rather than situates the problem of resistance, because it is not at all self-evident how the lack of an independent or external place from which to judge can also be termed a "purely external difficulty." In the succeeding sentences of the paragraph, however, the so-called external difficulty is drawn into the more purely internal question of analytic technique: "Nor can one do the latter [that is, practice psychoanalysis on someone else] without having acquired a specific and decidedly delicate technique."

If one reads this movement inward as an attempt to make good on a totalizing figure, then unmistakably technique becomes the key to translating rhetorical overstatement into something closer to referential accuracy. In effect, the resistant figure's alarming proportions are scaled down by the institution of technique, and with that institution comes a marked improvement in the position of psychoanalysis: "Until recently there was no easily accessible means of learning psychoanalysis and its technique. This position has now been improved by the foundation (in 1920) of the Berlin Psycho-analytic Clinic and Training Institute, and soon afterwards (in 1922) of an *exactly similar institute* in Vienna" (222; italics added). The exact similarity of these institutes, guaranteeing the repetition or reproduction of a technique, seems to advance the position of psychoanalysis beyond the stalemated encounter with a figure of overwhelming resistance. But there has been in fact no improvement in the *rhetorical* position, which remains as tenuous as ever in its promise to deliver one from the alarming figure of the opposition of the "whole human race." Only another trope, the powerful trope of mimesis, can allow one to say that institutes of whatever sort are *exactly* similar. The mimetic institution, that is, the institution of mimesis as technique, appears to solve a difficulty, but in fact it swallows that difficulty whole.

A Lesson in Resistance

The narrative elements we have been considering in Freud's essay are assembled in similar sequence by Rousseau's account of the necessary primacy of figurative over denominative language. Both Jacques Derrida[17] and de Man have made this episode from the *Essay on the Origin of Languages* justly famous,

[17]See Derrida, *Of Grammatology*, 275ff.

the latter even returning to the text a second time. First, let us briefly recall the passage in question from Rousseau's essay:

> Upon meeting others, a savage man will initially be frightened. Because of his fear he sees the others as bigger and stronger than himself. He calls them *giants*. After many experiences, he recognizes that these so-called giants are neither bigger nor stronger than he. Their stature does not correspond to the idea he had initially attached to the word giant. So he invents another name common to him and to them, such as the name *man*, for example, and leaves the name *giant* to the fictitious object that impressed him during his illusion. This is how the figurative word is born before the literal word, when our gaze is held in passionate fascination.[18]

From de Man's reading of this passage and the consequences that must follow from it through the *Discourse on Inequality*, we lift the sequence that shows certain parallels with Freud's essay: (1) the fearful face-off with an overwhelming figure; (2) the reduction of the figure through a technical operation; (3) the substitution of a literal metaphor for the first, wild metaphor; (4) the institution or repetition of the mimetic figure as a proper denomination that can found a science: anthropology, sociology, political science, psychoanalysis.

De Man's rhetorical analysis of this sequence is laid out in two essays: "The Rhetoric of Blindness" in *Blindness and Insight* (1971) and chapter 7 of *Allegories of Reading*. The second of these is said to have been written to "cope" with the "inadequacies" of the first.[19] In both essays, the "giant" narrative is read in the sense of a demonstration of "the priority of metaphor over denomination." What shifts from one essay to the next, however, is the understanding of Rousseau's choice of fear as the passion with which to illustrate this priority. In the earlier essay, this reaction is aligned on the side of need rather

---

[18]Rousseau, *Essay*, 13.

[19]De Man, "Foreword to Revised, Second Edition," in *Blindness and Insight*, xi. De Man is referring to his first reading of the allegory in "Rhetoric of Blindness," 133ff.

than passion, a situation that places Rousseau in contradiction with his assertion that it is the passions that produce the first metaphors.[20] Thus Rousseau would have made a mistake. In the second essay, de Man realigns his own earlier reading when he addresses the choice of fear to illustrate the figurative source of denomination:

> [Fear] can only result from a fundamental feeling of distrust, the suspicion that, although the creature does not look like a lion or a bear, it nevertheless might act like one, outward appearances to the contrary. The reassuringly familiar and similar outside might be a trap. Fear is the result of a possible discrepancy between the outer and inner properties of entities. It can be shown that, for Rousseau, *all passions*—whether they be love, pity, anger, or even *a borderline case between passion and need such as fear*—are characterized by such a discrepancy; they are based not on the knowledge that such a difference exists, but on the hypothesis that it might exist, a possibility that can never be proven or disproven by empirical or by analytical means. A statement of distrust is neither true nor false: it is rather in the nature of a permanent hypothesis. (150; Italics added)

In this passage, a shift moves the reaction of fear from the side of need, to which it was consigned in the earlier essay. But this shift does not cross all the way over to the side of passion: it stays its movement at the borderline between the two. De Man, in other words, does not correct the "mistake" by reversing the distinction and calling fear a passion, although that might seem to offer the most obvious solution to the problem. By stopping *between* the terms of Rousseau's distinction (of need from passion), de Man's reading, in effect, suspends the textual metaphors in several senses at once. First, what is called fear is suspended in the hypothesis of "a possible discrepancy between

[20]"In Rousseau's vocabulary, language is a product of passion and not the expression of a need; fear, the reverse side of violence and aggression, is distinctively utilitarian and belongs to the world of 'besoins' rather than 'passions'" (De Man, "Rhetoric of Blindness," 134). De Man's revision of this distinction recalls Derrida's effacement of the limit between need and passion; see below, n. 21.

the outer and inner properties of entities." That is, when the metaphor "giant" accuses the possible discrepancy between the other's familiar exterior and bearlike or lionlike interior, it does so as well from a suspended position between the "exterior" and "interior" motives for the subject's acts, otherwise called need and passion. This is not all, however: the discrepancy is itself two-faced since it applies to *both* entities as they confront each other, the "creature" to be named no less than the naming subject. Thus the series of conceptual distinctions structuring this encounter—need/passion, outside/inside, other/self—are all suspended in a "strange unity."[21]

The shift onto the borderline between these suspended oppositions also brings into focus the other encounter in progress here, not between two men but between an act of reading and a text. Fear or anxiety provides a pivot on which the text can turn from the action represented to the action of representing, from, that is, one act of naming to another. The identification of the fearful reaction supplies something like a hook on which the reader can hang an identificatory interpretation of the text. At the same time, however, it is just such a precipitous identification or equalization of the two parties to the encounter (man/ giant but also reader/text) which is denounced by the allegory as a wishful but unreliable mode of reading. Reading by identification precipitates the same leap into the reassuring generality of "man" and the same forgetfulness of the metaphoric substitutions that allowed one to arrive there in the first place. Most important, such a reader forgets that he[22] has substituted the model of an intersubjective, face-to-face encounter for this other encounter with metaphor which, precisely, has no model.

---

[21]The term is Derrida's to describe the effaced limit between need and passion: "This incoherence would apply to the fact that the unity of need and passion (with the entire system of associated significations) constantly effaces the limit that Rousseau obstinately sketches and recalls. Rousseau *declares* this backbone, without which the entire conceptual organism would break up, and *wishes to think it* as a distinction; he *describes* it as a supplementary differance. This constrains in its graphics the strange unity of passion and need" (*Of Grammatology*, 238).

[22]Or she? The question of the gender of the reader is discussed below.

The reader's substitution reverses the order of substitution recounted by the allegory—the category of number or measure (a knowable, exteriorized quantity) for the category of intention (an unknowable, interiorized quality)—which allows for the crucial passage from metaphor to concept. Reading reverses this pattern when it reassures itself of its own understanding by interiorizing, turning the text's exterior into an intentional design of a subject: the text's author. The allegory, on the other hand, positions the necessary priority of an encounter with metaphor over any concept of subjectivity or intersubjectivity, showing, indeed, that metaphor gives the model to understanding based on intersubjective identifications. Nevertheless, a profound reading habit inverts this insight and misses the point of the allegory.

We can consider, through one brief example, how de Man's commentary effectively recovers the point that has been blunted by nonreading, or rather how it sticks the point to that nonreader par excellence which is the overarching subject of identification.

The passage we are concerned with sets a trap for this subject by means of its assumption that, in encounters with "giants," it is "we" men who have everything to fear. This assumption is vulnerable precisely in a reader's precipitous identification with the word "man" in the allegory, a move that erases the metaphorical interchangeability with the other word "giant." It begins thus: "The word 'man' is the result of a quantitative process of comparison based on measurement, and making deliberate use of the category of number in order to reach a reassuring conclusion." This reassuring process is then illustrated with recourse to the first person: "if the other man's height is numerically equal to *my own*, then he is no longer dangerous" (italics added). It is the words "my own" that form the hook for the reader's identification. Once hooked, this reader is caught in the trap to be sprung in the final sentence, which returns to the mode of commentary: "The conclusion is wishful and, of course, potentially in error—as Goliath and Polyphemos, among others, were soon enough to discover" (154). The reader, in effect, has been tricked into identifying with the overconfident calculations of the doomed giants. Like a rat in an experimenter's maze, he receives a shock that sends him back to find a safer exit. These sentences, in other words, perform an object lesson in the perils of hasty reading, which would be any reading that supplies an extratextual reference for the textual first person. That operation conceals a potential for error demonstrated in the very sentence one reads to its stinging conclusion. There, the names Goliath and Polyphemos, rather than the categories of giant and man, suddenly assume the force of proper names the reader has been led to substitute for "my own" name.[23] The point of the allegory will thus have been brought home: names are properly metaphorical, which is to say monstrous in their potential unreliability.

This reminder of the differences subsumed through a conceptual, categorical operation depends for its effect on a certain reversal of the substitutive process of generalization, a falling back into proper names. De Man recommends reading the allegory in the sense of the fate of proper names in a note that precedes the demonstration: "The actual word 'giant,' as we know from everyday usage, presupposes the word 'man' and is not the metaphorical figure that Rousseau, *for lack of an existing word*, has to call 'giant.' Rousseau's 'giant' would be more like some mythological monster; one could think of Goliath or Polyphemos" (153; italics added). To accept this suggestion entails certain consequences for Rousseau's tale of man's name. When these myths are superimposed on the allegory, another

---

[23]The substitution of a proper name for the common noun *giant* as the instance of metaphoric or improper denomination is consistent with Derrida's description of this moment in the "Essai": "What we interpret as literal expression in the perception and designation of giants, remains a metaphor that is preceded by nothing either in experience or in language. Since speech does not pass through reference to an object, the fact that 'giant' is literal as sign of fear not only does not prevent, but on the contrary implies that it should be nonliteral or metaphoric as sign of the object. It cannot be the idea-sign of the passion without presenting itself as the idea-sign of the presumed cause of that passion, opening an exchange with the outside. This opening allows the passage to a savage metaphor. No literal meaning precedes it" (*Of Grammatology*, 276). "Goliath" or "Polyphemos" would be something like the improper name of the self as outside itself.

moral can emerge beside the one that appears to lift the word "man" out of a gigantic error: it is not just that one man's triumph is another man's fall, but that the same name has to be made to stand for one and the other sense. The measure of this predicament is taken by Rousseau's allegory when, "for lack of an existing word" to represent properly the impropriety of names, it falls victim to the categorical error it also denounces.

Pièce de résistance

Rousseau's choice of fear should perhaps be read as the fear of never owning "my own" name. Such is also the anxiety that fuels resistance to a theory whose "main theoretical interest lies in the impossibility of its definition." Faced with an insistent reminder of the name's unreliability, one may, like Rousseau's man when faced with the "giant" or like Rousseau himself when faced with the deviations of his signature, alternately magnify and minimize the risk posed by the unnamable other. "It is," writes de Man in "Resistance to Theory," "a recurrent strategy of any anxiety to defuse what it considers threatening by magnification and minimization, by attributing to it claims to power of which it is bound to fall short" (5). De Man then proceeds to illustrate this assertion in a manner that I cannot help wondering how to read:

> If a cat is called a tiger it can easily be dismissed as a paper tiger; the question remains however why one was so scared of the cat in the first place. The same tactic works in reverse: calling the cat a mouse and then deriding it for its pretense to be mighty. Rather than being drawn into this polemical whirlpool, it might be better to try to call the cat a cat and to document, however, briefly, the contemporary version of the resistance to theory in this country.

It would be foolish, no doubt, to take such a light moment too seriously. But how seriously is too seriously? We are still trying to read in the absence of a measure of too fast or too slow, too big or too small. Since the passage in question qualifies such alternative errors as the recurrent strategy of anxiety, a mimicking effect is set off between the cat as metaphor *in* the text (which someone with an irrational fear of cats calls a tiger) and the cat as metaphor *of* the text one is trying to read. One's anxious question about how to read the cat in the text or the text in the cat already figures there precisely as the motive of rhetorical distortion. Whatever check the question seemed to offer on excesses of interpretation is overturned, mocked by a doubling reversal.

Like all acts of denomination, calling *the* cat *a* cat substitutes for the concept of difference (the singularity of the thing named) the concept of similarity (resemblance within a class or species). It would thus be sheerest delusion to believe that, having called the cat a cat, one has corrected the fundamental error of denomination. What is more, although the illustration moves to correct aberrant metaphors that try to pass themselves off as referential, it can make this adjustment only by leaving untouched the initial aberration that consists in giving that "something called literary theory" the other name of "cat." The thorough arbitrariness of this substitution (it is the substitution of allegory, more precisely of cat-egory) is not hidden behind any appeal to some natural resemblance between cats and theories (which is why it is hard to take the example seriously).

Finally, however, the evident arbitrariness of the latter substitution (cat for theory) undoes the apparent tautological self-evidence of the former one (the name cat for the thing cat). It does so when it suspends at the limit of the example the question of why one was so scared of the cat in the first place. Not only, then, does the example illustrate the decision of the suspended state of anxiety through aberrant acts of naming; it remarks as well that an essentially linguistic predicament—the impossibility of proper names—has been displaced onto the psychology of a subject. Since replacing the aberrant metaphors of tiger and mouse with the referential figure that calls the cat a cat can hardly be of any comfort to anyone who is scared of cats, the suspended question can be answered only by an identificatory leap of some sort. But precisely this unnamed, unnamable cat poses the limit of reading by identification. Like a signature—a *griffe*—its mark retracts from conceptual measure.

Unmanned Resistance

In tracing the pattern of reading by identification, we spoke of "the reader . . . he." Is there a reason for this deliberate sexism? The two ways of answering that question are seemingly incompatible and yet equally necessary.

1. "He" remarks the mark of gender on the general concept "man." If we choose to read Rousseau's (or de Man's) allegory of man's name as an allegory of reading by identification, with all of the potential for error that it entails, then we also take it as pointing to a crucial condition of that reading habit: the exclusion of sexual difference. The exclusive condition is confirmed by the patterns that have determined literary study in the age of its institutionalization, where the two parties to the encounter—reader and text—largely continued to play out the allegory of primitive man meeting other men and measuring himself through identification.[24] On the one hand, even after women were finally admitted to these institutions as coequal students of reading, the grid of a presumed transparency between subjects identified as men remained in place as the unacknowledged prescriptive filter of measured understanding. On the other hand, the same prescriptive grid continued to shape and select the canon of texts to be studied according to the privilege granted men's signatures. This exclusive pattern of identification can be made to appear as so much playing with mirrors when a critical stance steps to one side of the mirrored field, into the beveled edge where the identificatory path is distorted or deflected. To read as a woman is to remark this unreflecting frame of reflection, to uncover its limits, and to overturn its exclusions.[25]

---

[24]It is finally this version of the institution of literary studies that is upheld by theories of mimetic desire such as that of René Girard in *Deceit, Desire, and the Novel: Self and Other in Literary Structure,* trans. Yvonne Freccero (Baltimore, 1965) and elsewhere. For a critique of Girard, see Sarah Kofman, *The Enigma of Woman: Woman in the Text of Freud,* trans. Catherine Porter (Ithaca, N.Y., 1985), 59–65; also see Philippe Lacoue-Labarthe, "Typographie," in *Mimesis: Des articulations,* ed. Sylviane Agacinski et al. (Paris, 1975), 231–51.

[25]In a chapter titled "Reading as a Woman," in his *On Deconstruction*

2. "He" effaces the mark of gender on the reader by identification. It insists, in other words, that whenever reading projects a model of identification, the model is masculine—not, obviously, in an empirical sense but in a structural one. To retain this structural sense means to recall that the effacement of difference is a conceptual violence whose effects can be all the more insidious when they are too quickly denied any political pertinence. If it leaves intact the identificatory structure, then the program of "reading as a woman" *in itself* will not end conceptual violence, but only redistribute its effects more equitably. The preserved structure presents little resistance to the institutionalized model of reading. Resistance, in other words, that takes the form of identifying (with) some feminine subject or essence puts nothing essential at risk and even provides the reassuring comfort of an essential likeness with already institutionalized methods of reading.

Far riskier, it seems, would be reading in the absence of a model subject engendered by the *classification* (or cat-egorization) of differences. This is not, however, to suggest a program to be institutionally adopted—for the obvious reason that reading in the absence of a model cannot, by definition, supply a model. But also for the equally undeniable reason that no reading is possible in the absence pure and simple of identificatory impulses. It is still a problem of reading too slowly *or* too quickly, *either* resisting those patterns of metaphorical sameness that allow reading to take some shortcuts *or* overlooking the marks of sheer difference that slow reading down and can bring it to a standstill altogether. The pedagogical enterprise will remain a critical one only so long as it is practiced within the space of a double stricture where both the conceptual gener-

---

(Ithaca, N.Y., 1982), Jonathan Culler chronicles three moments in the development of American feminist literary criticism, each of which is formed around the experience of woman reading. Culler's synthesis is especially valuable in that it isolates the ambiguous place of this appeal to experience: "it has always, already occurred and yet is still to be produced—an indispensable point of reference, yet never simply there. . . . The noncoincidence reveals an interval, a division within woman or within any reading subject and the 'experience' of that subject" (62).

ality of the text and the singular difference of the reader can encounter their limits.

And this is to say not only that readers, too, must sign but that my signature, any signature, takes place as an effect of reading.

Works Cited

Abrams, M. H. "Construing and Deconstructing." In *Romanticism and Contemporary Criticism*, ed. Morris Eaves and Michael Fischer. Ithaca, N.Y., 1986.

Baker, Felicity. "Remarques sur la notion de dépôt." *Annales Jean-Jacques Rousseau* 37 (1966– 68).

Barthes, Roland. "The Death of the Author." In *Image-Music-Text*, trans. and ed. Stephen Heath. New York, 1977.

———. *A Lover's Discourse: Fragments*. Trans. Richard Howard. New York, 1978.

Baudelaire, Charles. *Oeuvres complètes*. Ed. Claude Pichois. Paris, 1975.

Baudrillard, Jean. *Oublier Foucault*. Paris, 1977.

Bell, Quentin. "Critical Response." *Critical Inquiry* 11 (March 1985).

———. *Virginia Woolf: A Biography*. London, 1973.

Benjamin, Walter. *Charles Baudelaire: A Lyric Poet in the Age of High Capitalism*. Trans. Harry Zohn. London, 1973.

Bennington, Geoffrey. *Sententiousness and the Novel: Laying Down the Law in Eighteenth-Century French Fiction*. Cambridge, 1985.

Benrekassa, Georges. *Fables de la personne: Pour une histoire de la subjectivité*. Paris, 1985.

Blum, Carol. *Rousseau and the Republic of Virtue: The Language of Politics in the French Revolution*. Ithaca, N.Y., 1986.

Bonnet, Jean-Claude. "Le Fantasme de l'écrivain." *Poétique* 63 (September 1985).

Bordo, Susan. "The Cartesian Masculinization of Thought." *Signs* 11(3).

Buttrick, G. A., et al., eds. *The Interpreter's Bible*. New York, 1952.

Chase, Cynthia. *Decomposing Figures: Rhetorical Readings in the Romantic Tradition.* Baltimore, 1986.

Colombet, Claude. *Propriété littéraire et artistique.* 2d ed. Paris, 1980.

Culler, Jonathan. "Criticism and Institutions: The American University." In *Post-Structuralism and the Question of History,* ed. Derek Attridge, Geoffrey Bennington, and Robert Young. Cambridge, 1987.

——. *On Deconstruction: Theory and Criticism after Structuralism.* Ithaca, N.Y., 1982.

——. "Reading Lyric." *Yale French Studies* 69 (1985).

Deguy, Michel. "Le Corps de Jeanne." *Poétique* 3 (1970).

De Man, Paul. *Allegories of Reading: Figural Language in Rousseau, Nietzsche, Rilke, and Proust.* New Haven, Conn., 1979.

——. *Blindness and Insight.* 2d ed. Minneapolis, 1983.

——. *The Resistance to Theory.* Minneapolis, 1986.

——. *The Rhetoric of Romanticism.* New York, 1984.

——. "Sign and Symbol in Hegel's *Aesthetics.*" *Critical Inquiry* 8 (Summer 1982).

Derathé, Robert. *Jean-Jacques Rousseau et la science politique de son temps.* Paris, 1970.

Derrida, Jacques. "Cogito and History of Madness." In *Writing and Difference,* trans. Alan Bass. Chicago, 1978.

——. "Des Tours de Babel." In *Difference in Translation,* ed. and trans. Joseph F. Graham. Ithaca, N.Y., 1985.

——. *Glas.* Trans. John P. Leavey, Jr., and Richard Rand. Lincoln, Nebr., 1986.

——. "Introduction." In *The Origin of Geometry.* Trans. John P. Leavey, Jr. Stony Brook, N.Y., 1978.

——. "Limited Inc abc . . ." Trans. Samuel Weber. *Glyph* 2 (1977).

——. "My Chances/*Mes Chances*: A Rendezvous with Some Epicurean Stereophonies." In *Taking Chances: Derrida, Psychoanalysis, and Literature,* ed. Joseph H. Smith and William Kerrigan, trans. Irene Harvey and Avital Ronell. Baltimore, 1984.

——. *Of Grammatology.* Trans. Gayatri Chakravorty Spivak. Baltimore, 1976.

——. *The Post Card: From Socrates to Freud and Beyond.* Trans. Alan Bass. Chicago, 1987.

——. "Signature Event Context," in *Margins of Philosophy.* Trans. Alan Bass. Chicago, 1982.

——. *Signéponge/Signsponge.* Trans. Richard Rand. New York, 1984.

——. *Speech and Phenomena.* Trans. David B. Allison. Evanston, Ill., 1973.

——. "Title (to be specified)." Trans. Tom Conley. *Sub-stance* 3 (1981).

——. *The Truth in Painting.* Trans. Geoffrey Bennington and Ian Mc-Leod. Chicago, 1987.

Dickinson, Emily. *Poems.* Ed. Thomas H. Johnson. Cambridge, Mass., 1955.

Diderot, Denis. *Lettre sur le commerce de la librairie.* Ed. Bernard Grasset. Paris, 1937.

Dock, Marie-Claude. *Etude sur le droit d'auteur.* Paris, 1963.

Drexler, K. Eric. *Engines of Creation.* New York, 1986.

Falk, Henri. *Les Privilèges de librairie sous l'Ancien Régime: Etude historique du conflit des droits sur l'oeuvre littéraire.* Geneva, 1970.

Foucault, Michel. *The Archaeology of Knowledge.* Trans. Alan Sheridan. New York, 1972.

———. *L'Historie de la folie.* 2d ed. Paris, 1972.

———. *The History of Sexuality.* Vol. 1. Trans. Robert Hurley. New York, 1978.

———. "Introduction." In *Rousseau juge de Jean-Jaques.* Paris, 1962.

Françon, Marcel. "La Condemnation de l'*Emile.*" *Annales de la Société Jean-Jacques Rousseau* 31 (1946–49).

Freud, Sigmund. "The Resistances to Psychoanalysis." In *The Standard Edition of the Complete Psychological Works of Sigmund Freud,* trans. James Strachey et al., ed. James Strachey, vol. 19. London, 1961.

Gasché, Rodolphe. "Joining the Text." In *The Yale Critics: Deconstruction in America,* Ed. Jonathan Arac, Wlad Godzich, and Wallace Martin. Minneapolis, 1983.

Gearhart, Suzanne. *The Open Boundary of History and Fiction: A Critical Approach to the French Enlightenment.* Princeton, N.J., 1984.

Gibaldi, Joseph, ed. *Introduction to Scholarship in Modern Languages and Literatures.* New York, 1979.

Gilbert, Sandra, and Susan Gubar. *The Madwoman in the Attic: The Woman Writer and the Nineteenth-Century Literary Imagination.* New Haven, Conn., 1979.

Girard, René. *Deceit, Desire, and the Novel: Self and Other in Literary Structure.* Trans. Yvonne Freccero. Baltimore, 1965.

Godfrey, Sima. "'Mère des souvenirs': Baudelaire, Memory, and Mother." *L'Esprit Créateur* 25(2).

Hamilton, George Heard. *Manet and His Critics.* New York, 1969.

Hartman, Geoffrey. "Paul de Man's Proverbs of Hell." *London Review of Books,* 15 March 1984.

Heine, Elizabeth. "Postscript to the *Diary of Virginia Woolf,* Vol. I: 'Effie's Story' and *Night and Day.*" *Virginia Woolf Miscellany* 9 (Winter 1977).

Hernadi, Paul. "Literary Theory." In *Introduction to Scholarship in Modern Languages and Literatures,* ed. Joseph Gibaldi, New York, 1979.

Herrmann-Mascard, Nicole. *La Censure des livres à Paris à la fin de l'Ancien Régime (1750– 1789)*. Paris, 1968.

Hirsch, E. D., Jr. *Validity in Interpretation*. New Haven, Conn., 1967.

Hodge, Jane Aiken. *Only a Novel: The Double Life of Jane Austen*. New York, 1972.

Jardine, Alice. *Gynesis: Configurations of Women and Modernity*. Ithaca, N.Y., 1985.

Jarrell, Randall. *Pictures from an Institution: A Comedy*. Chicago, 1986.

Johnson, Barbara. "Apostrophe, Animation, and Abortion." *Diacritics* 16 (Spring 1986).

Juhl, P. D. *Interpretation: An Essay in the Philosophy of Literary Criticism*. Princeton, N.J., 1980.

Kamuf, Peggy. *Fictions of Feminine Desire: Disclosures of Heloise*. Lincoln, Nebr., 1982.

———. "Replacing Feminist Criticism." *Diacritics*, Summer 1982.

———. "Writing Like a Woman." In *Women and Language in Literature and Society*, ed. Sally McConnell-Ginet, Ruth Borker, and Nelly Furman. New York, 1981.

Kase, Francis J. *Copyright Thought in Continental Europe: Its Development, Legal Theories, and Philosophy*. South Hackensack, N.J., 1967.

Kavanagh, Thomas M. *Writing the Truth: Authority and Desire in Rousseau*. Berkeley, 1987.

King, Russell S. "Dialogue in Baudelaire's Poetic Universe." *L'Esprit Créateur* 13(2).

Klein, Richard. "The Blindness of Hyperboles: The Ellipses of Insight." *Diacritics*, Summer 1973.

Knapp, Steven, and Walter Benn Michaels. "Against Theory 2: Hermeneutics and Deconstruction." *Critical Inquiry* 14 (Autumn 1987).

Kofman, Sarah. *The Enigma of Woman: Woman in the Text of Freud*. Trans. Catherine Porter. Ithaca, N.Y., 1985.

Lacoue-Labarthe, Philippe. "Typographie." In *Mimesis: Des articulations*, ed. Sylviane Agacinski et al. Paris, 1975.

Lalande, André, ed. *Vocabulaire technique et critique de la philosophie*. 9th ed. Paris, 1962.

Launay, Michel, and Gunnar Von Proschwitz. *Index du "Contrat social."* Paris, 1977.

Leavey, John P., Jr., ed. *Glassary*. Lincoln, Nebr., 1987.

Lebensztejn, Jean-Claude. "Esquisse d'une typologie." *La Revue de l'art* 26 (1974).

Lejeune, Philippe. *Le Pacte autobiographique*. Paris, 1975.

McDonald, Christie. *The Dialogue of Writing: Essays in Eighteenth-Century French Literature*. Waterloo, Ont., 1984.

——. "En-harmoniques: L'Anagramme de Rousseau." *Etudes Françaises* 17 (October 1981).

——, ed. *The Ear of the Other: Texts and Discussions with Jacques Derrida.* Trans. Peggy Kamuf and Avital Ronell. New York, 1985.

Maclean, Ian. "Un Dialogue de sourds? Some Implications of the Austin-Searle-Derrida Debate." *Paragraph* 5 (March 1985).

Marcus, Jane. "Critical Response." *Critical Inquiry* 11 (March 1985).

Masson, Pierre-Maurice. "Le Séjour de J.-J. Rousseau à l'Hospice du Spirito Santo." *Revue d'Histoire Littéraire de la France* 21 (1914).

Mély, Benoît. *Jean-Jacques Rousseau: Un intellectuel en rupture.* Paris, 1986.

Miller, J. Hillis. "Ariachne's Broken Woof." *Georgia Review* 30 (Spring 1977).

——. "On Edge: The Crossways of Contemporary Criticism." In *Romanticism and Contemporary Criticism,* ed. Morris Eaves and Michael Fischer. Ithaca, N.Y., 1986.

Mitchell, W. J. T., ed. *Against Theory: Literary Studies and the New Pragmatism.* Chicago, 1985.

Nancy, Jean-Luc. *La Communauté désoeuvrée.* Paris, 1986.

——. *Le Partage des voix.* Paris, 1982.

Nehamas, Alexander. "Untheory." *London Review of Books,* 22 May 1986.

Prévost, Jean. *Baudelaire.* Paris, 1953.

Recht, Pierre. *Le Droit d'auteur, une nouvelle forme de propriété: Histoire et théorie.* Gembloux, Belgium, 1969.

Rousseau, Jean-Jacques. *The Confessions of Jean-Jacques Rousseau.* Trans. J. M. Cohen. London, 1953.

——. *Correspondance complète.* Ed. R. A. Leigh. Madison, Wis., 1969.

——. *Correspondance générale.* Ed. Théophile Dufour and Pierre-Paul Plan. Paris, 1924.

——. *Essay on the Origin of Languages.* In *On the Origin of Language: Two Essays,* ed. and trans. John H. Moran and Alexander Gode. Chicago, 1966.

——. *The Miscellaneous Works of Mr. J. J. Rousseau.* London, 1767; rpt. New York, 1972.

——. *Oeuvres complètes.* Ed. Bernard Gagnebin and Marcel Raymond. Paris, 1959–69.

——. *Oeuvres inédites.* Ed. V. D. Musset-Pathay. Paris, 1824.

——. *Of the Social Contract.* Trans. G. D. H. Cole. London, 1973.

Searle, John R. "Reiterating the Differences: A Reply to Derrida." *Glyph* 1 (1977).

Stamelman, Richard. "The Shroud of Allegory: Death, Mourning, and Melancholy in Baudelaire's Work." *Texas Studies of Literature and Language* 25(3).

Stendhal. *Red and Black.* Trans. Robert M. Adams. New York, 1969.

Todorov, Tzvetan. *Frêle Bonheur, essai sur Rousseau.* Paris, 1985.

——. *Pensée de Rousseau.* Paris, 1985.

Trombley, Stephen. *All That Summer She Was Mad: Virginia Woolf: Female Victim of Male Medicine.* New York, 1981.

Ulmer, Gregory. *Applied Grammatology: Post(e)-Pedagogy from Jacques Derrida to Joseph Beuys.* Baltimore, 1985.

——. "Sounding the Unconscious." In *Glassary,* ed. John P. Leavey, Jr., Lincoln, Nebr., 1987.

Unger, Robert Mangabeira. *The Critical Legal Studies Movement.* Cambridge, Mass., 1986.

Wilson, Duncan. *Leonard Woolf: A Political Biography.* London, 1978.

Woolf, Leonard. *Beginning Again: An Autobiography of the Years 1911–1918.* London, 1964.

Woolf, Virginia. *The Diary of Virginia Woolf.* Ed. Anne Olivier Bell. New York, 1979.

——. *A Room of One's Own.* New York, 1929.

Index

Library of Congress Cataloging-in-Publication Data

Kamuf, Peggy, 1947–
   Signature pieces.

   Bibliography: p.
   Includes index.
   1. Authorship. I. Title.
PN145.K36   1988   801.9   88 47731
ISBN 0-8014-2209-4 (alk. paper)